IMAGES
of America

LINCOLN COUNTY

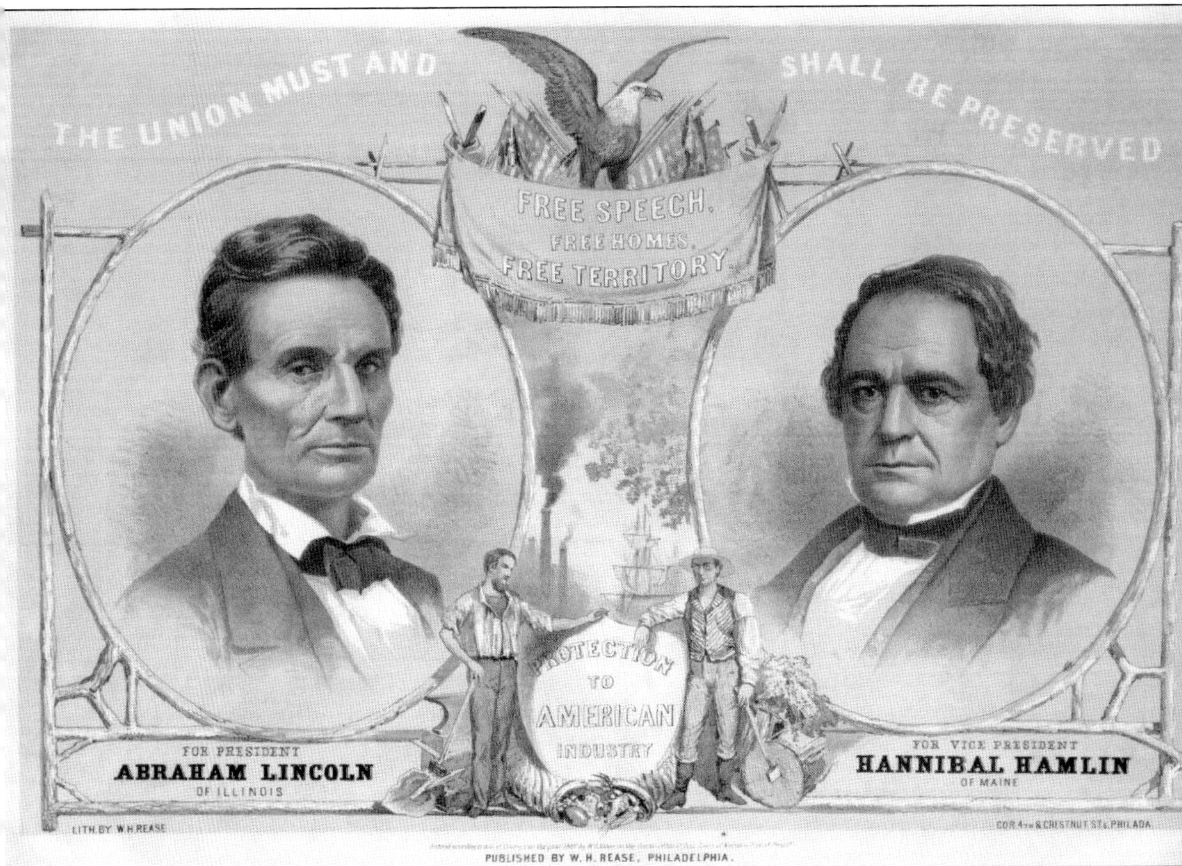

Republican Party presidential candidate Abraham Lincoln and his running mate, Hannibal Hamlin, are shown in this 1860 lithograph. Hamlin is the county seat of Lincoln County. (Courtesy of Library of Congress.)

On the Cover: Students from Harts Creek and Laurel Hill Districts were transported to Guyan Valley High School on this bus in 1928. (Courtesy of Marshall University Libraries, Fred Lambert Collection, Accession Number 236, Box 14, Folder 1.)

IMAGES
of America

LINCOLN COUNTY

Ralph D. Triplett and Boone Triplett

ARCADIA
PUBLISHING

ISBN 978-0-7385-9825-3

Published by Arcadia Publishing
Charleston, South Carolina

Printed in the United States of America

Library of Congress Control Number: 2012945994

For all general information, please contact Arcadia Publishing:
Telephone 843-853-2070
Fax 843-853-0044
E-mail sales@arcadiapublishing.com
For customer service and orders:
Toll-Free 1-888-313-2665

Visit us on the Internet at www.arcadiapublishing.com

To Dee-Dee and Kathleen

Contents

ACKNOWLEDGMENTS

Space limits our ability to thank everyone who contributed to this project. The good citizens of Lincoln County stepped up in a big way, and for that the authors are humbly grateful. Since all submissions are credited in the text, we would like to recognize those individuals whose assistance was especially invaluable: Billy Adkins, Randy Davidson, Lucian Isaacs, Donna Martin, Gary McClure, and Jim Ryan. We sincerely hope that the latter finds our efforts to be "in good taste."

Prof. Lisle Brown and the staff at the Marshall University Libraries Special Collections Department were highly cooperative in permitting access to the papers and photographs of Fred Lambert, Accession Number 236. For the sake of brevity, those images are cited in the captions as (MU-Lambert). Abbreviations are also used for the Lincoln County Friends of the Arts (LCFOA) and the Hamlin-Lincoln County Public Library (HLCPL), two more organizations that were helpful in obtaining images. We would also like to acknowledge the *Lincoln Journal* for allowing us to pick through their archives. Images from the authors' collection are denoted as (AC).

Primary sources of information are listed in the bibliography on page 127. Without the research efforts of these historians, this book would not be possible. While we have tried hard to "get it right," we apologize in advance for any historical inaccuracies. By no means is this volume intended to be a definitive, comprehensive history of Lincoln County. It is more of a photo album to be pulled off the shelf every now and then to relive some good memories about the place we all call home. Enjoy.

Introduction

Lincoln County may be the only place in the United States that was born of the Civil War twice over. Consider the tale of John Chapman, who lived above the falls of the Guyandotte in Cabell County, Virginia, on the eve of that conflict. After joining the Confederate army, he wrote letters home about how "we whiped [*sic*] them in every fight." After his cause was lost, Chapman returned home to what was now Lincoln County, West Virginia. Only a decade earlier, Abraham Lincoln had been an obscure politician from Illinois, but on February 23, 1867, the "Restored Government of the State of Virginia" recognized a new county in honor of the martyred president. They would also see fit to name its seat of government for Lincoln's first vice president, Hannibal Hamlin. (Although some maintain that the Virginia General Assembly established Hamline at the site in 1853.) The organization of townships with names such as Sheridan and Union, in what had recently been part of the Confederacy, left no doubt about allegiances. So, from the very beginning, Lincoln County has been an orphan county in an orphan state.

The strangeness of this is captured on modern maps. West Virginia is probably America's most irregularly shaped state. A glance at an outline map of West Virginia's 55 counties will reveal a peculiar, mitten-shaped blob in the southwestern part of the state: this is Lincoln. Cobbled out of Boone, Cabell, Kanawha, and Putnam Counties, it is characterized by another geographic oddity—three north-flowing rivers: Guyandotte, Mud, and Coal. Even before there was a Lincoln County, these water highways floated goods and people in and out of the area. Lock and dam navigation systems operated on both the Guyandotte and the Coal in pre–Civil War days.

Mary Draper Ingles is thought to have crossed near the falls of the Guyandotte while escaping from captivity by Shawnee Indians in 1755. France had first claimed the region, but its defeat in the French and Indian War assured English dominance west of the Appalachian Mountains. The "shot heard 'round the world" signaled the start of another war, and after Great Britain lost this one to the upstart rebels, Americans pushed westward across the mountains. The first ones to settle in Lincoln County were the McComas family in 1799. They resided at the falls of the Guyandotte, where William McComas established a mill around 1808. By then, others had followed. That list of early pioneer surnames reads like a modern telephone directory: Adkins, Brumfield, Burns, Cremeans, Elkins, Fry, Hatfield, Lucas, Midkiff, Parsons, Smith, and Spurlock.

Transportation routes were established in pioneer days. In addition to the rivers, a crude road was cut along the east side of the Guyandotte River between Barboursville and Logan Court House. A postman, who traveled its 60-mile distance twice a week, delivered mail along this road. Another road led eastward to the important saltworks beyond Charleston. The main north-south transportation axis through Lincoln County would eventually become West Virginia State Route 10, while the east-west road evolved into Routes 3 and 214. These highways are named today after Dr. Gilmer Odell McClellan and Gen. Charles Elwood "Chuck" Yeager, two of Lincoln County's most famous citizens. When the Chesapeake and Ohio (C&O) Railroad came through during 1903 and 1904, it paralleled the old Barboursville-Logan Road and the Guyandotte River.

The Civil War found Lincoln County evenly divided. Local historian Harold "Hal" Ray Smith has determined that just over 50 percent of its residents fought for the North and 49 percent for the South. Three engagements, all involving the 3rd West Virginia Cavalry (Union) commanded by John Seashoal Witcher, were fought within the borders of Lincoln County. Two of these skirmishes, which claimed four killed and six wounded on both sides, were Union defeats. At the lone Union victory (which occurred on the Curry farm near modern Hamlin on May 29, 1864), the commander of the losing Confederate forces was none other than Maj. John Chapman.

"Unreconstructed" types may not want to admit it, but West Virginia—and especially Lincoln County—was organized by Yankees. General Witcher's father-in-law, William C. Mahone, could be regarded as the "Father of Lincoln County." Mahone, who circulated the petition to organize a county named Lincoln, was voted president of the first board of supervisors. That initial gathering of county officers was held in a church on the Curry farm battlefield. They subdivided the new county into three townships, which were aligned along the three north-flowing rivers: Sheridan to the west, Carroll in the center, and Duval to the east. There was some shifting of county boundaries as the townships of Union, Jefferson, Washington, Harts Creek, and Laurel Hill were created, but by 1871 the traditional county map of eight magisterial districts was complete. It remained that way until 1986, when Jefferson and Union Districts were dissolved. The other six were merged by the Lincoln County Commission into the rather generic Districts One, Two, and Three in 2011.

In the years since 1867, Lincoln County has followed a pattern typical of rural Appalachia, whereby wealthy out-of-state investors have taken freely from the land and given back little or nothing in return. This cycle began with excessive deforestation during the late 1800s and continued with mining and drilling industries into the 20th century. While large-scale coal mining operations never did take root in Lincoln County, and oil drilling was greatly scaled back after the Great Depression, hundreds of active natural gas wells still dot the landscape. In the search for alternative fuel sources, the Marcellus formation, with its rich natural gas reserves, could hold the key to the state's economic future. But this cycles back to the same jobs versus environment debate that has gone on in West Virginia throughout its history.

Outsiders call Lincoln County rural and depressed, a conclusion disputed by anyone who has ever lived here. Rural is accurate. Depressed? Perhaps it is, economically, but not in the spirit of its people. This spirit was best exemplified on October 14, 1947, when a farm boy from Mud River became the first human being ever to fly faster than the speed of sound. This made General Yeager the county's singular claim to fame. Ironically, the man who broke the sound barrier hails from a place where the pace of life is decidedly slow. And that is what "foreigners" just do not understand. Residents here are tough, honest, God-fearing, and, above all, proud. There is an understated elegance to this way of living that has been a constant throughout the years. This quality is symbolically reflected by the area's hills and streams, which also hardly change. Like a security blanket, people find comfort in them. They define a population.

One

Along the Guyandotte Valley

What does the name Guyandotte mean? It could be from the Shawnee "Gee-an-do-tee." Or maybe it is Iroquois. There were tons of variations on early maps: "Guiandot," "Kayendode," "Kiandot," and "Kyandot." Some claim that the name comes from the Wyandotte Indian tribe, while others cite a French fur trader named Henry Guyan. It will remain one of history's mysteries.

It is known that the area was first settled at "Guyandott Falls" in 1799 by the McComas family, and that this spot, south of modern West Hamlin, was a focal point during the early pioneer era. Tributaries south of the former falls are named for their distance from it; for example, Four Mile Creek or Ten Mile Creek. The 37 miles of river in Lincoln County provided the area's primary transportation route for a century, and a string of communities developed along this relatively narrow and steep-walled valley: (from north to south) West Hamlin, Pleasant View, Sheridan, Branchland, Hubball, Midkiff, and Ranger. Residents of these towns attended Guyan Valley High School, which opened in 1926.

The Guyandotte River Navigation Company was put out of business by the Civil War, but vast amounts of timber, and coal to a lesser extent, were moved along the river during the last half of the 19th century until the C&O Railroad was completed in 1904. Nearly "killed" by excessive sediment and acid runoff from these industries, the Guyandotte River is poised today to make a comeback. In recognition of its varied recreational opportunities, local groups are currently seeking scenic waterway designation for development of the Guyandotte Water Trail.

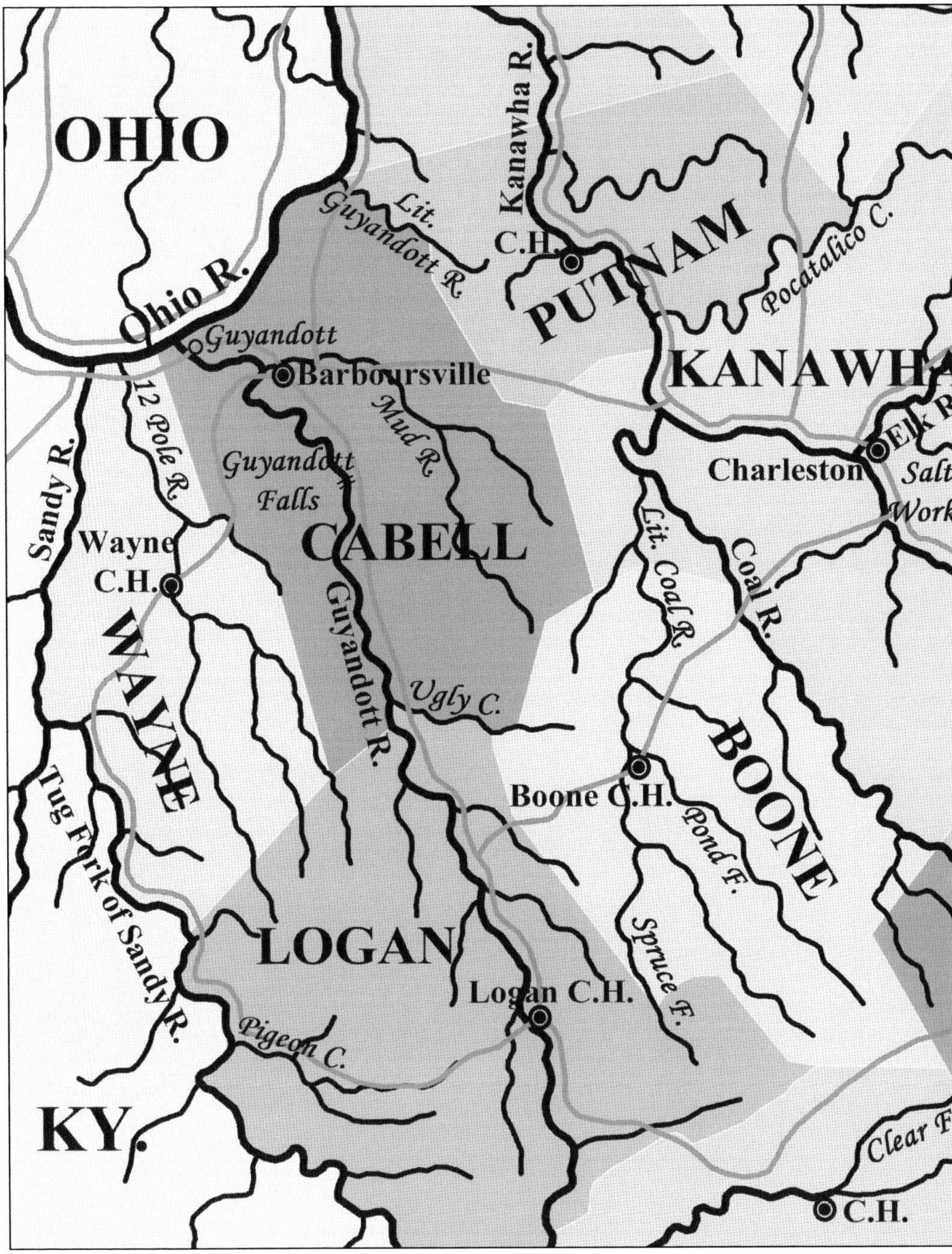

Adapted from Thomas Cowperthwaite's 1850 "New Map of the State of Virginia," this map shows the area before Lincoln County was created out of Boone, Cabell, Kanawha, and Putnam Counties in 1867. The most significant geographic feature in what would become Lincoln County was "Guyandott Falls." While the Barboursville-Logan Road is also identified (note its location on the east side of the river, opposite modern Route 10), the major transportation artery in the 1800s was the Guyandotte River. There are no railroads, and the hub city of Huntington does not yet exist. (AC.)

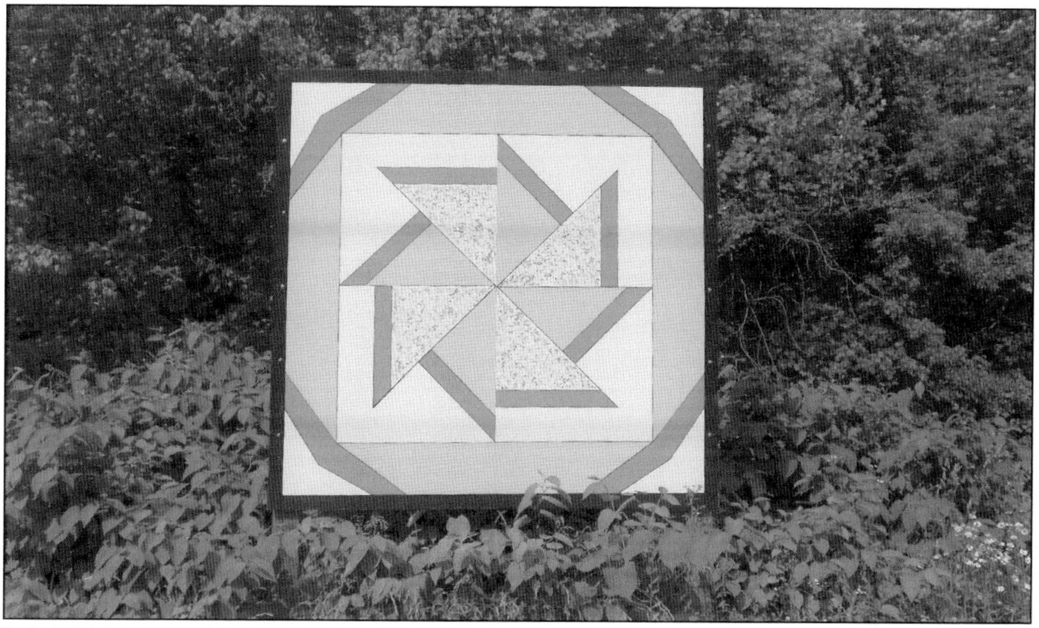

Labeled "the worst slackwater system ever built," the ill-fated Guyandotte River Navigation Company opened a series of six locks and dams in the 1850s. One of the dams along its 36-mile length was located at the falls of the Guyandotte. The falls are now gone, and all that marks the location today is this quilt square. Quilt squares were erected by Lincoln County Parks and Recreation in the early 2000s to recognize historically significant sites across the county. (AC.)

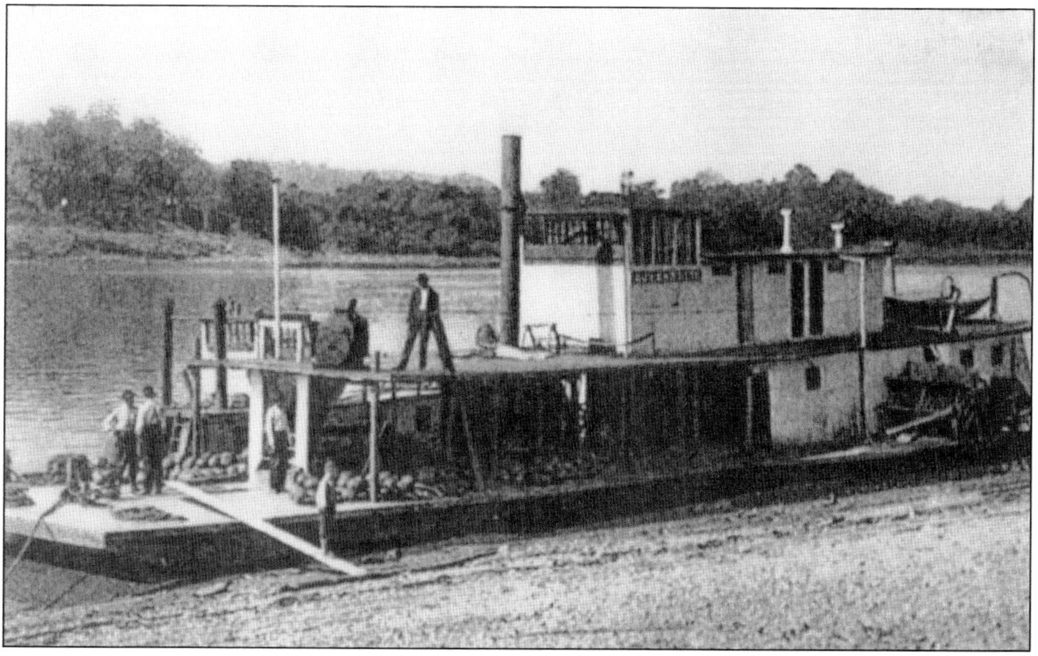

Typical of the steamers that once ran along the Guyandotte River is the (appropriately named) *Guyandotte*, built at Guyandotte in Cabell County. This little steamboat once made it all the way to Logan by running the river during a spring flood. This boat hauled supplies for the C&O Railroad. (Courtesy of US Army Corps of Engineers.)

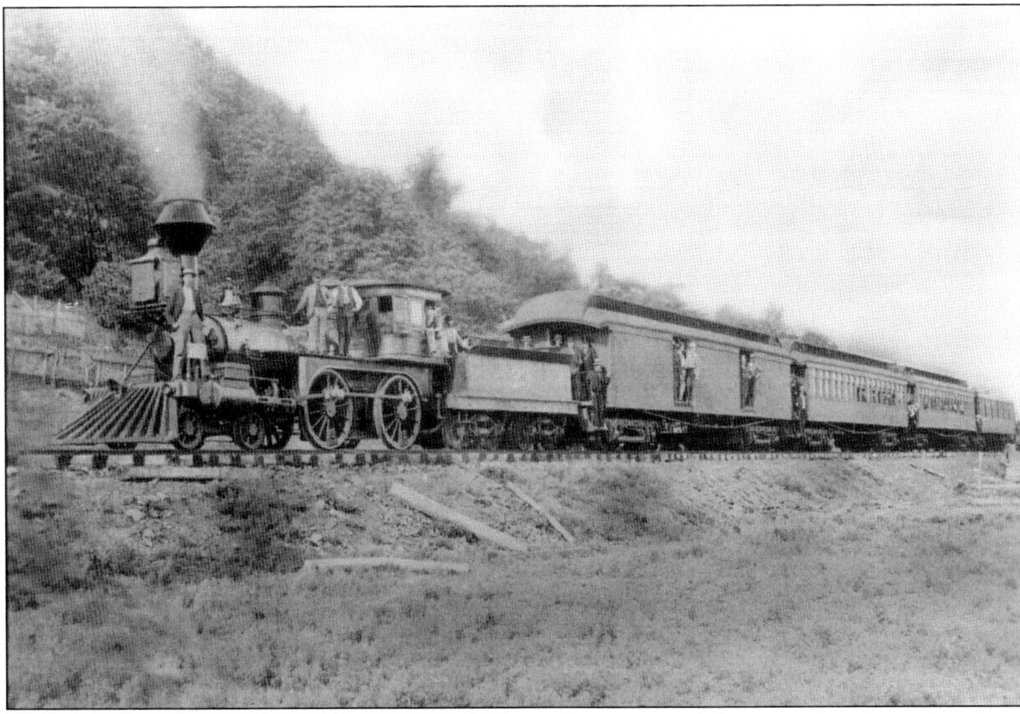

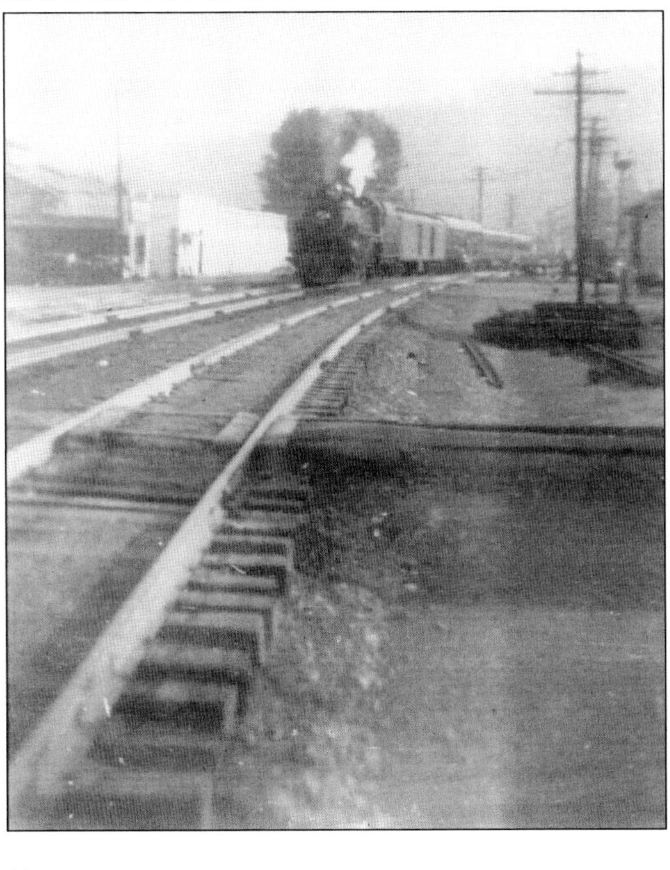

The arrival of the railroad facilitated the movement of people and goods through Lincoln County, cutting travel times from days to hours. Pictured here is one of the earliest passenger trains to pass through the region. C&O Railroad tracks were laid along the east side of the Guyandotte River during 1903 and 1904. (MU-Lambert.)

West Hamlin, the only incorporated municipality along the Guyandotte River in Lincoln County (founded in 1871 and incorporated in 1947), was a key stop on the C&O Railroad. A southbound train is pictured here blowing off steam at the passenger depot, a place where travelers from all over the county boarded trains headed for Huntington or Logan. (Courtesy of Edna Messinger Burger.)

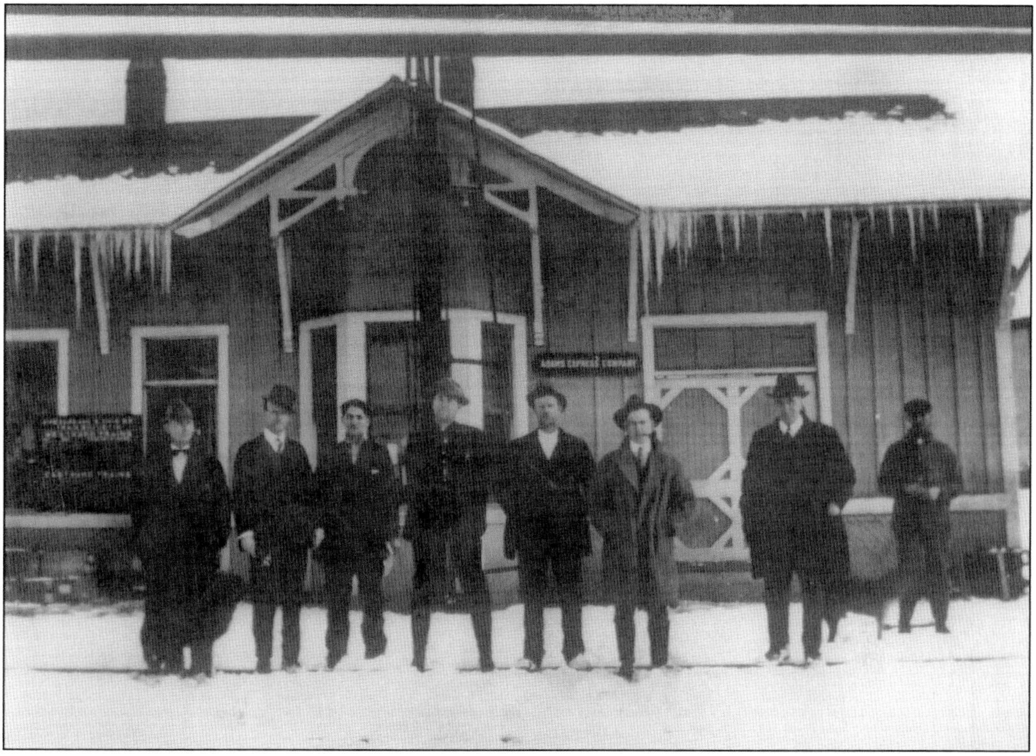

Pictured is the West Hamlin freight depot in winter. In addition to transferring cargo, steam engine trains frequently stopped here to take on water and coal. Both the freight depot and water tower are gone, but the coal tipple still stands. (Courtesy of Walter Midkiff.)

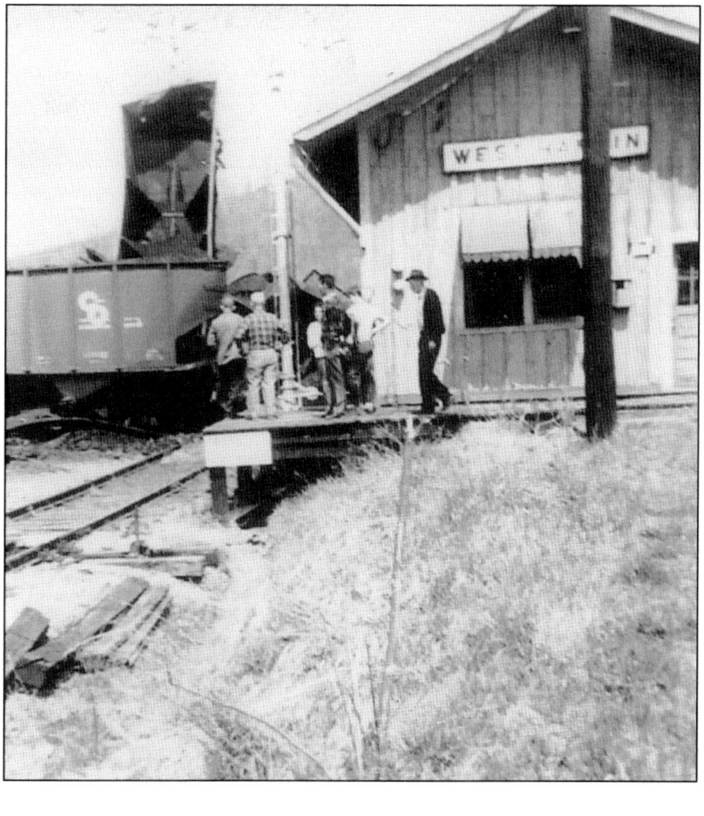

While trains fundamentally changed the quality of life, usually for the better, they were sometimes the source of inconvenience for county residents. This derailment at West Hamlin forced citizens to make a long detour. Onlookers view the wreck from the C&O passenger depot. (Courtesy of Lynda Lou Gibson Overbaugh.)

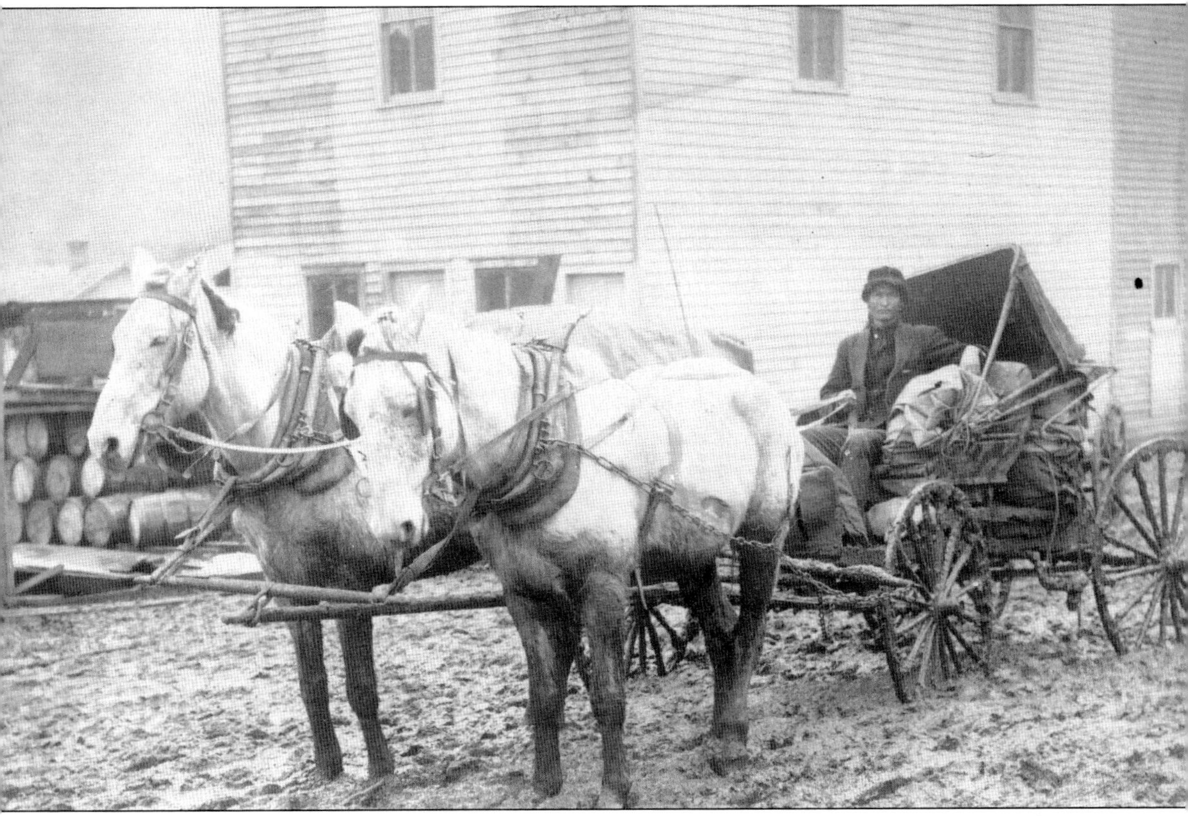

Getting around by any means other than water or rail during the early part of the 20th century was no easy task, as the mud on the horses' hooves and the wagon wheels of this West Hamlin mail carrier will attest. Before the arrival of the railroad, mail was carried on horseback 60 miles between Barboursville and Logan Court House twice a week. This road later provided a convenient right-of-way for the C&O Railroad. As a result of the way these transportation corridors developed along the Guyandotte Valley, post offices and towns were located almost exclusively on the east, or railroad side, of the river. But, when Route 10 was constructed during the 1920s, it was built primarily on the more sparsely populated west side. This highway remains the county's main north-south transportation corridor and is named in honor of West Hamlin physician Dr. Gilmer Odell McClellan. (MU-Lambert.)

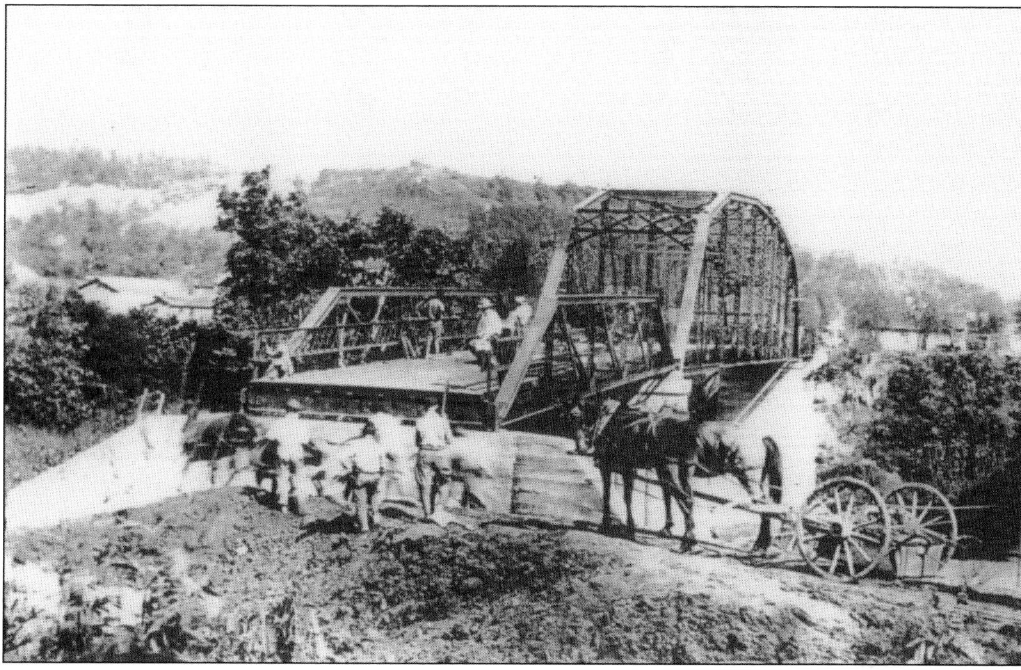

The bridge at West Hamlin was opened to traffic in 1919. Like all of the bridges along the Guyandotte River, it was an iron truss design with a wooden deck floor. As these bridges were of the one-lane variety, countless hours were spent by Lincoln County commuters waiting for traffic to clear from the other side. (Courtesy of Edna Messinger Burger.)

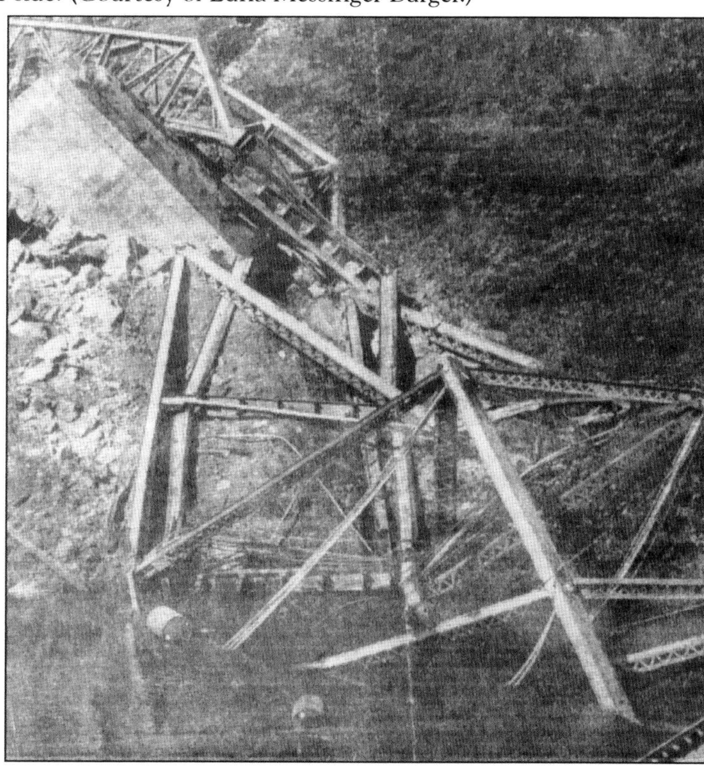

None of the Guyandotte River's signature bridges remain. The West Hamlin Bridge served for 60 years, but after a new two-lane span was opened, the old bridge was dropped into the river on October 18, 1979. All of the other spans met a similar fate. (Courtesy of Debbie Vance.)

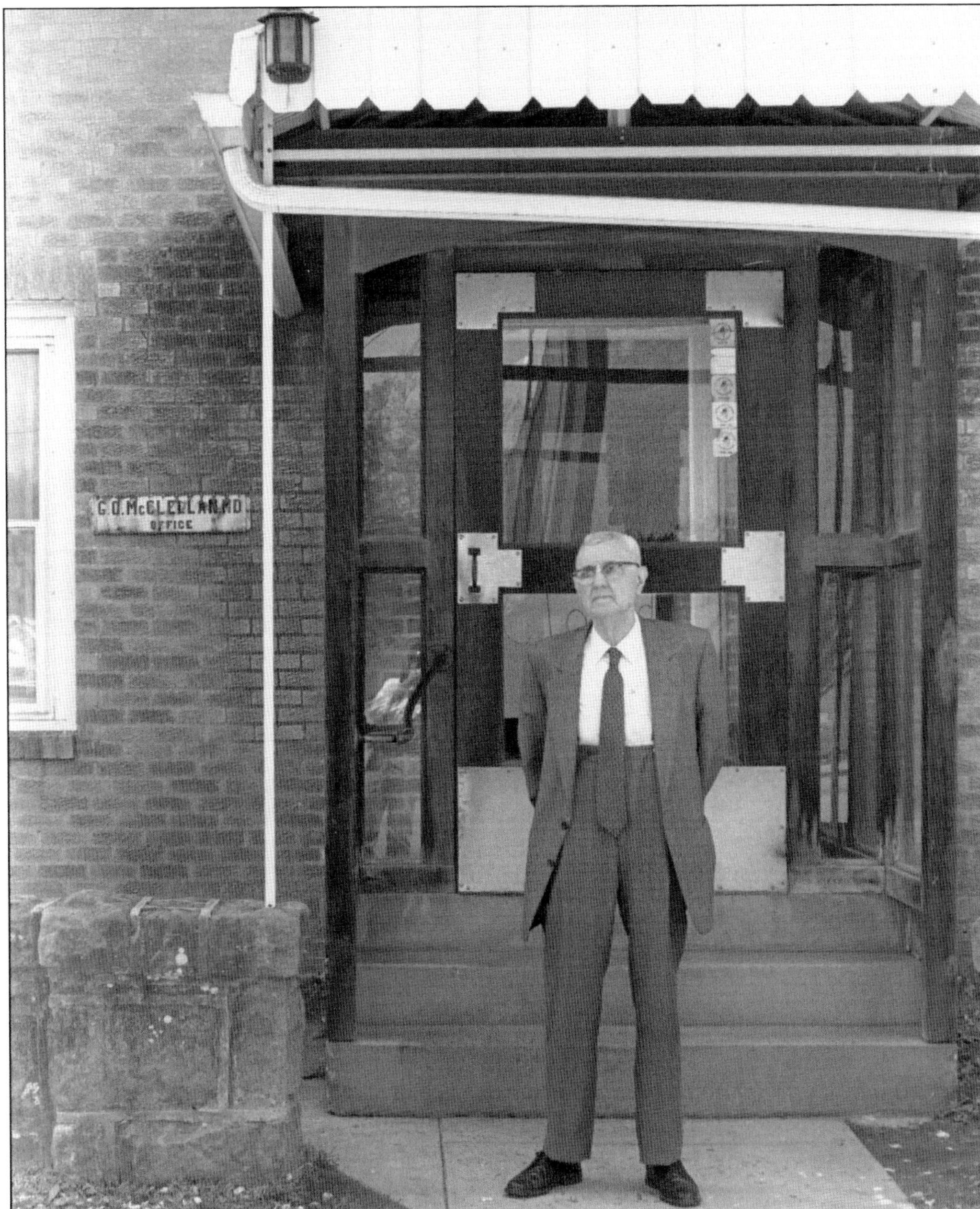

Several thousand Lincoln Countians received their welcome into this world with a firm slap to the backside by Dr. Gilmer Odell McClellan in this unassuming office on Shelton Street in West Hamlin. McClellan was born at Branchland in 1910, was a member of Guyan Valley High School's first graduating class in 1929, graduated from the University of Tennessee's Memphis College of Medicine in 1936, interned at the old C&O Hospital in Huntington, was the first mayor of West Hamlin (1947–1957), practiced at West Hamlin from 1937 to 1989, and died in 1995. A long-standing member of the West Hamlin United Methodist Church, "Doc" McClellan was no ordinary country doctor, as it is estimated he delivered about 10,000 babies during his 52-year medical career. (Courtesy of *Lincoln Journal*.)

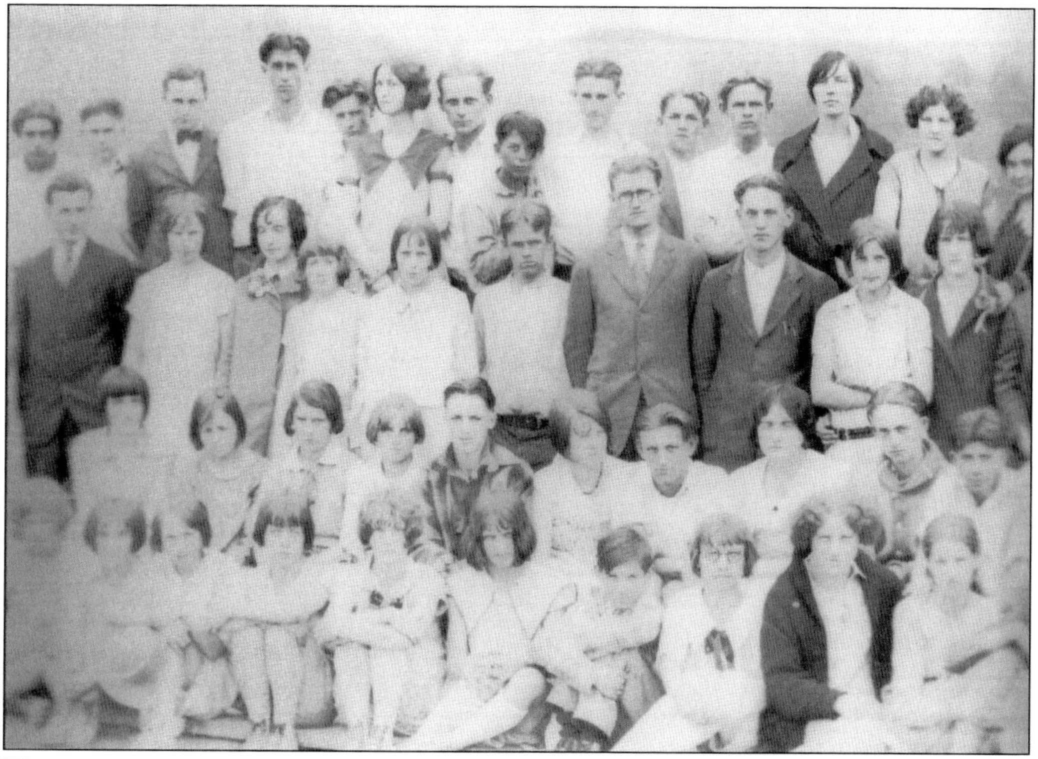

The conspicuous young man in a suit and tie near the center of this 1928 photograph is Dr. McClellan. Both the gymnasium at Guyan Valley Middle School and a street in West Hamlin are named in his honor. So are Route 10 and an apartment building at Lincoln Plaza. Nearly everyone living along this road between Cabell and Logan Counties has a "McClellan Highway" address. (MU-Lambert.)

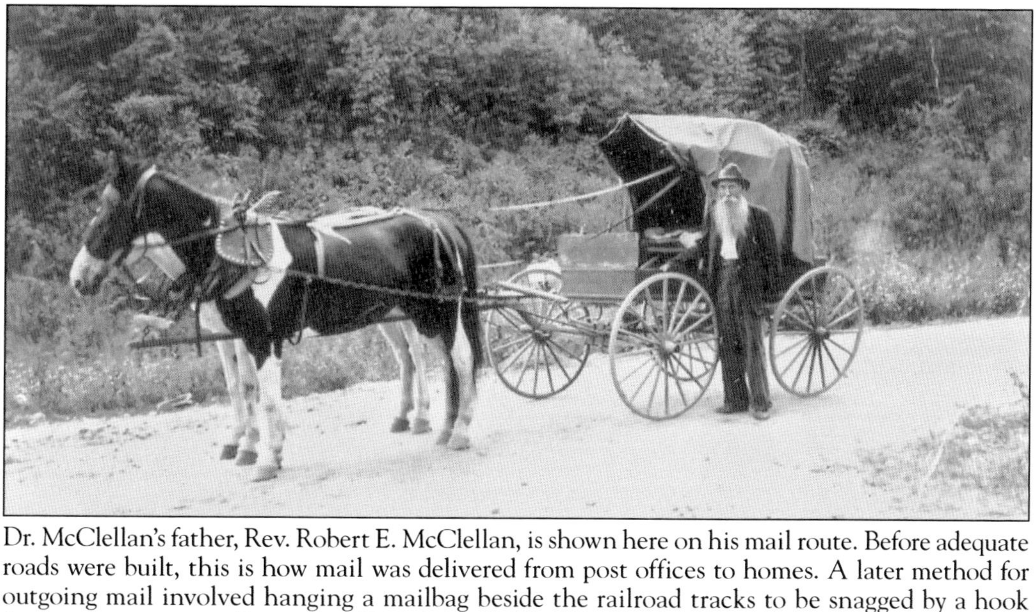

Dr. McClellan's father, Rev. Robert E. McClellan, is shown here on his mail route. Before adequate roads were built, this is how mail was delivered from post offices to homes. A later method for outgoing mail involved hanging a mailbag beside the railroad tracks to be snagged by a hook from a passing train. (Courtesy of Lottie Midkiff.)

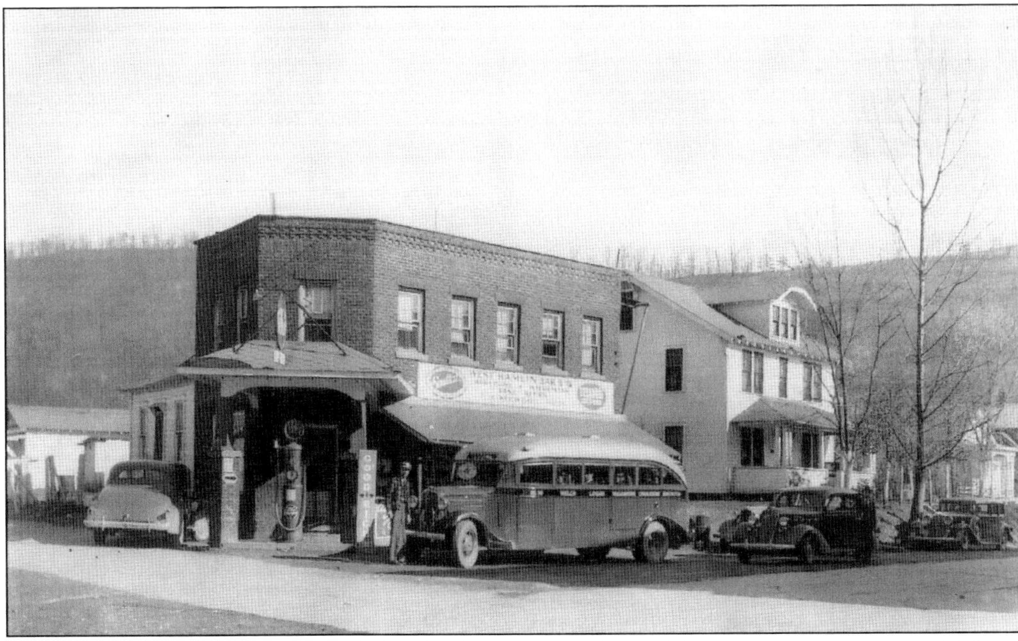

When this c. 1940 photograph of "The Ritz" was taken, the building was serving as a combination barbecue restaurant, beer joint, gas station, and bus depot. It has also been a hotel, grocery store, and gaming hall over the years. It still stands at the corner of Sheridan Street and Virginia Street (Route 10) in West Hamlin and operates as a taxidermy shop. (Courtesy of Edna Messinger Burger.)

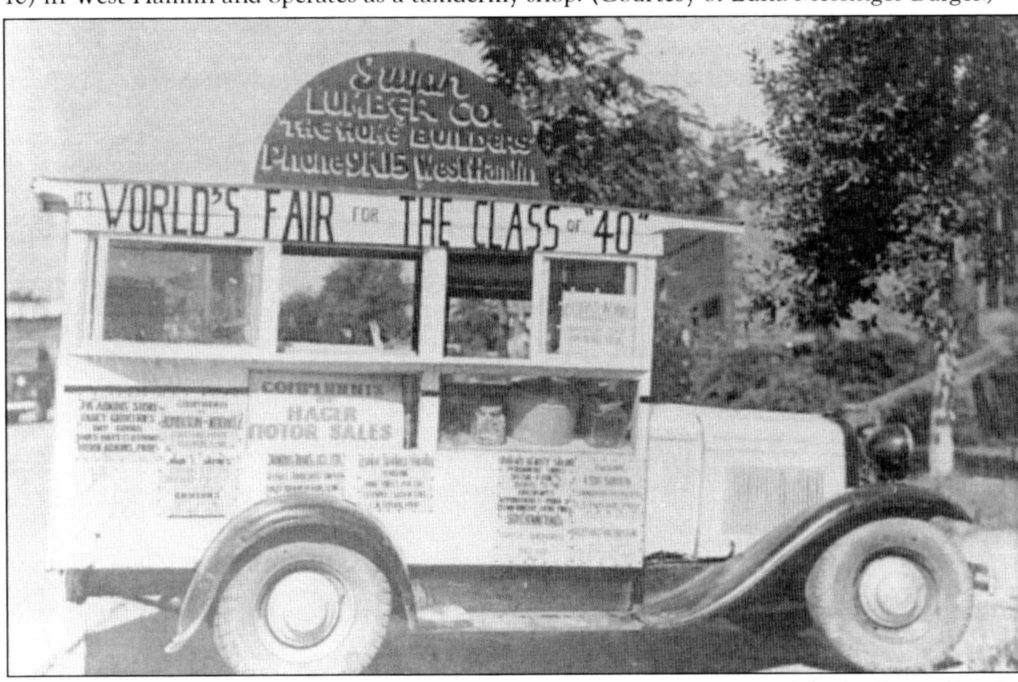

This catering truck in West Hamlin is covered with advertising, most notably for Guyan Lumber Company and Hager Motor Sales. The "World's Fair for the Class of 1940" refers to a Guyan Valley High School senior class trip to New York City. A donation jar may be seen in the counter window. (Courtesy of Debbie Pennington.)

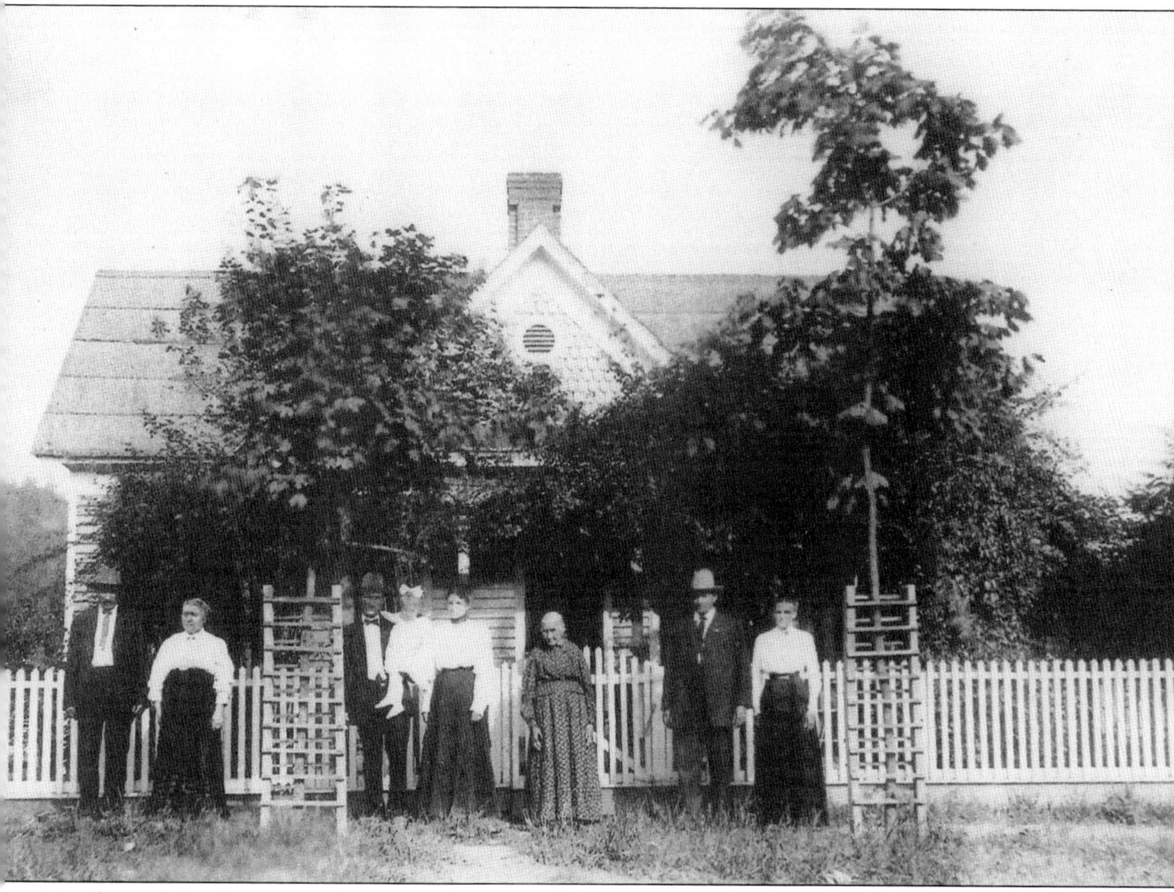

Members of the Covey family occupied this residence at West Hamlin, which was located along Sheridan (now McClellan) Street. The Sheridan Street dogleg through town was eliminated when the new bridge opened in 1979. Significant businesses over the years along this former strip of Route 10 included Payne's General Store, McGhee Funeral Home, Triplett's Shoe Store, White's Trailways Bus Stop, Spencer's Hardware and Furniture, Lincoln Dry Goods, and the First National Bank of West Hamlin. The Coveys owned prime bottomland about one mile south of town and transferred lots to the State of West Virginia around 1922 for the construction of Route 10 and a state highway maintenance garage. The farmhouse there was remodeled to face the new road, which bisected the farm. Still a valuable piece of real estate in an otherwise narrow valley, the land was later developed into the Lincoln Plaza shopping area. A few scattered remnants of the Covey farm survive into the present day. (Courtesy of Edna Messinger Burger.)

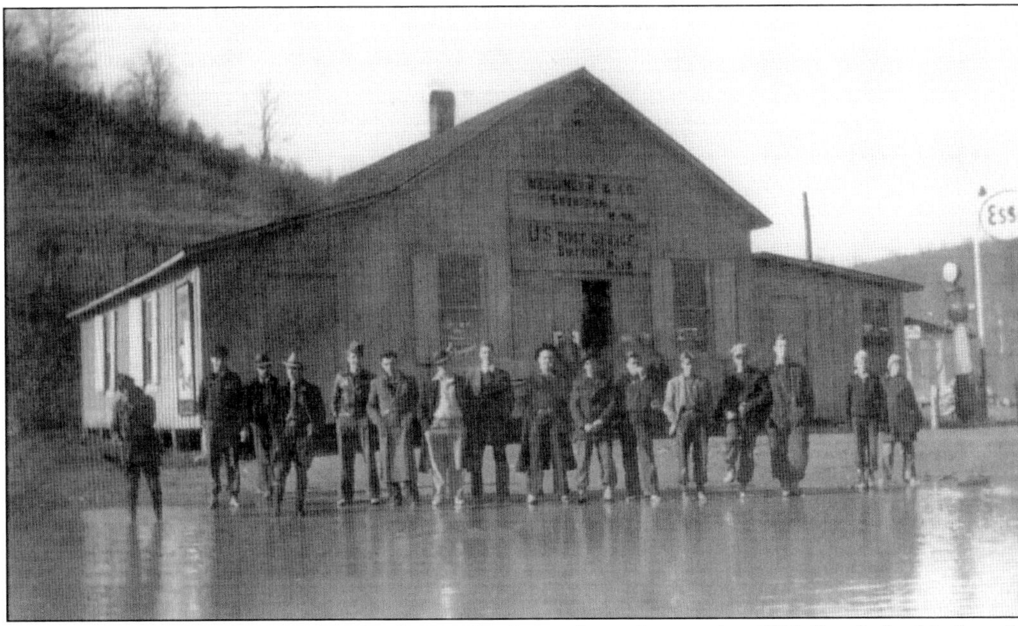

Messinger's Store at the mouth of Falls Creek, shown here during the 1937 flood, doubled as the Sheridan Post Office. Originally called McComas, the township was renamed after Gen. Philip Sheridan when Lincoln County was organized. Part of McComas Township in Cabell County was renamed for Gen. Ulysses S. Grant. (Courtesy of Lottie Midkiff.)

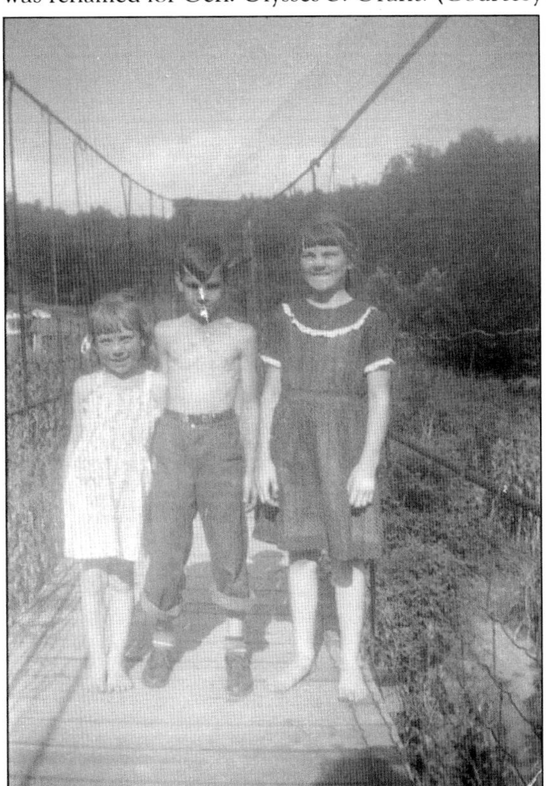

Technically a suspension bridge, the Lincoln County variety was called a "swinging bridge" because of the rocking motion caused by crossing one of these rickety structures. Since the railroad and highway were on opposite sides of the river, students crossed these bridges to catch the bus or board a train. Swinging bridges at Sheridan and Hubball rotted away during the 1980s. (Courtesy of Francis Wrenn Porter.)

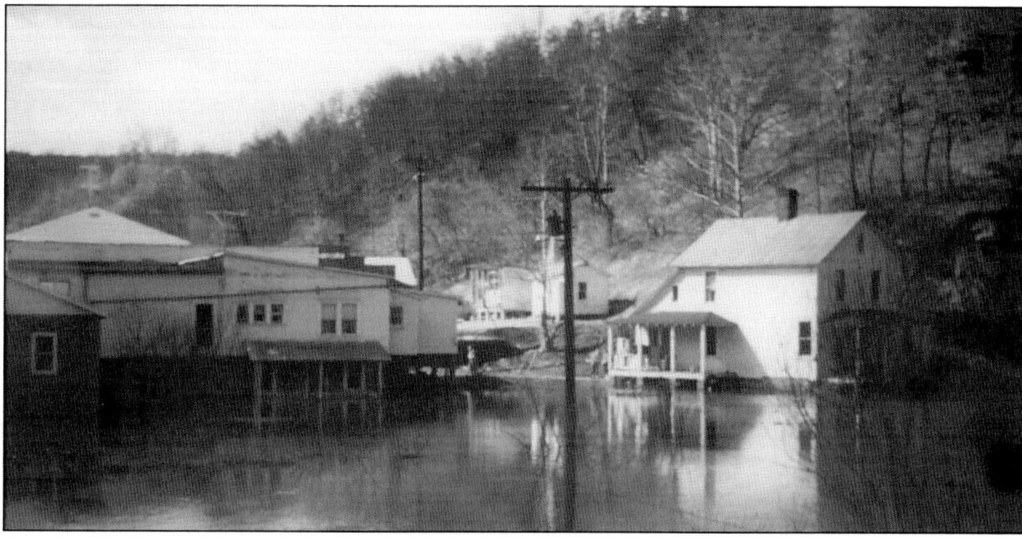

Spring flooding was an annual occurrence along the Guyandotte River. The 44-foot crest at Branchland in 1963 (pictured) was the second-highest on record. Originally called Hadley, the community was renamed after coal developer James Ransom Branch, a banker from Richmond. In addition to mining interests, Colonel Branch also dabbled in Thoroughbred racehorses and financed a succession of theaters. (Elba Davidson collection.)

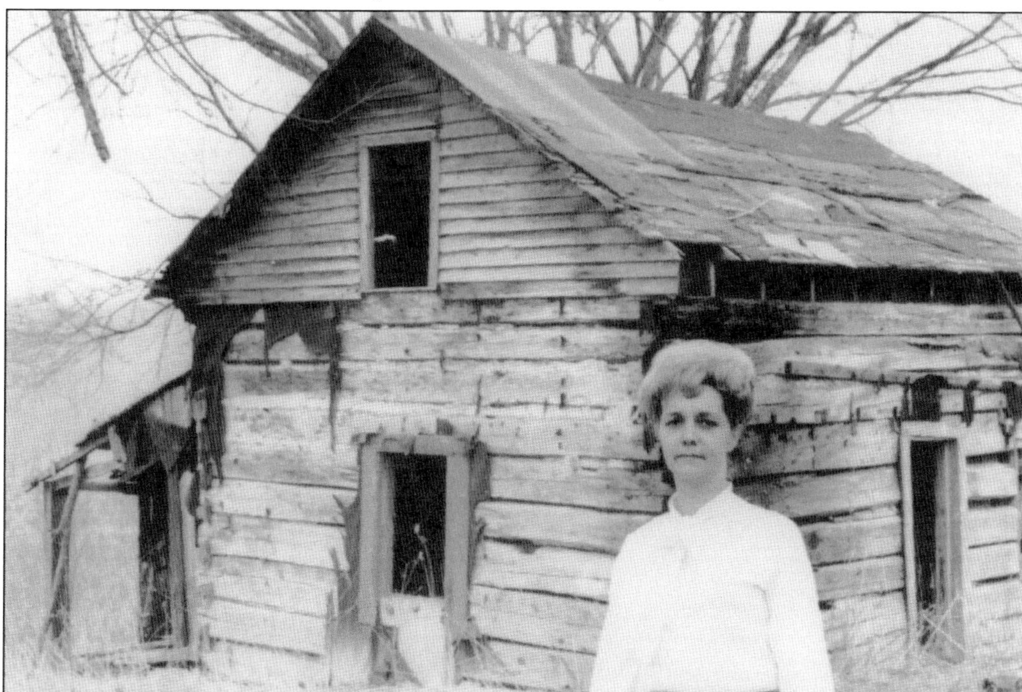

Razed during the early 1970s, the John Chapman house at the mouth of Four Mile Creek in Branchland was once the site of an important ferry crossing. Chapman served in the 34th Battalion Virginia Cavalry, a unit loosely attached to Gen. Albert Gallatin Jenkins's brigade, and fought for the Confederacy at Gettysburg. After the war, Chapman was a Sheridan District justice, and his son was constable. (Elba Davidson collection.)

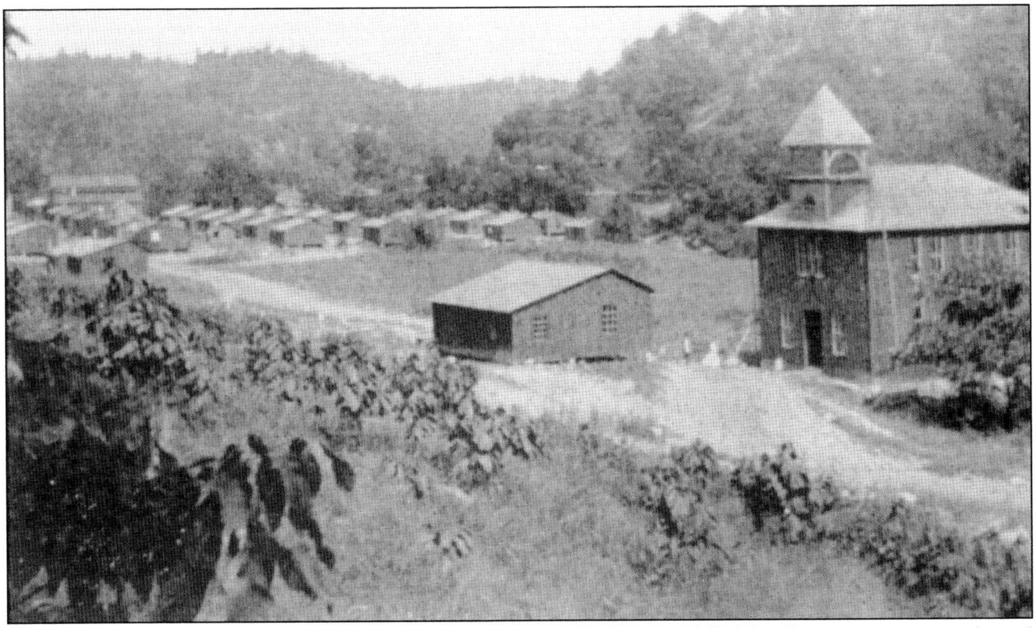

The post office on the west side of the river was called Branchfield, where neat rows of coal company houses (back center) sit behind the school building (front right). Coal was first mined here during the 1880s. During the early 20th century, Branchfield was home to a Republican voting precinct, while Hadley (now Branchland) on the railroad side of the river voted Democratic. (Elba Davidson collection.)

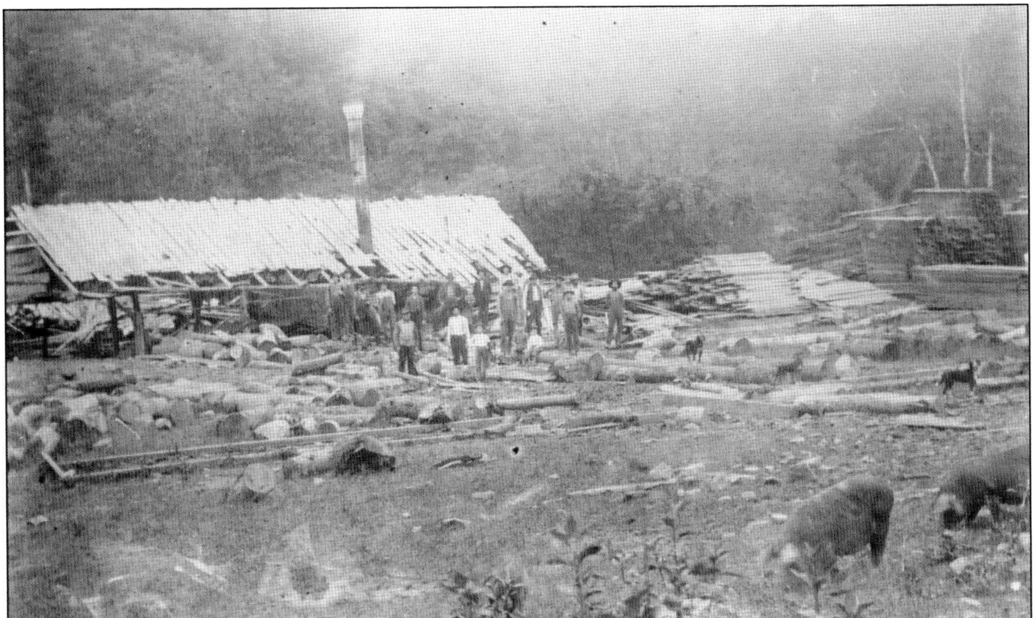

While fossil fuels have been the backbone of Branchland's economy, some timbering and farming have also been done in the area. This is the Greeley Isaacs sawmill on Red River Fork of Four Mile Creek. Tobacco was shipped down the Guyandotte River as early as 1871, when tobacco warehouses were built at West Hamlin for storing that commodity. (MU-Lambert.)

The store of the Branchland Coal Company was built around 1900. Miners were paid in company-issued scrip and purchased everything here, including clothing, food, furniture, tools, and so on. It was the "big-box" retailer of its day. Along with the Chapman House, this building was torn down in the early 1970s when the bridge (back right) over Four Mile Creek on Route 10 was replaced. (Elba Davidson collection.)

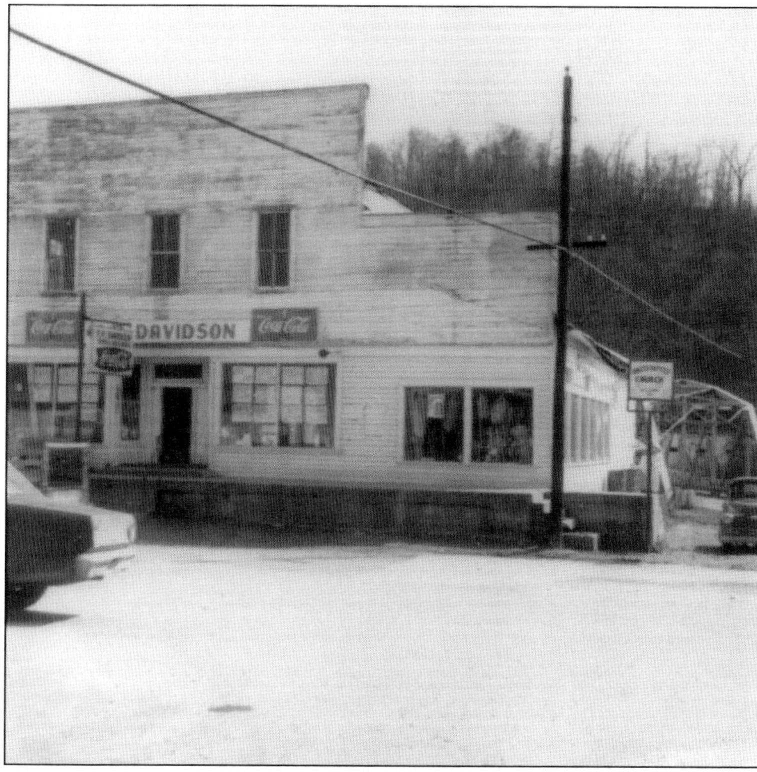

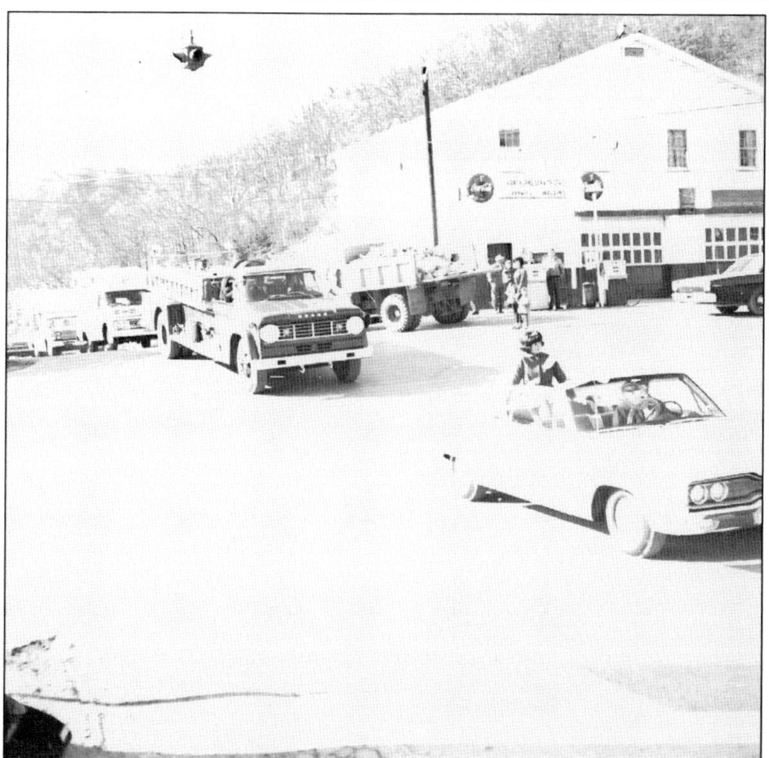

This is a view of the same intersection as above (Route 10 and Four Mile Creek Road), but looking in the opposite direction. The occasion was a Branchland-Midkiff Public Service District parade celebrating the arrival of "city water" in 1964. The infamous flashing caution light (top left) was a favorite target of vandals, who repeatedly shot it out—much to the frustration of state road repair crews. (Photograph by Gene Brewer, courtesy of Lucian Isaacs.)

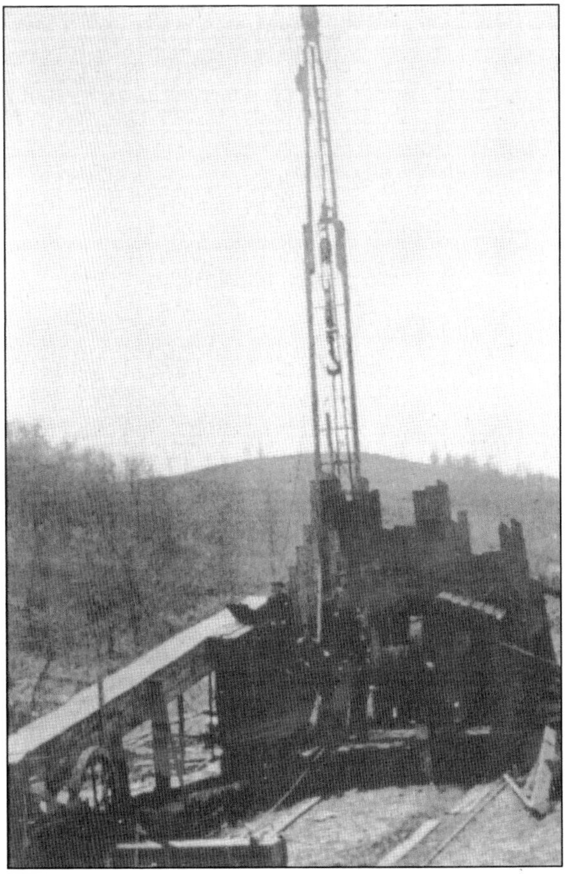

Shown is a natural gas well drilling rig. Over 4,000 gas wells have been drilled in Lincoln County since 1861. The Columbia Gas and Electric Company, doing business locally as United Fuel Gas Co. (UFG), was organized in 1906 to take advantage of rich deposits of high-Btu gas found underground in the "Big Injun" sandstone formation. Many roustabout jobs were also associated with the maintenance of wells and pipelines. (AC.)

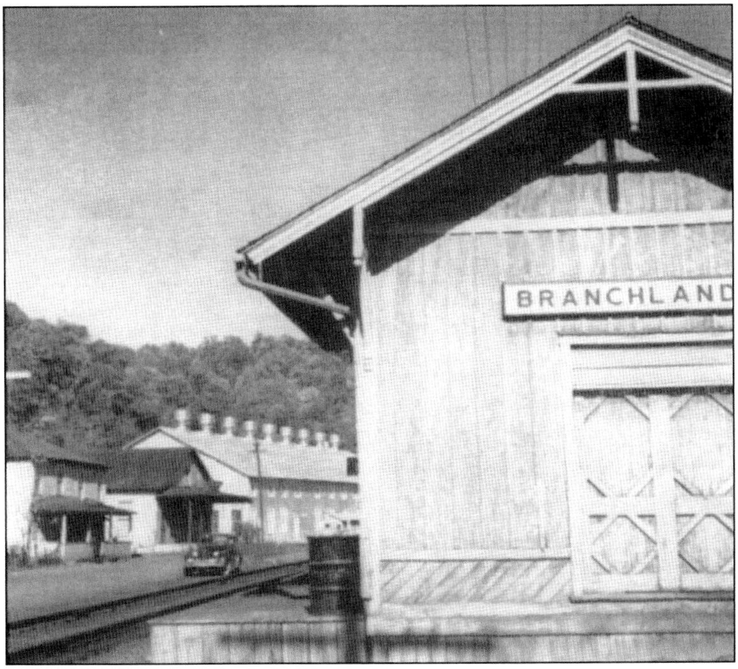

Pictured is the C&O Railroad passenger depot at Branchland. A UFG compressor station is in the background. Initially chartered as the Guyandotte Valley Railroad by an act of the West Virginia Legislature in 1868, C&O took over in 1903 when construction actually began on the line in Lincoln County. C&O became Chessie System in 1972 and CSX Transportation in 1989. (AC.)

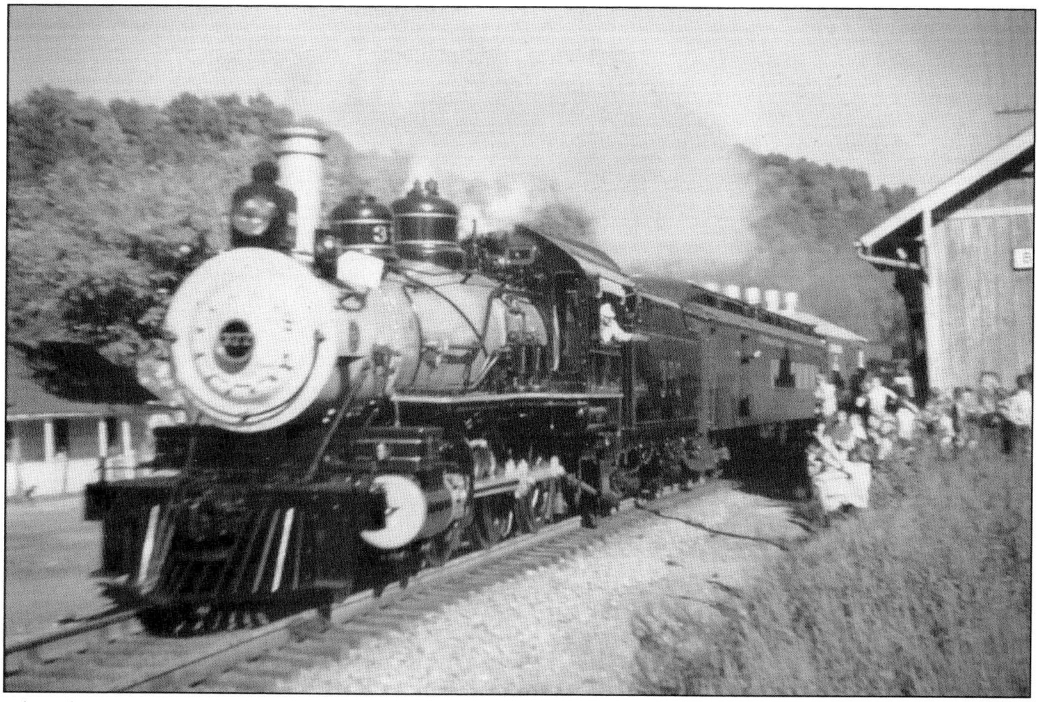

The plaintive wail of a steam locomotive, heard throughout the valley, announced the arrival of a train at one of the Guyandotte Valley's C&O Railroad stations. Shown here is the West Virginia Centennial Train at Branchland in 1963, one of the last steam engine passenger trains to pass through the county. By the 1970s, diesel had completely replaced steam, and passengers were traveling almost exclusively by automobile. (Elba Davidson collection.)

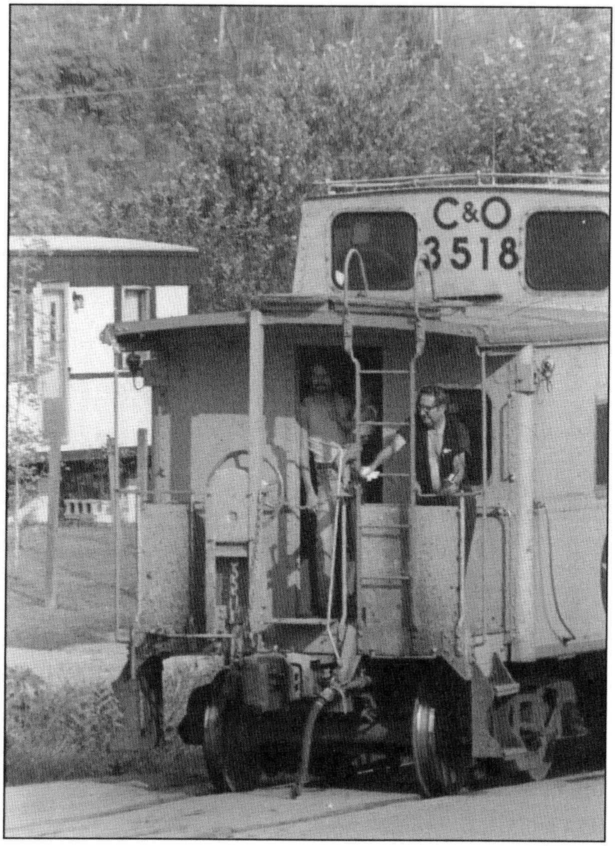

Generations of Lincoln County children would flock trackside to wave at the man in the caboose. He almost always waved back. Alas, the friendly caboose has gone the way of the steam engine. A flashing light affixed to the last car on the train is a poor substitute. (AC.)

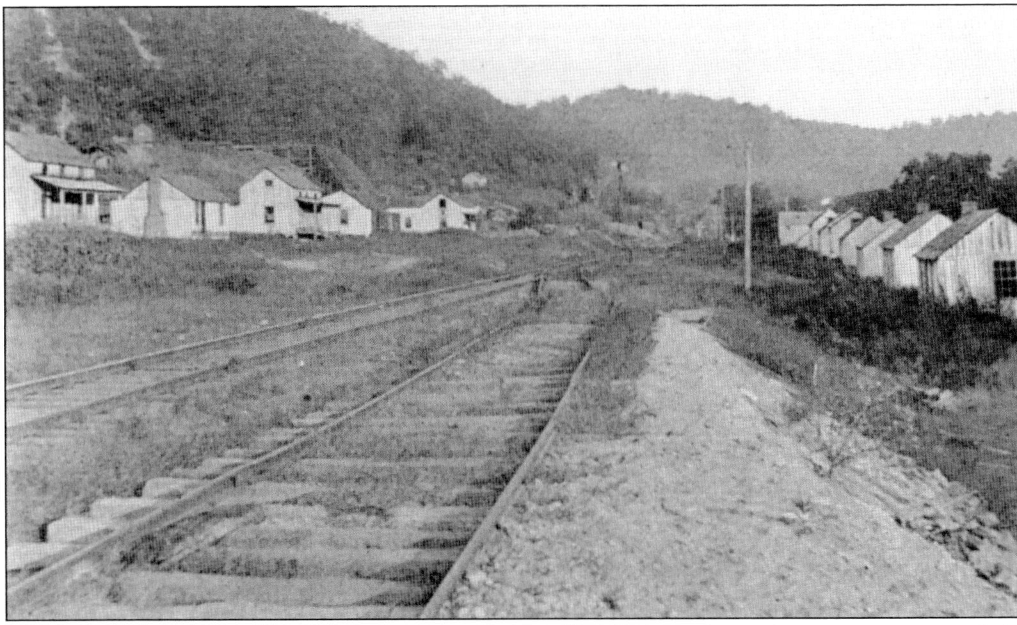

South of Branchland was the mining community of Rochester. Once thriving, it now qualifies as a legitimate ghost town. Developed by J.X. Hill (who would later meet his fate at Eden Park), the Rochester mines produced 10,000 tons of coal in 1904. The line of company homes on the right was called "Pumpkin Row." Rochester was largely abandoned after the mines petered out. (Elba Davidson collection.)

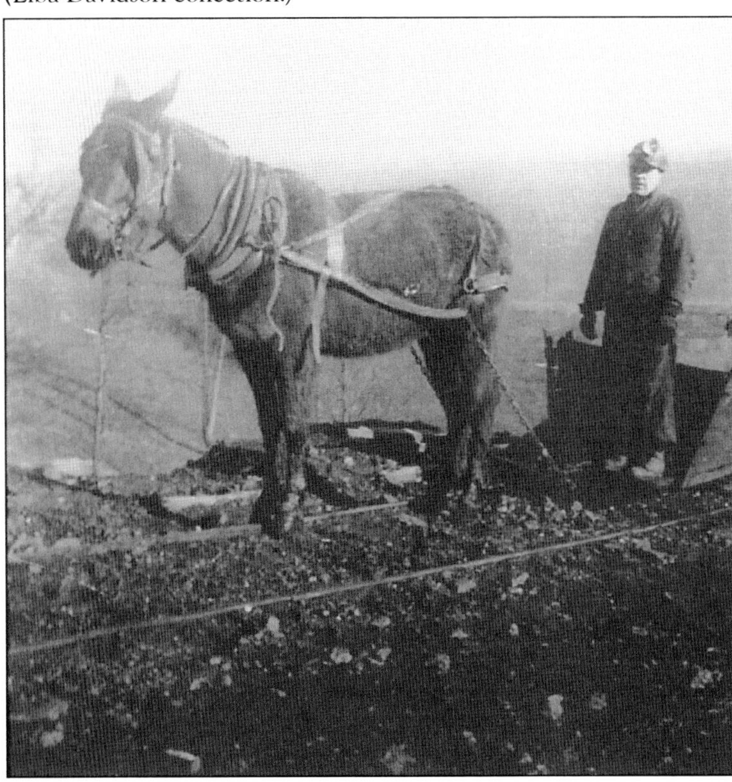

Miner Hal Pritchard and his mule Jess are shown with the tools of their trade at a Branchland mine. Their work was highly hazardous. Working underground, with only a carbide lamp for illumination, miners like Pritchard dug coal out of the ground with a pick and shovel. The coal was then loaded onto carts, which were pulled to the river or railroad for loading. (Courtesy of Imogene and Kathleen Pritchard.)

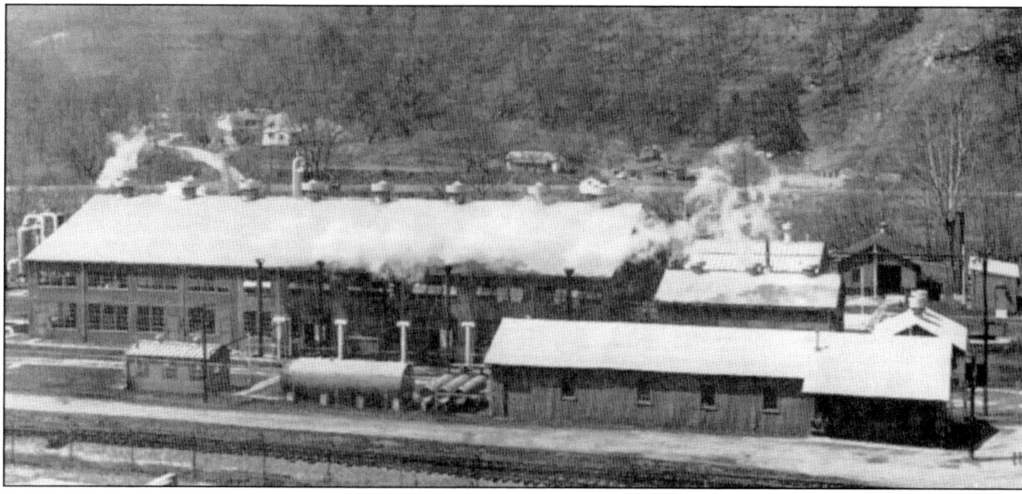

Built in 1915, the compressor station at Hubball is still in operation today. (So is another one at Nye, on Trace Fork of Mud River, near the Putnam county line.) Across the river are the right-of-way for a major transmission pipeline (back right) and Camp Branch Road (back left). Hubball was originally called "Brown City" but was renamed after Mary Lillian Hubball, wife of Colonel Branch. (AC.)

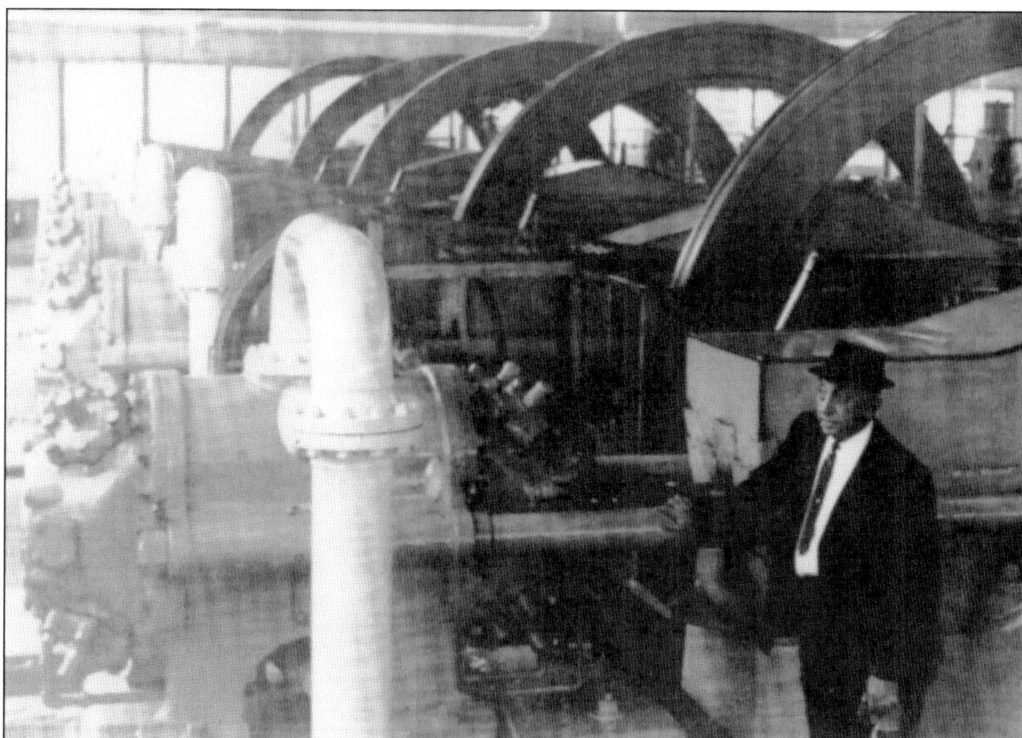

By 1955, UFG employed over 200 Lincoln County residents, and its compressor station at Hubball, near the mouth of Six Mile Creek, was capable of pumping 43 million cubic feet of gas a day. Such facilities were needed to pressurize gas in the pipelines so it could be easily transported to large East Coast markets, such as Baltimore and Washington, DC. A gasoline plant was also located here. (AC.)

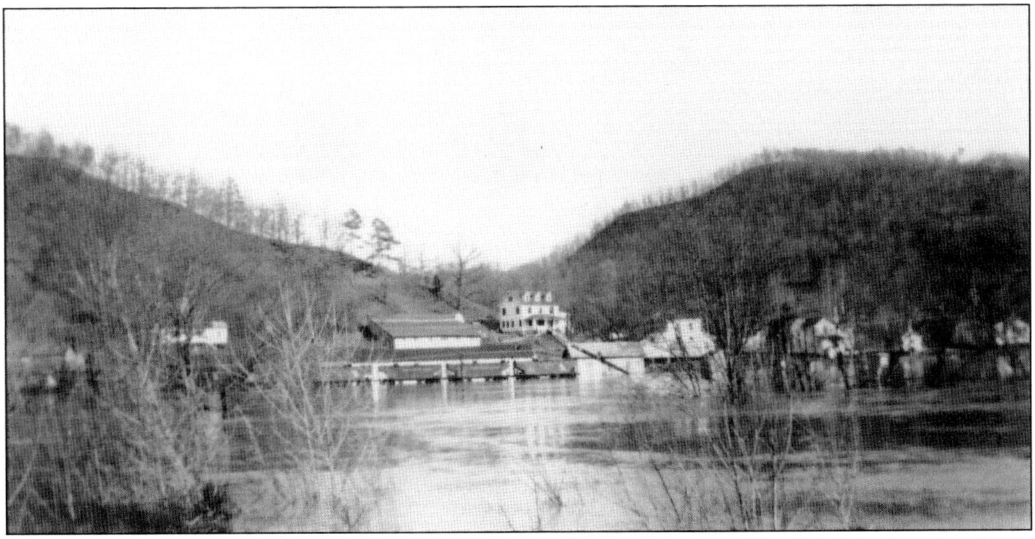

Midkiff, at the mouth of Nine Mile Creek, was the southern terminus of the C&O Railroad in 1903. Spurlock's General Store was a fixture here for many years and a focal point for the community. Spurlock's warehouse and family home are also visible in this photograph, taken during a flood in 1955. Midkiff also once had a movie house, the Guyan Theater. (Courtesy of Howard Elkins Jr.)

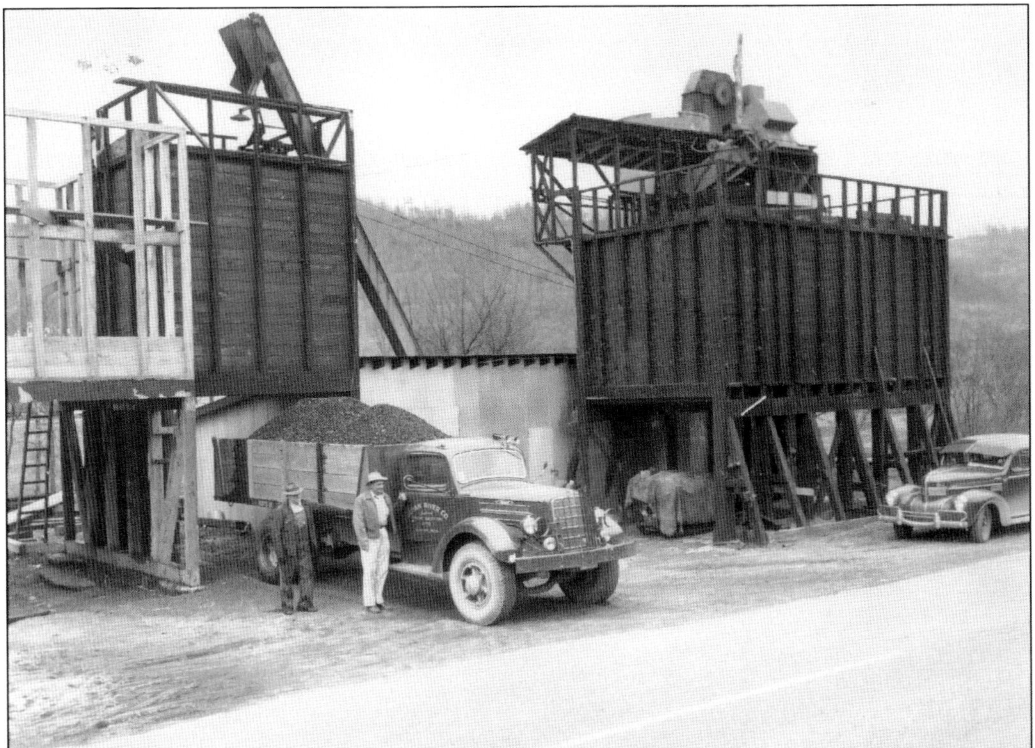

Midkiff also supported some industrial ventures, as indicated by this Guyan River Company plant beside Route 10. This business, established by Howard Elkins in 1946, recovered "supreme quality coal and sand" from the river and trucked it across the region. Furnaces were required to sufficiently dry the sand before shipment. (Courtesy of Howard Elkins Jr.)

Tipples, like this one at Brady, were once staples along the Guyandotte River. Sediment from the river was pumped to the top where a "stick picker" manually removed waste materials. A large vibrating sifter sorted product by size, while a water-fed sluice at the bottom separated fine coal particles from sand. The sand was used in mining and masonry applications. (Courtesy of Howard Elkins Jr.)

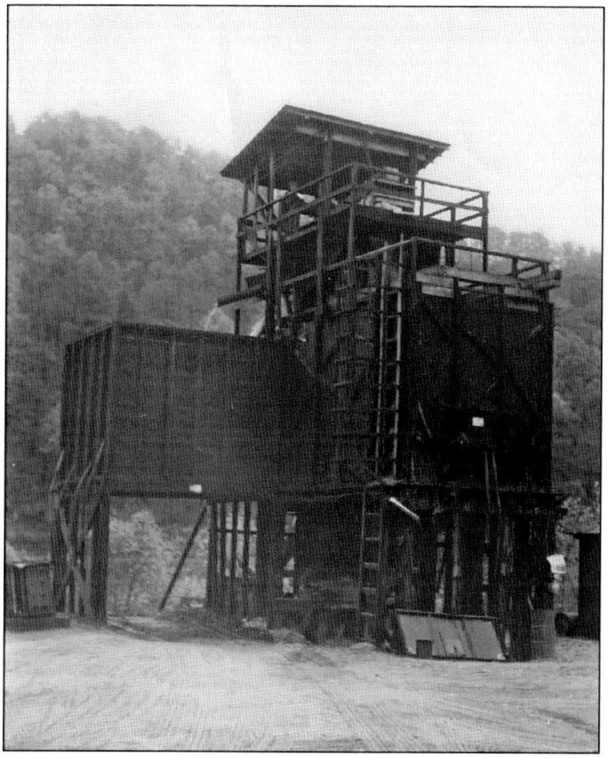

Dredges were tied in an X to trees on the riverbank. An agitator lowered to the river bottom stirred up sediment, which was then pumped back to the tipple. Pumps were powered by either gasoline or natural gas. Such operations took advantage of plentiful amounts of coal waste, which washed into the river from large-scale production mines upstream in Logan County. (Courtesy of Howard Elkins Jr.)

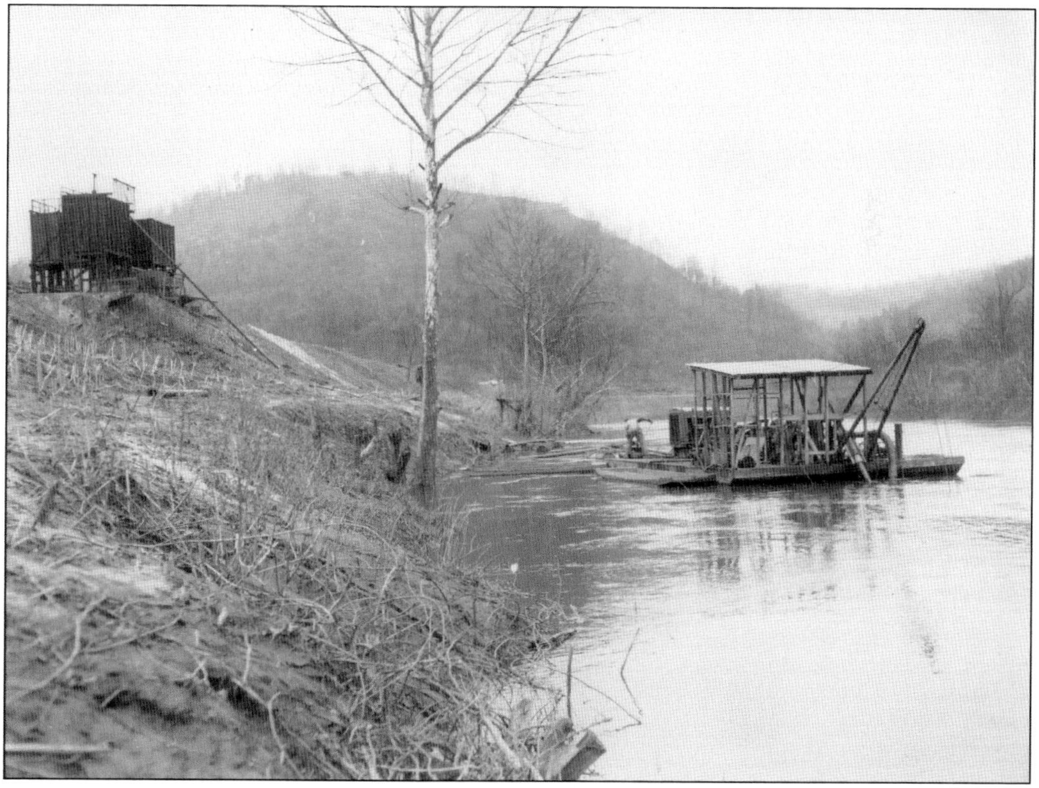

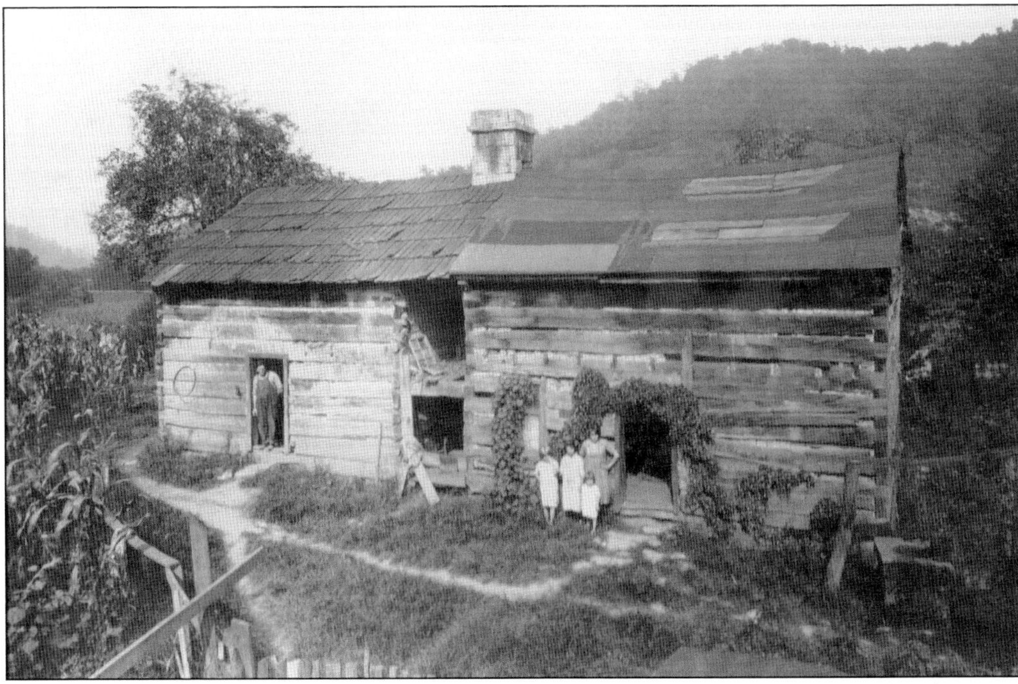

Brady was a whistle-stop community along the C&O Railroad between Midkiff and Ranger. Today, signs along Route 10 mark its general location. This is the McComas family home at Brady, photographed on September 17, 1926. (MU-Lambert.)

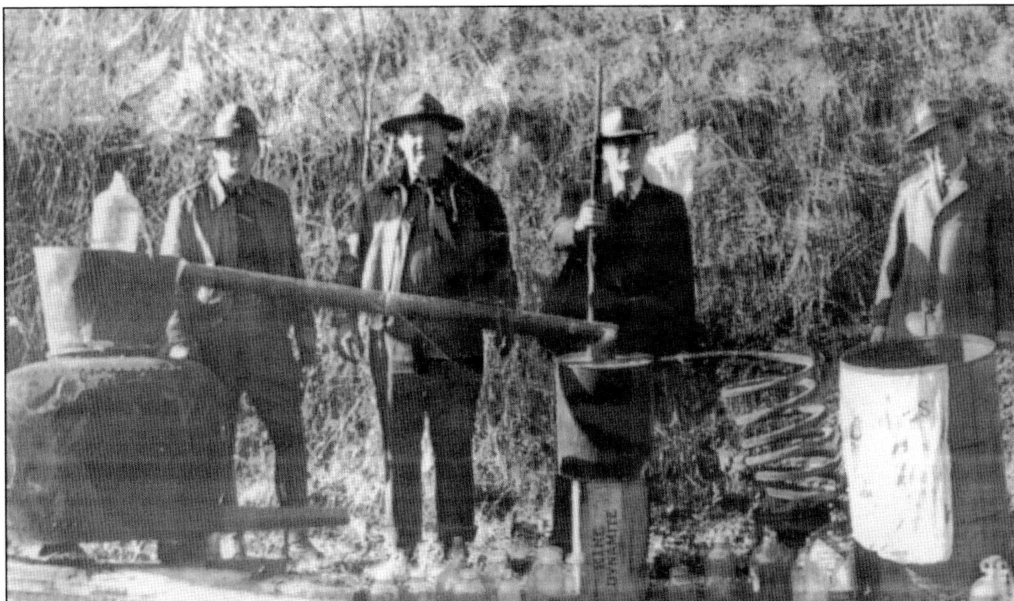

Proving that there might be a little truth in the moonshining hillbilly stereotype, authorities break up a distillation apparatus on Ranger Ridge in 1943. From left to right are Trooper Carl Nutt, Cpl. Dallas Wilfong, Dep. Jim Toppings, and prosecuting attorney Huston Smith. Production of illegal spirits is an Appalachian tradition that some maintain goes on to this day in the more remote hills and "hollers." (Courtesy of Harold Ray Smith.)

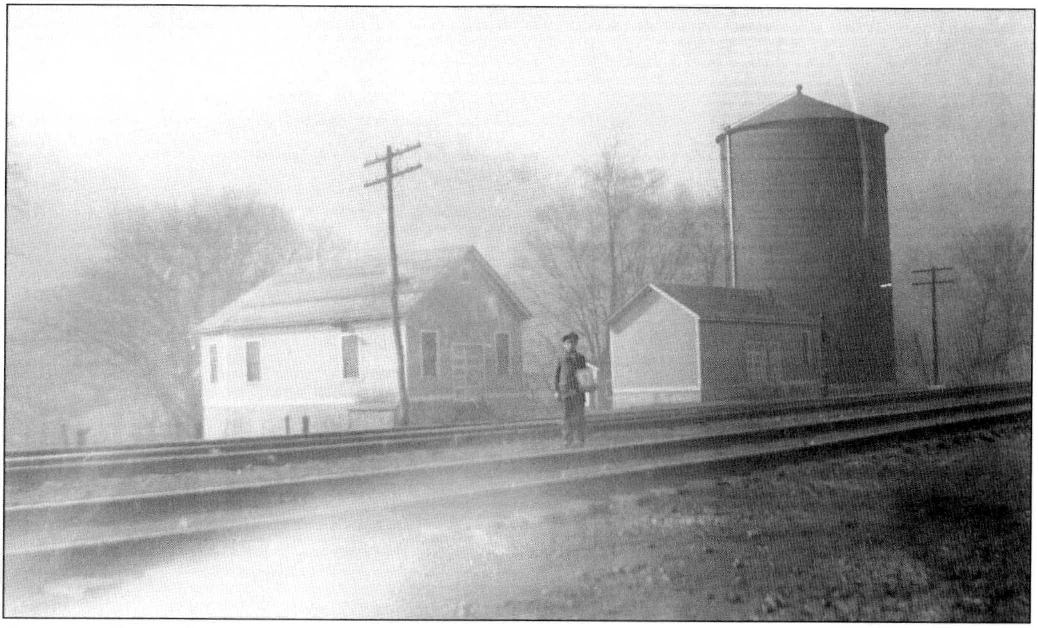

A gristmill was first established on Fourteen Mile Creek by William C. Smith around 1825. Also known as Laurel Hill, a post office called Fourteen was established here in 1877. The C&O Railroad paid the Smith family $700 for the purchase of land to be used for a right-of-way, where passenger and freight depots, a water tower, and switching yard were constructed. The depot was called Fourteen Station. (Courtesy of Harold Ray Smith.)

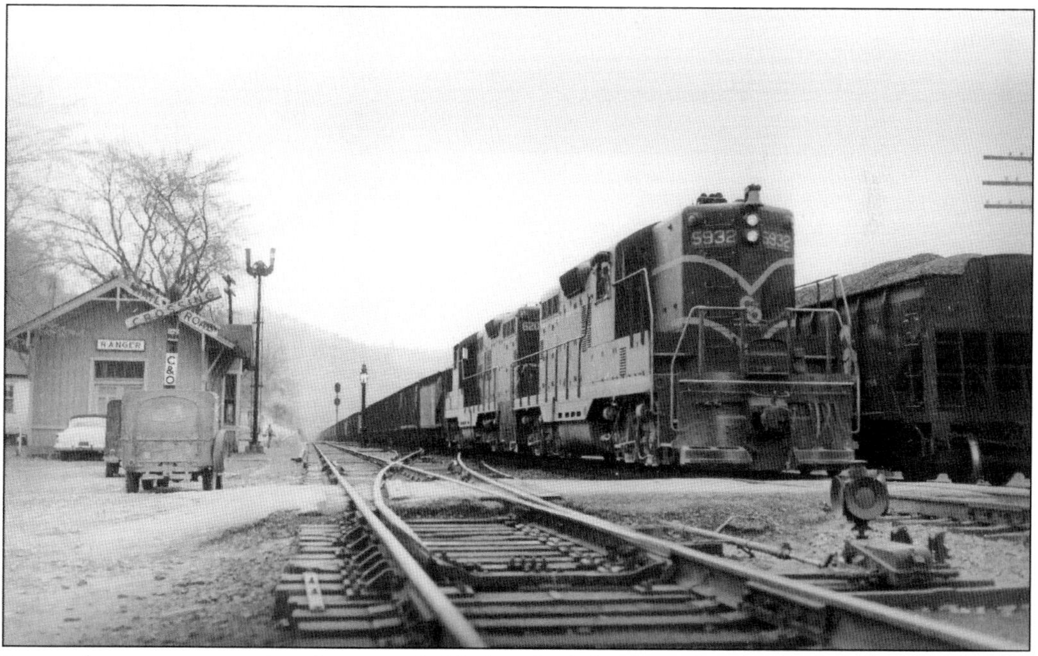

Ranger became a true railroad town in 1904 after the C&O line was extended south from Midkiff. Local businessman Theodore B. Hatfield purchased a railroad lot and relocated his store and post office to Fourteen Station. Hatfield's post office was called Ranger, named after the family dog. (Courtesy of Harold Ray Smith.)

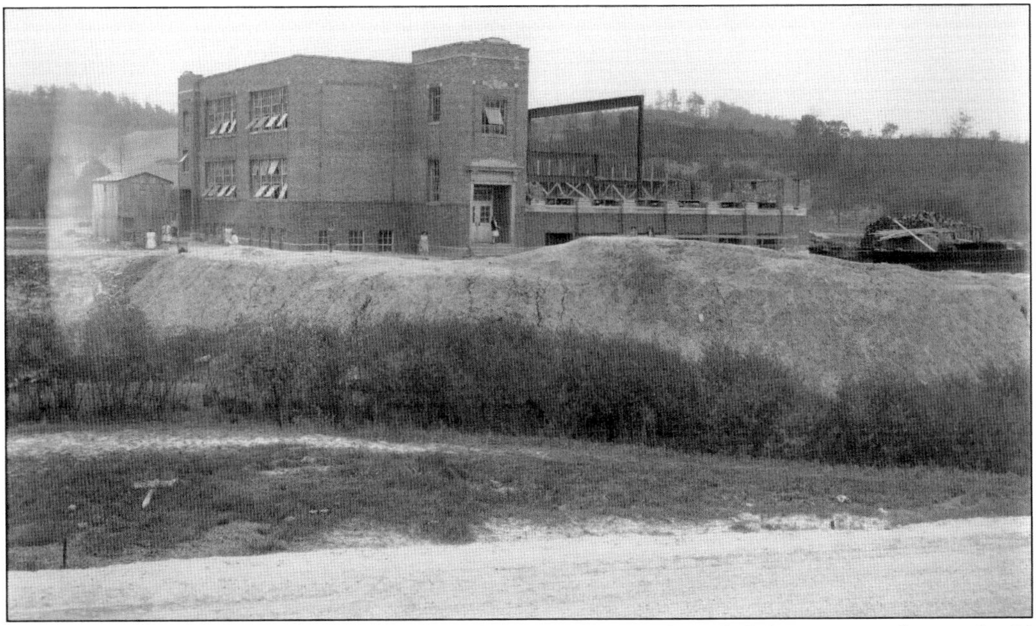

Five elections were held in Sheridan District between 1920 and 1925, defeating a tax levy to build a new high school along Guyandotte River. Undeterred, residents petitioned the state legislature, where a bill was passed authorizing the construction of Guyan Valley High School (GVHS). The new school building at Pleasant View, selected for its location near the center of the district, was opened on September 5, 1927. (MU-Lambert.)

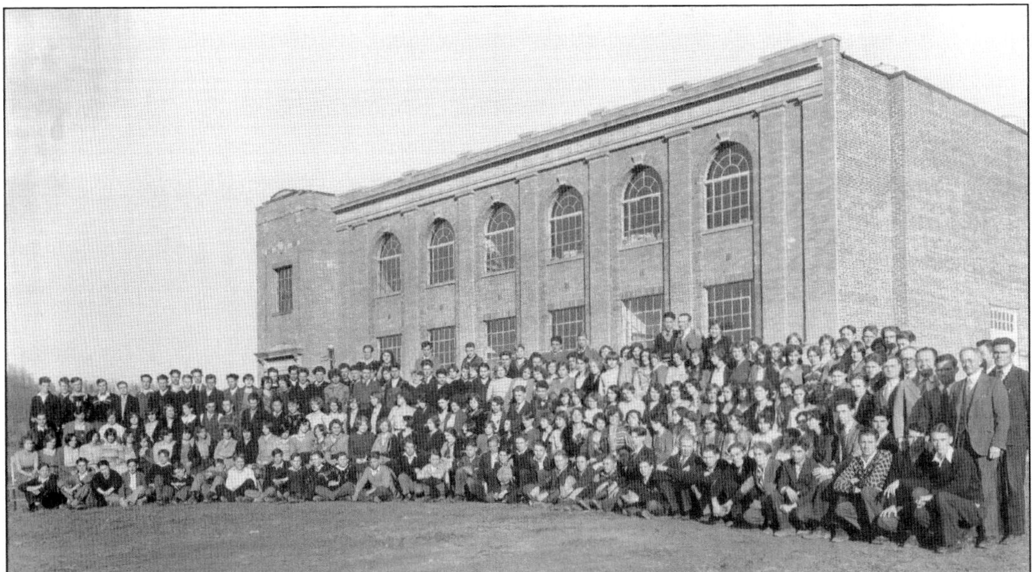

This image was made a year after Guyan Valley's first class graduated in May 1929. Those first eight graduates were Shirley Adkins, Gilmer Odell McClellan, Rhoda Messinger, Jennings O. Midkiff, Ray Midkiff, Dennis Roy, Glenna Roy, and Maude Triplett. J.O. Midkiff would go on to serve as GVHS principal. Wings were later added to the building, and further remodeling in 1979 and 1980 added a junior high and eliminated the old auditorium. The building functions today as a middle school. (MU-Lambert.)

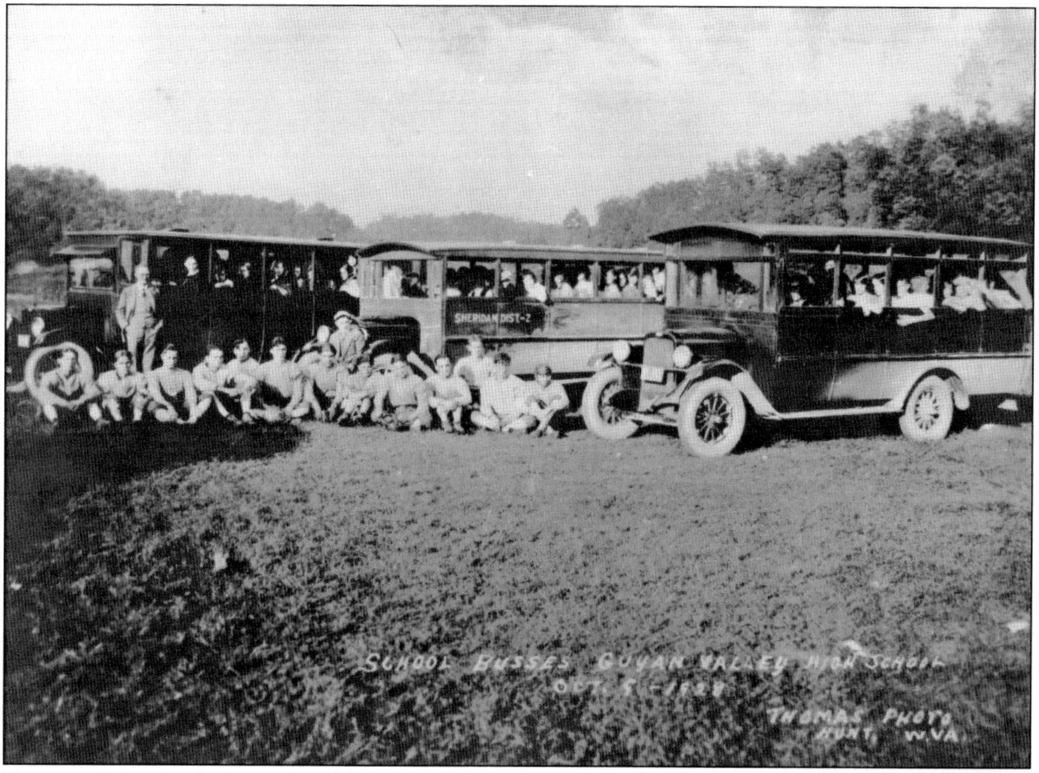

Frustrated by the failing school levies, ordinary citizens made the unprecedented move of purchasing a $2,500 school bus to send students to Carroll District High School in Hamlin. When Guyan Valley High School finally opened, more buses were acquired to transport students from Sheridan, Laurel Hill, and Harts Creek Districts in Lincoln County, as well as from McComas District in Cabell County. (MU-Lambert.)

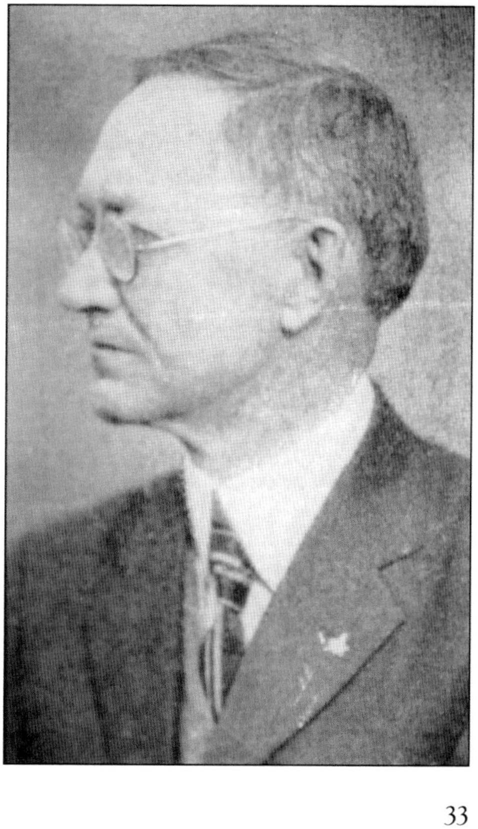

Fred Lambert, who called Guyan Valley the "finest and most outstanding rural high school ever erected in West Virginia," was its first principal. He was also principal at Carroll High School, where he published *The Llorrac* (*Carroll* backwards), an early definitive history of Lincoln County. Upon his passing in 1967, Lambert's entire collection was donated to Marshall University. All modern local historians are indebted to his work. (MU-Lambert.)

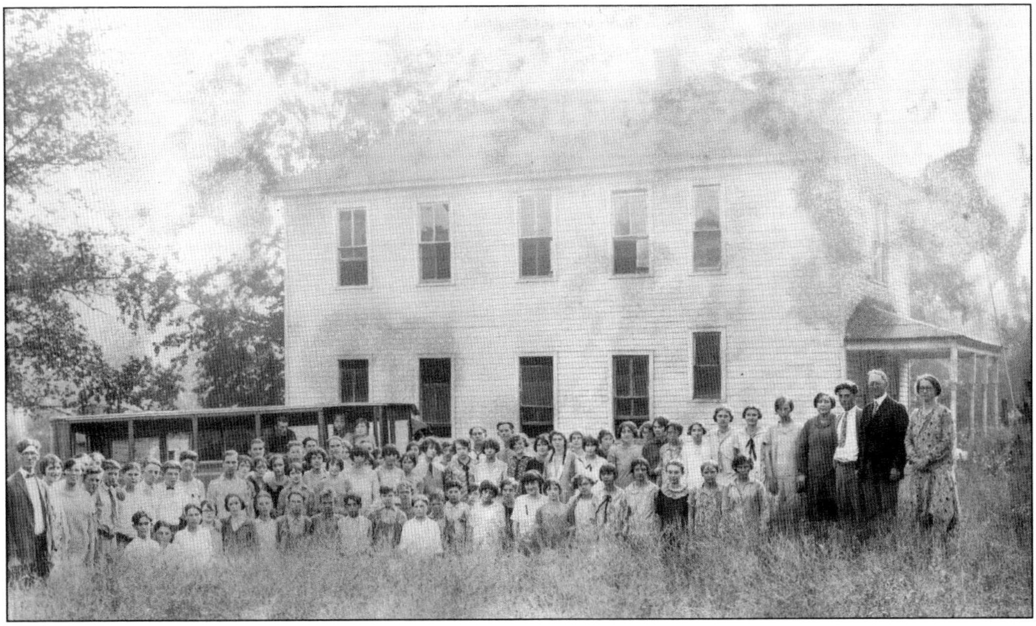

Classes for the Guyan Valley school term of fall 1926 to spring 1927 were held in the Branchfield Grade School, where students pose with Sheridan school bus No. 1. Enrollment increased even further when the school on the east side of the river at Hadley (now Branchland) was closed. The top story of this frame structure was removed, and it was eventually replaced by a new brick building in 1949. (MU-Lambert.)

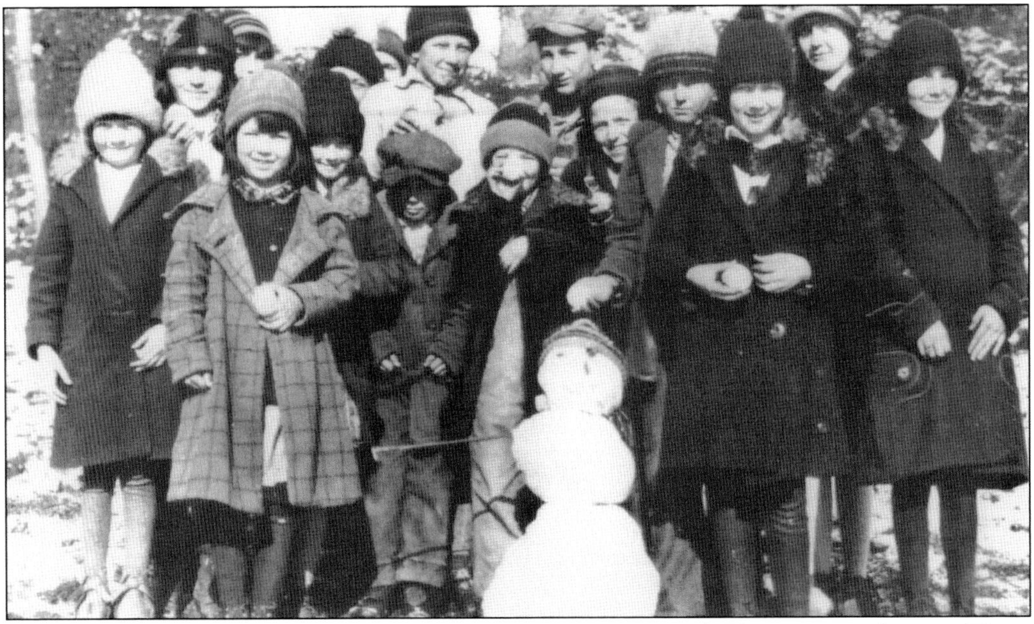

Students (and their snowman) pose for the camera at Betty's Branch Elementary in Ranger. There were once nearly 40 schools in the Guyandotte Valley's Sheridan and Laurel Hill Districts. A sampling of these includes Bear Creek, Beech Grove, Burger, Childers, Coleman, Cuzzie, Hamilton, Hubball, Isaacs, Lick Fork, Messinger, Midkiff, Orchard Branch, Pine Grove, Pleasant View, Sias on Sulphur Fork, and Vernatter (Furnetts) Creek. (Courtesy of Harold Ray Smith.)

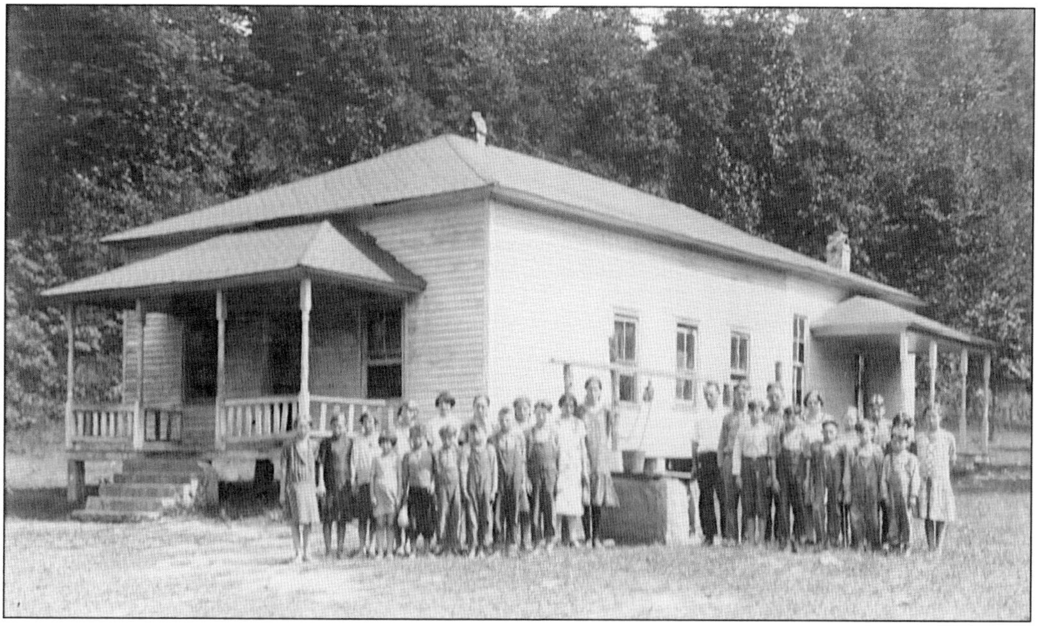

With 62 students during the 1948–1949 academic year, Dial School was the largest of several grade schools once located along Four Mile Creek. Others were at Harless Fork (23 students), Kentuck Fork (19), Red River (53), and Trace Fork (21). With an enrollment of 296, West Hamlin Elementary was then the largest school in the county, according to a census conducted by local historian Harold Ray Smith. (MU-Lambert.)

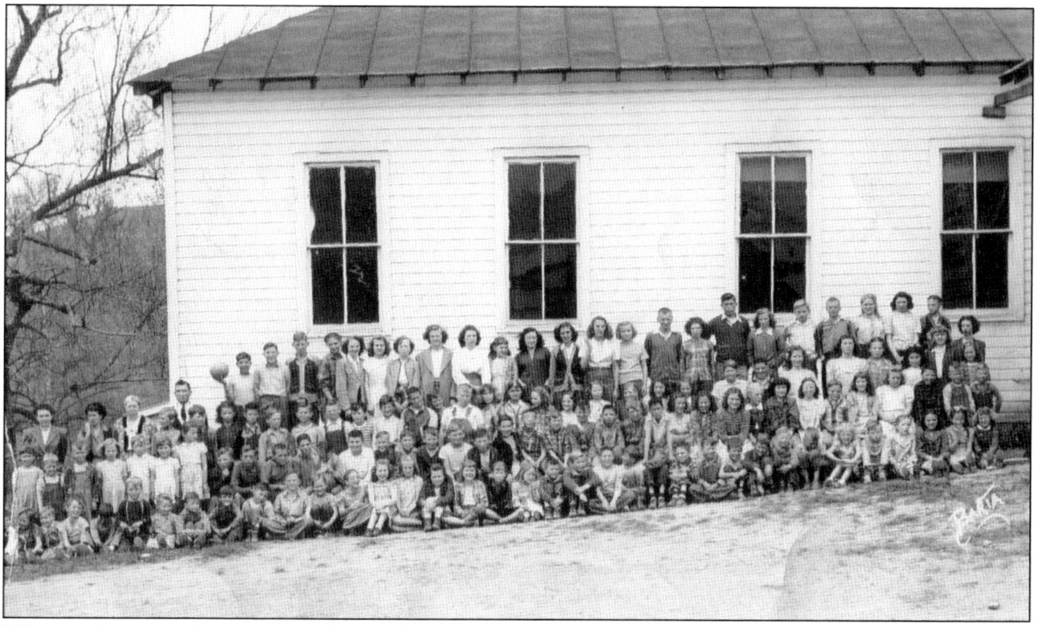

This is the school on Two Mile Creek, so named because its mouth at Sheridan Station is two miles above the falls of the Guyandotte. Other "mile" creeks include One Mile, Four Mile, Six Mile, Nine Mile, Ten Mile, and Fourteen Mile with outlets at Pleasant View, Branchland, Hubball, Midkiff, Brady, and Ranger, respectively. Dozens of one-room schoolhouses once lined these tributaries. (Courtesy of Lucian Isaacs.)

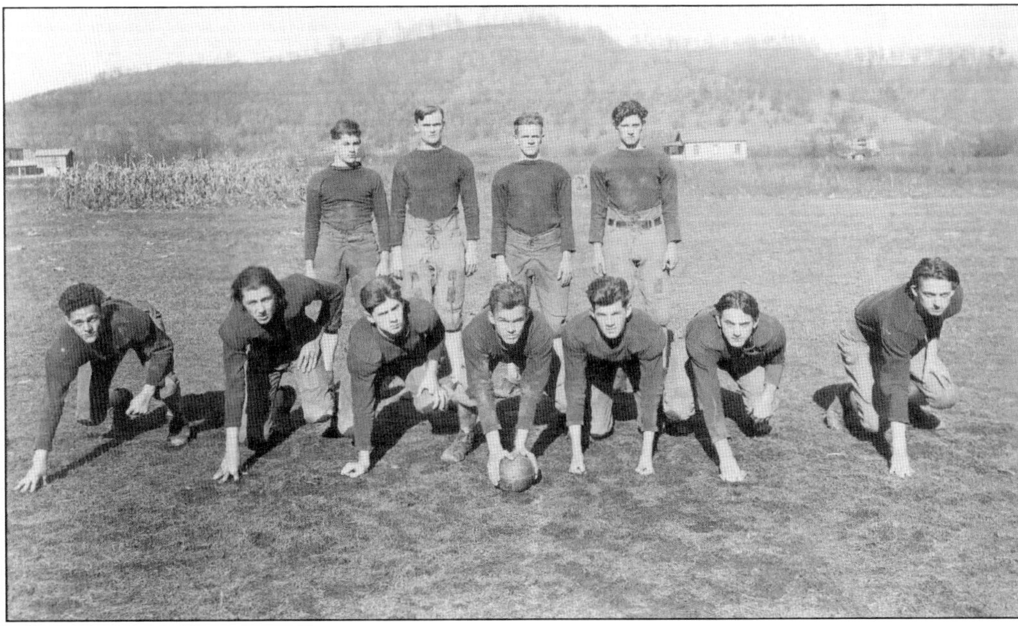

"Hit 'em high, / Hit 'em low, / Go! Guyan Valley! Go!" was the official school cheer for the Guyan Valley High football team. Pictured is the 1930 squad; the first team was fielded in the fall of 1928. The boys in blue and gold were nicknamed Wildcats, a name possibly derived from the famed Logan County Confederate fighting unit. County rivals derisively called them "River Rats." (MU-Lambert.)

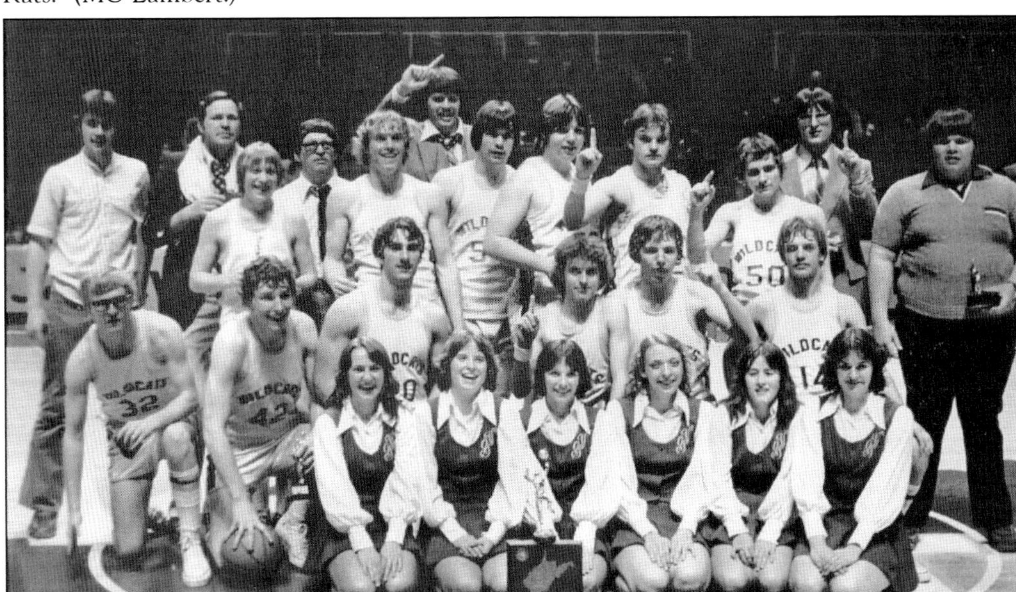

Guyan Valley won its only high school state championship in any sport when the Wildcats defeated heavily favored Morgantown St. Francis by one point in the 1979 West Virginia Class A basketball title game. Trailing by 14 points late in the game, GVHS capped an improbable comeback on a basket by Justin Huffman (kneeling, with ball in hand) with only three seconds remaining. (AC.)

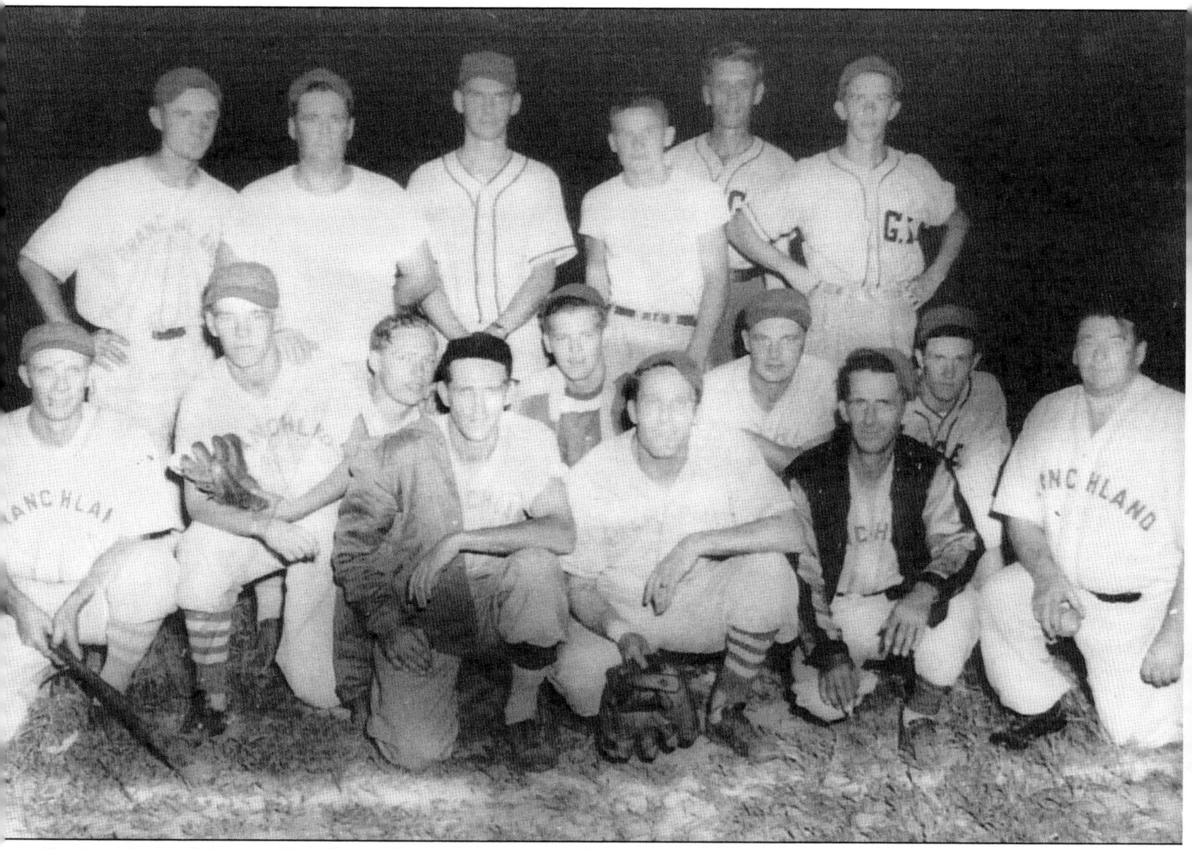

Barber Verlin "Scrump" Adkins (far right) managed the Branchland Bombers independent league baseball team. His advertisement in a 1939 edition of the *Watchman*, a Branchland newspaper, reads: "The whiskers grown and look a sight, / The missus says: 'You look a fright; / And you can't kiss these lips of mine / With whiskers like a porcupine.' / Smooth faces make happy homes. / Come in to-day." Adequate local ball fields were lacking during the 1930s and 1940s, which sometimes forced teams to jump county lines to play "home" games at Salt Rock. Before other facilities were eventually constructed (at the Covey farm or the often flooded "Hole" at West Hamlin), games were often played at Guyan Valley High School's Sheridan Field. A makeshift baseball diamond with lights, it could be difficult for visiting opponents to find since the similarly named Sheridan Post Office was at Falls Creek curve on Route 10, and Sheridan Station was on the railroad side of the river near the mouth of Two Mile Creek. This rare night photograph of the Bombers was taken at Sheridan Field. (Elba Davidson collection.)

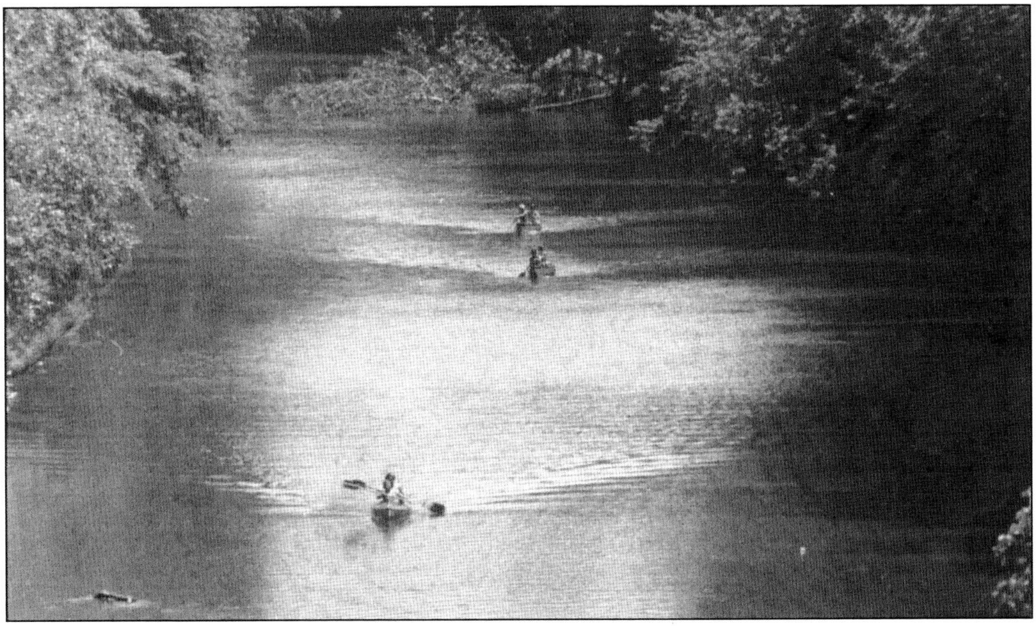

The Greater Guyan branch of the US Junior Chamber, or Jaycees, sponsored river regatta races. Participants started at Branchland and raced six miles downriver to the West Hamlin Bridge. Racers were entered in categories such as one-man kayak, two-man canoe, or johnboat. All boats were oar-powered. (Elba Davidson collection.)

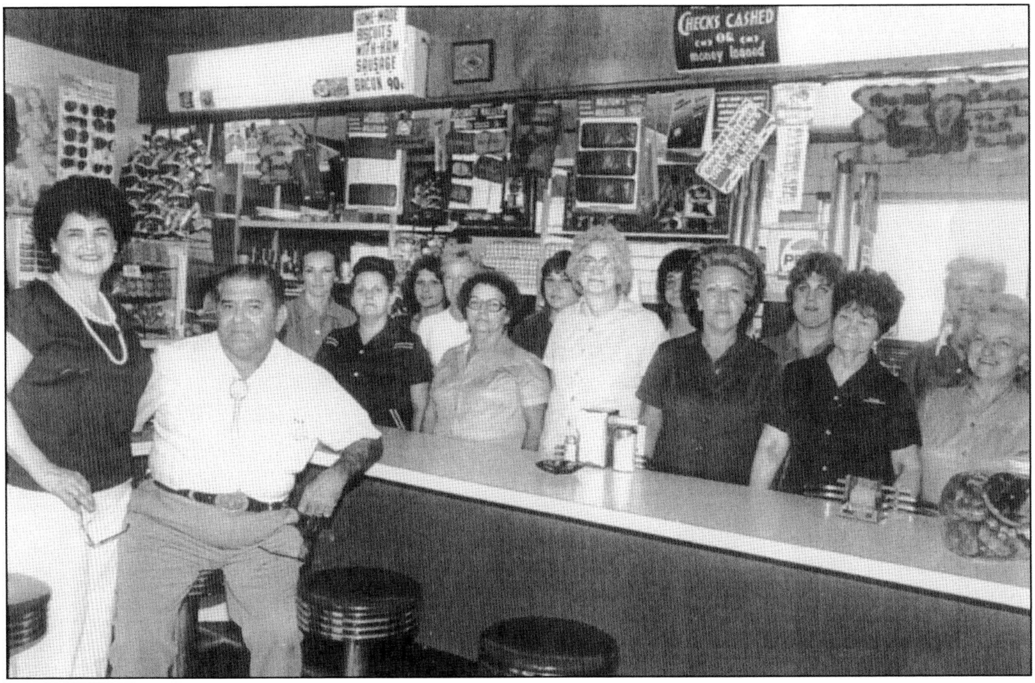

Proprietors Pearl and Louis Abraham (left) are pictured with their staff around 1965 at Annette's Drive Inn. Before the onslaught of modern fast-food restaurants, Annette's was perhaps the most popular place along Route 10 between Huntington and Logan to grab a hot meal. It was known for good food and friendly service. (Courtesy of Debbie Vance.)

Film actor Paul Newman (right) visited the James Cummings farm near Ranger in 1966 while researching for the title role of Lucas Jackson in the motion picture *Cool Hand Luke*. One local resident is said to have asked, "Nice to meet you, Mr. Newman. What do you do for a living?" (Courtesy of Angie Cummings Urling.)

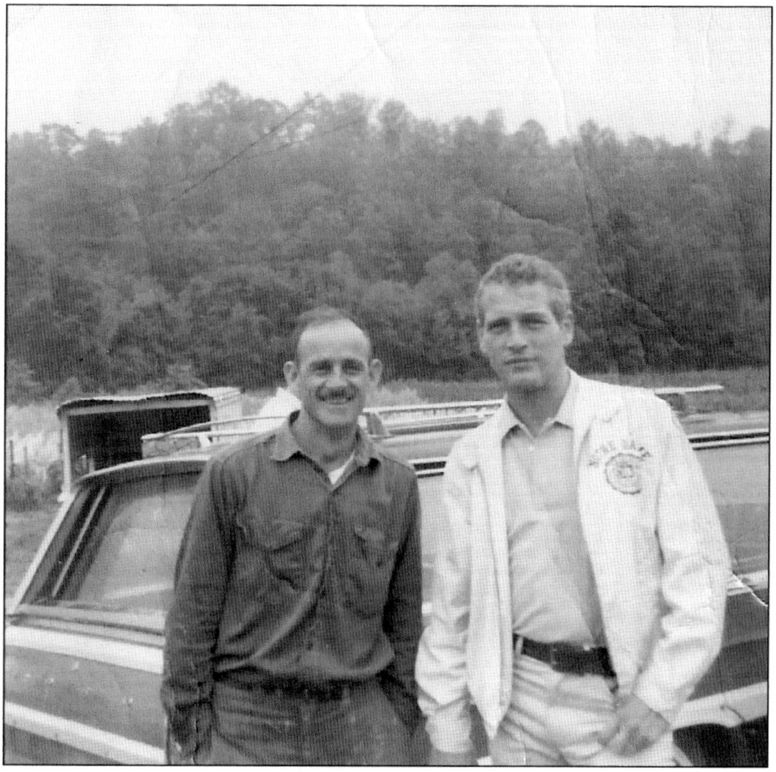

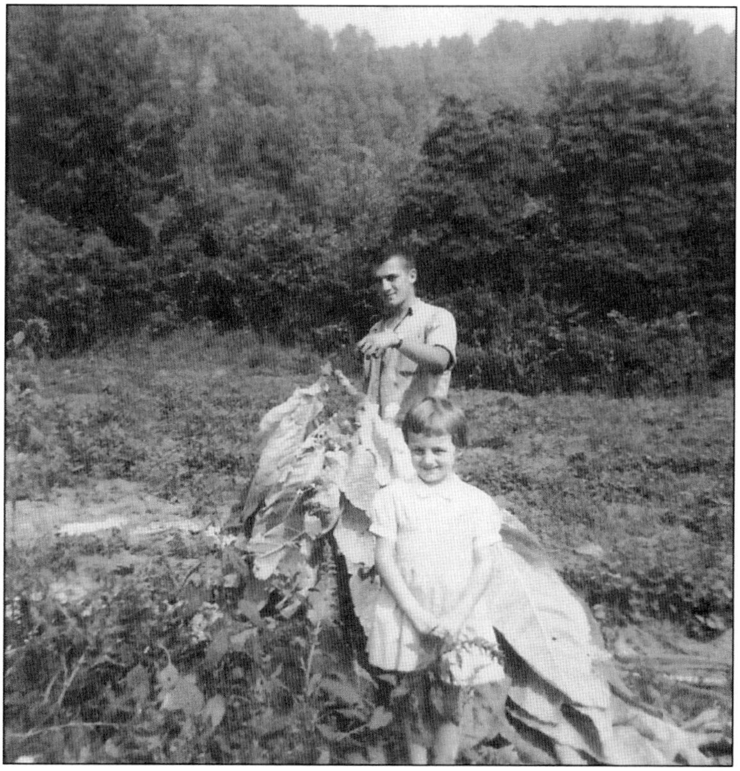

A family operation, the Cummings farm was acknowledged far and wide as the best place along the Guyandotte River to purchase strawberries. Working the fields are eldest son Jimmy Cummings and his little sister Pam. The Cummings family also operated a sawmill. This farm has been recognized with a Parks and Development quilt square. (Courtesy of Angie Cummings Urling.)

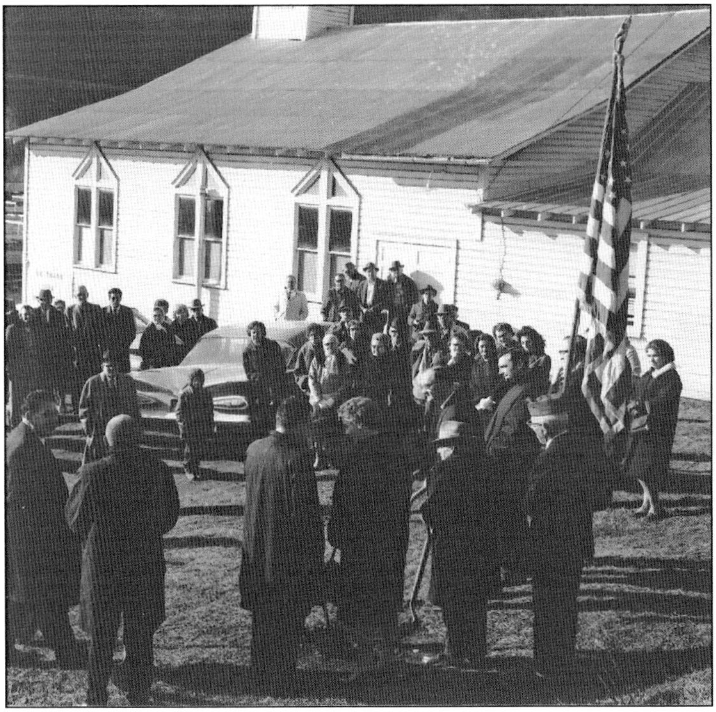

Dignitaries from the Farmers Home Administration, including future West Virginia secretary of state and treasurer A. James Manchin, gathered at Branchland on January 18, 1964, for the groundbreaking ceremony for a new water line running along the Guyandotte River from Branchland to Midkiff. After a parade, closing ceremonies were conducted at the Branchland United Baptist Church. (Photograph by Gene Brewer, courtesy of Lucian Isaacs.)

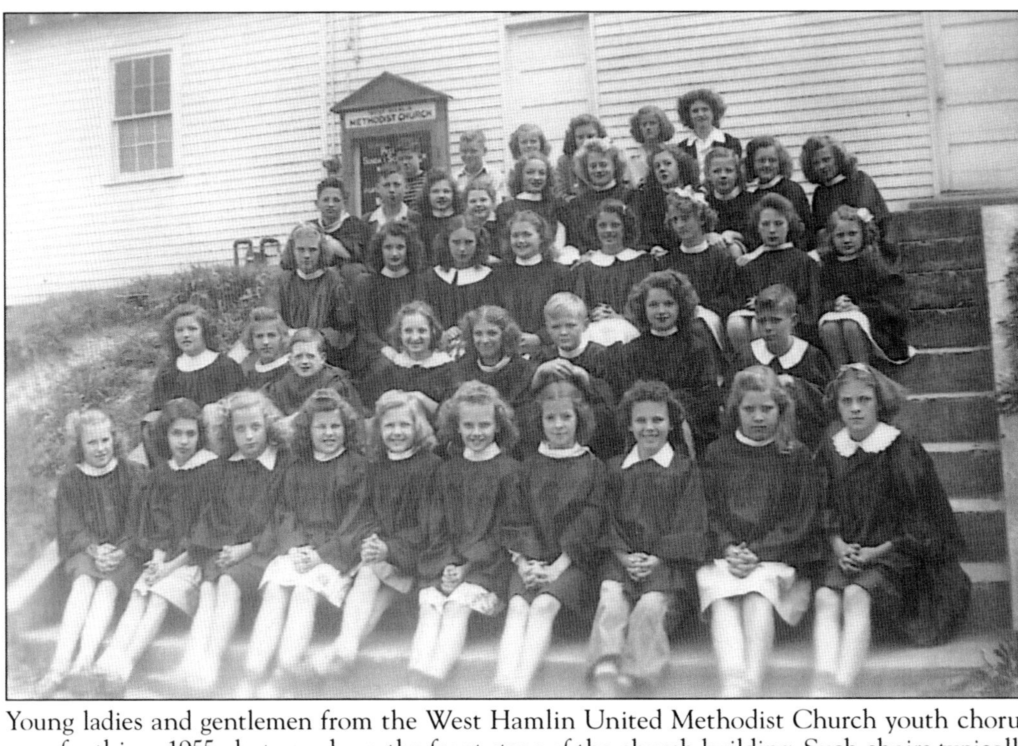

Young ladies and gentlemen from the West Hamlin United Methodist Church youth chorus pose for this c. 1955 photograph on the front steps of the church building. Such choirs typically practiced during the week and sang during Sunday services. (Courtesy of Debbie Pennington.)

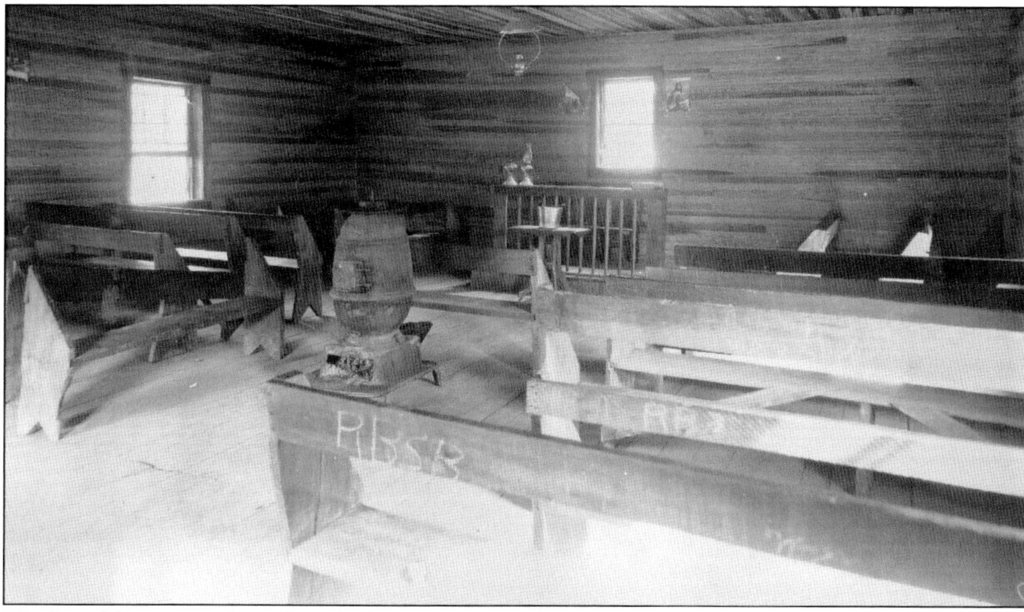

The humble interior furnishings of Four Mile United Baptist Church on Harless Fork of Four Mile Creek are shown here in 1926. Organized in 1850, the famed log church is one of the county's oldest and still holds services today. An annex has been added, but the original log structure remains. (MU-Lambert.)

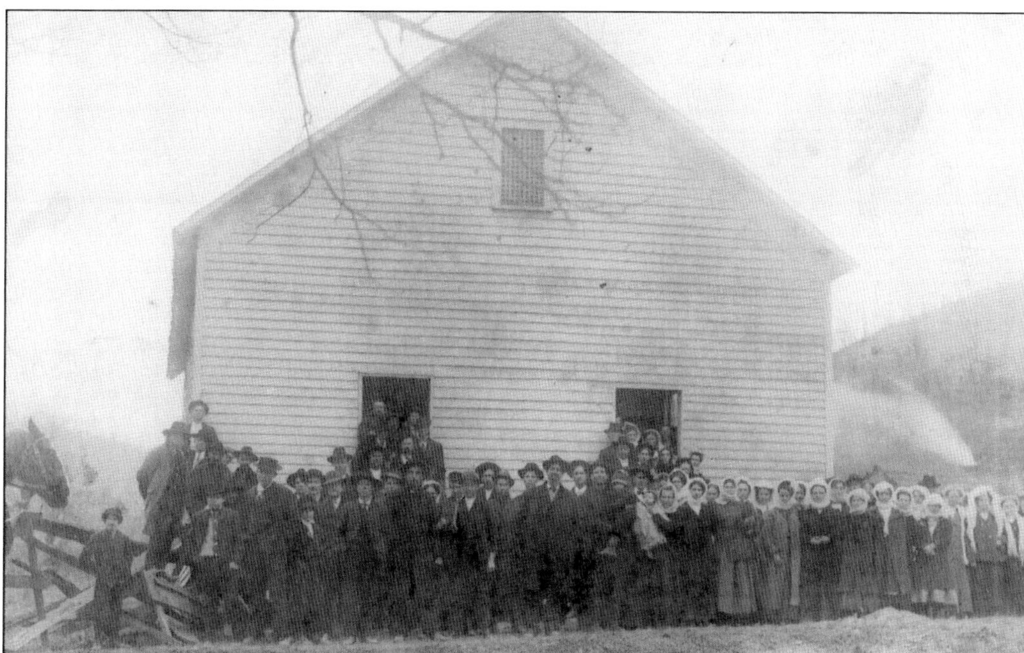

Another notable Guyandotte Valley house of worship is Mount Moriah United Baptist Church, located along Falls Creek Road. A Right Hand of Fellowship was granted to the congregation by the Bethlehem Association in 1875, and the current building (pictured here) dates to 1905. Center Point United Baptist Church in West Hamlin was founded in 1927 as an offshoot of Mount Moriah. (Courtesy of Debbie Pennington.)

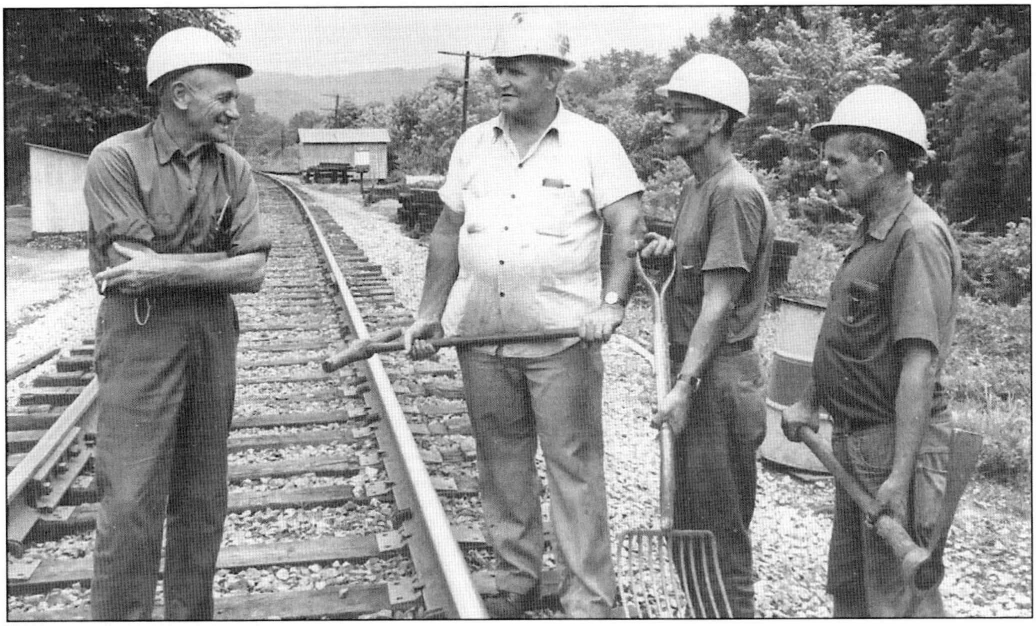

Education, farming, and the fossil fuel industry are traditional fields of employment in Lincoln County. So, too, is the railroad. Pictured from left to right, Floyd Pennington, David Aldridge, Calvin Porter, and Etsel Hurst represent a combined 137 years of service with C&O Railroad. C&O employed hundreds of Lincoln Countians engaged in the business of delivering coal to world markets. (Elba Davidson collection.)

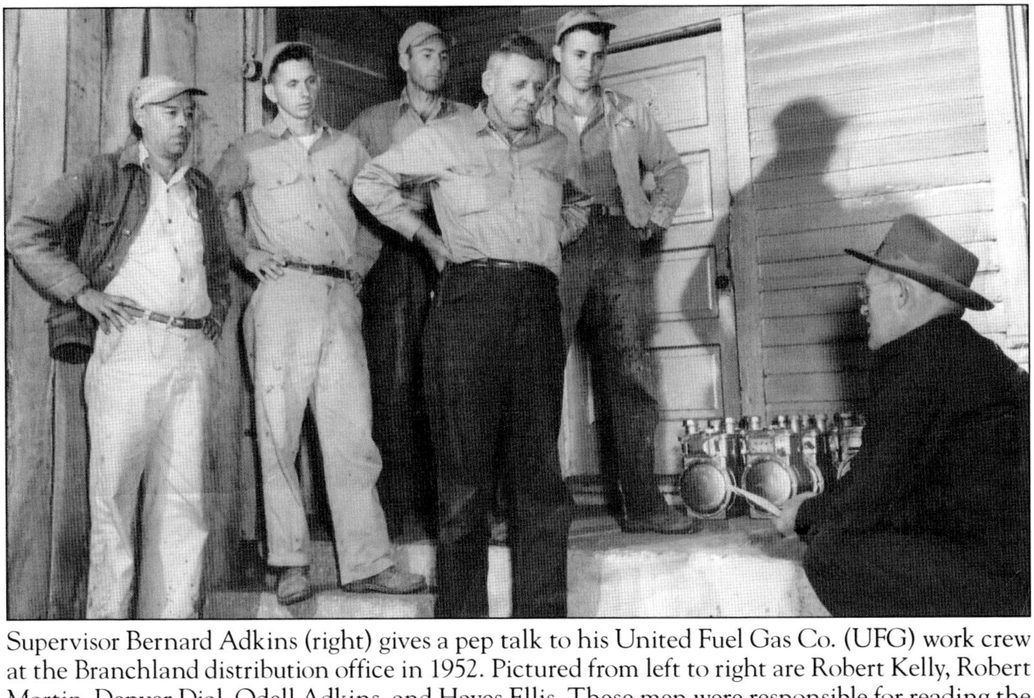

Supervisor Bernard Adkins (right) gives a pep talk to his United Fuel Gas Co. (UFG) work crew at the Branchland distribution office in 1952. Pictured from left to right are Robert Kelly, Robert Martin, Denver Dial, Odell Adkins, and Hayes Ellis. These men were responsible for reading the gas meters of over 2,000 UFG customers in Lincoln County and are emblematic of America's "greatest generation." (Courtesy of Richard "Dickie" Adkins.)

Two

Up Harts Creek Way

If Lincoln County is a microcosm of West Virginia, then Harts Creek is a microcosm of Lincoln County. It is the most geographically isolated part of a geographically isolated county in a geographically isolated state. An independent spirit has always existed here. While loyalties in what would become Lincoln County were split nearly evenly during the Civil War, over 85 percent of Harts Creekers fought for the South. Perhaps Fourteen Mile Mountain was the real Mason-Dixon Line. Even in 2006, when Harts High was closed, residents opted to send their students to Chapmanville Regional High School in nearby Logan County rather than face the prospect of unreasonably long bus rides to the new high school at Hamlin.

Harts Creek is one of the Guyandotte River's largest tributaries, draining an area of 45 square miles. It was named for pioneer outdoorsman Stephen Hart, a legendary Indian fighter, ginseng digger, and deer hunter. The region shares a history with the rest of the Guyandotte Valley, albeit with some more colorful elements, as demonstrated by the Brumfield-McCoy Feud or Big Ugly Creek. Frequently lampooned in national headlines (and, most notably, on NBC's *The Tonight Show* with Johnny Carson), Big Ugly Creek was supposedly named for the ruggedness of the local terrain.

Besides Harts and Big Ugly, other communities in the former Harts Creek District include Atenville, Ferrellsburg, Gill, Leet, and Sand Creek.

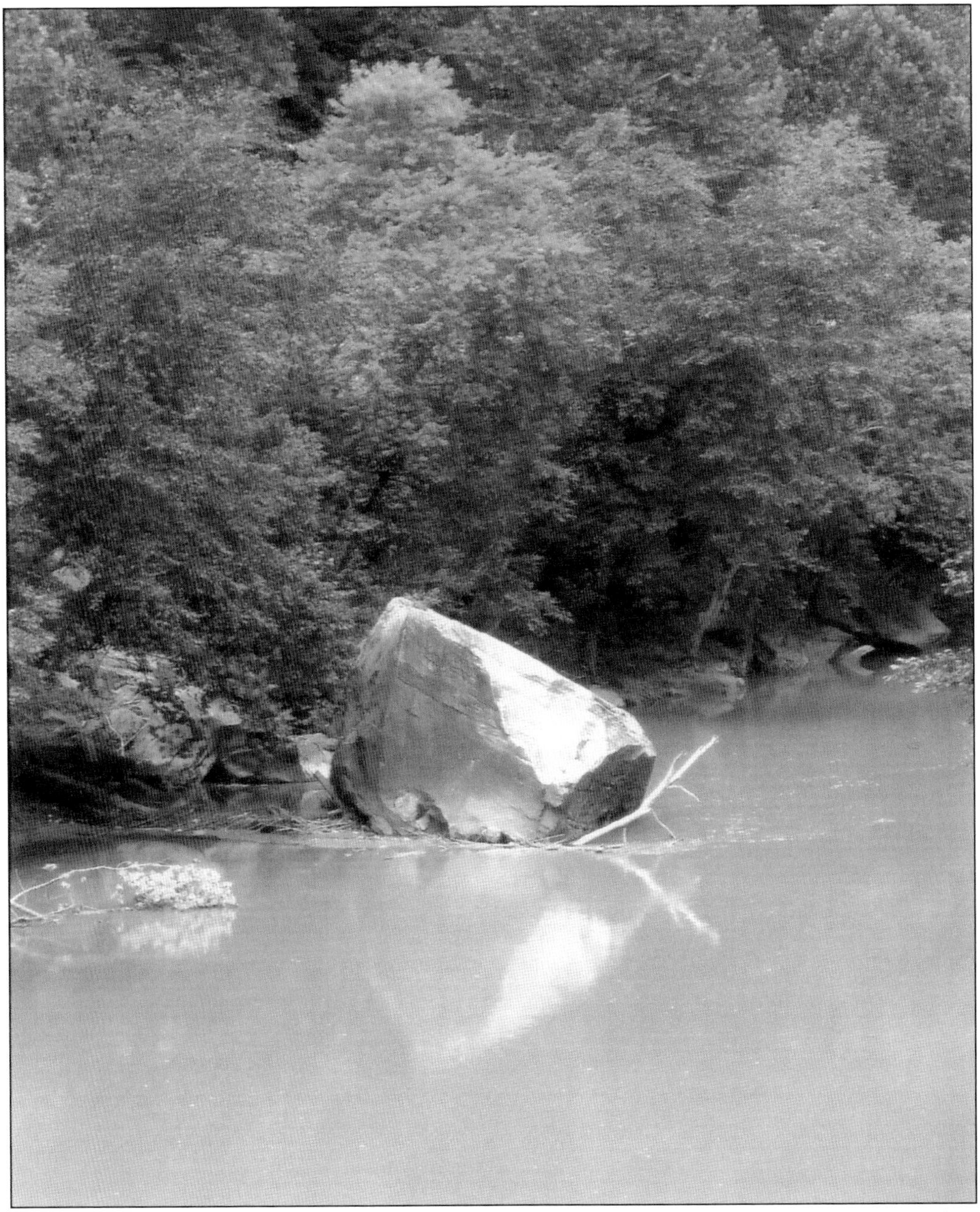

Early pioneer Stephen Hart left more than just his name in the community. Legend states that Hart lived in a cave along the Guyandotte River, at the mouth of Harts Creek. When blasting was done during the construction of Route 10 in the 1920s, this gigantic boulder tumbled off the hillside and into the river. Divers have reported that markings at the entrance to Hart's cave remain on the underside of the rock, which is just north of the Harts Bridge. Hart was a transient sort who left the area around 1800. (Reportedly, he believed that a neighbor was living too close if he could see their chimney smoke.) William Wirt Brumfield first settled at the mouth of Big Ugly Creek (later Gill) in 1801, while Harts's first permanent resident was Richard Elkins, in 1815. (AC.)

Calvin Cyfers, was a blacksmith and first sergeant in Company E of the 16th Virginia Cavalry. This Confederate regiment was formed in part from Col. Milton J. Ferguson's Guyandotte Battalion, was associated with Gen. Albert Gallatin Jenkins's brigade, and saw action alongside the 34th Battalion Virginia Cavalry at Gettysburg. (Courtesy of Harold Ray Smith.)

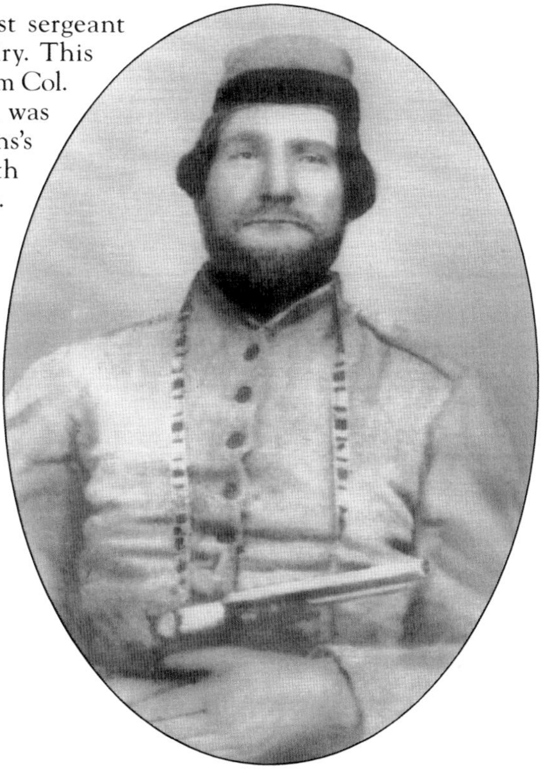

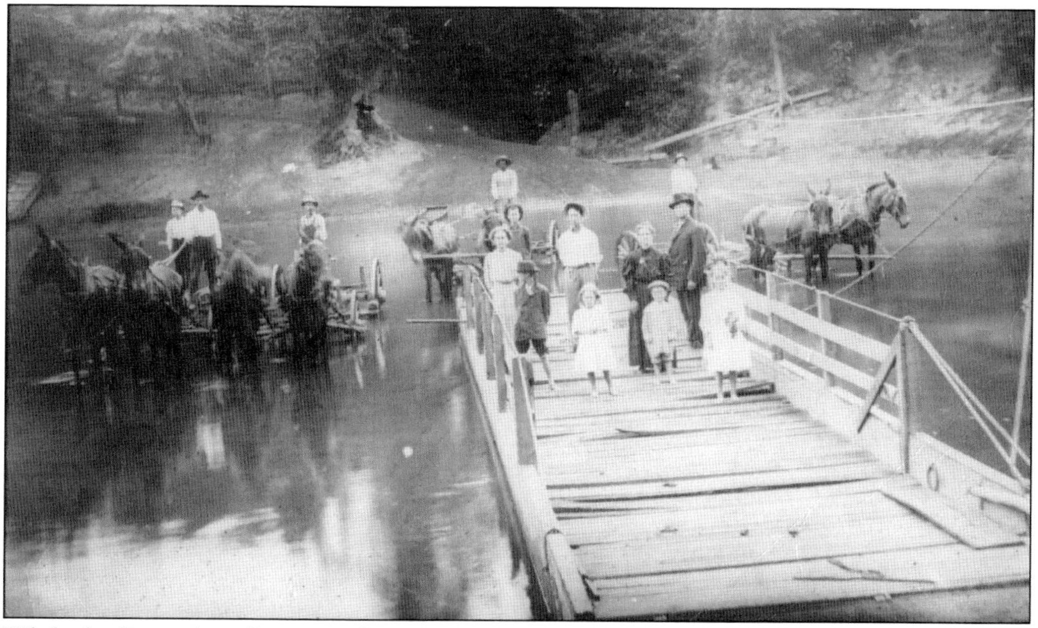

While the Guyandotte River was the primary transportation route through Lincoln County during the 19th century, there also was a crude road cut along the east bank of the river connecting Barboursville and Logan Court House. A shortcut across Low Gap via this ferry at Ferrellsburg accessed an even more primitive mountaintop trail on the west side that terminated near the falls of the Guyandotte. (Courtesy of Ralph Smith.)

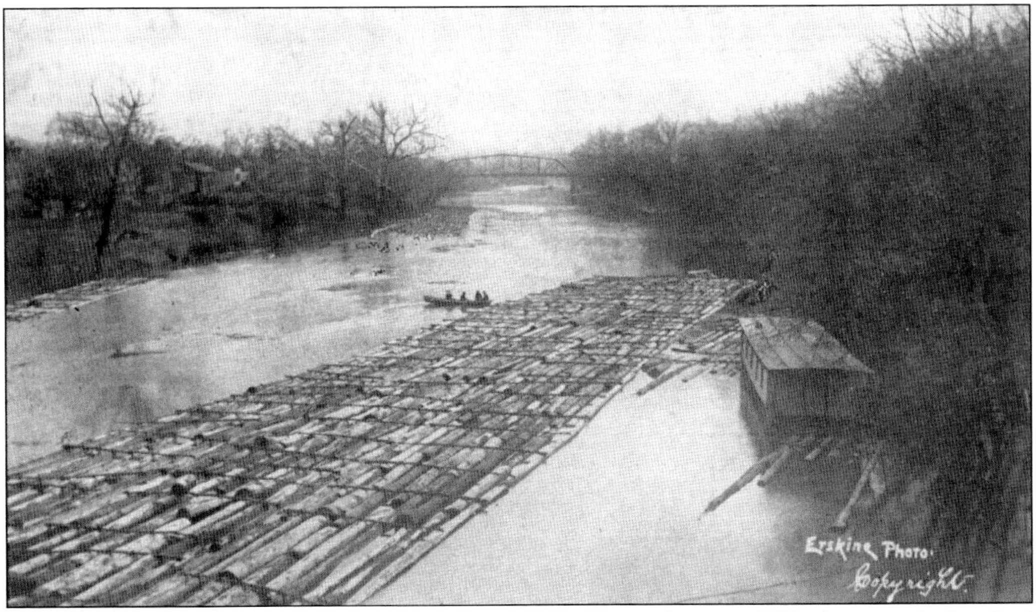

Removal of the old Guyandotte River Navigation Company dams in 1878 eliminated what had been a significant barrier to the transportation of timber. Rafts such as these were tied together in sections and sometimes comprised thousands of logs. Both a canoe (center) and a push boat (right) were used to handle this particular shipment. Cole and Crane Company was a major player in the local timber industry. (MU-Lambert.)

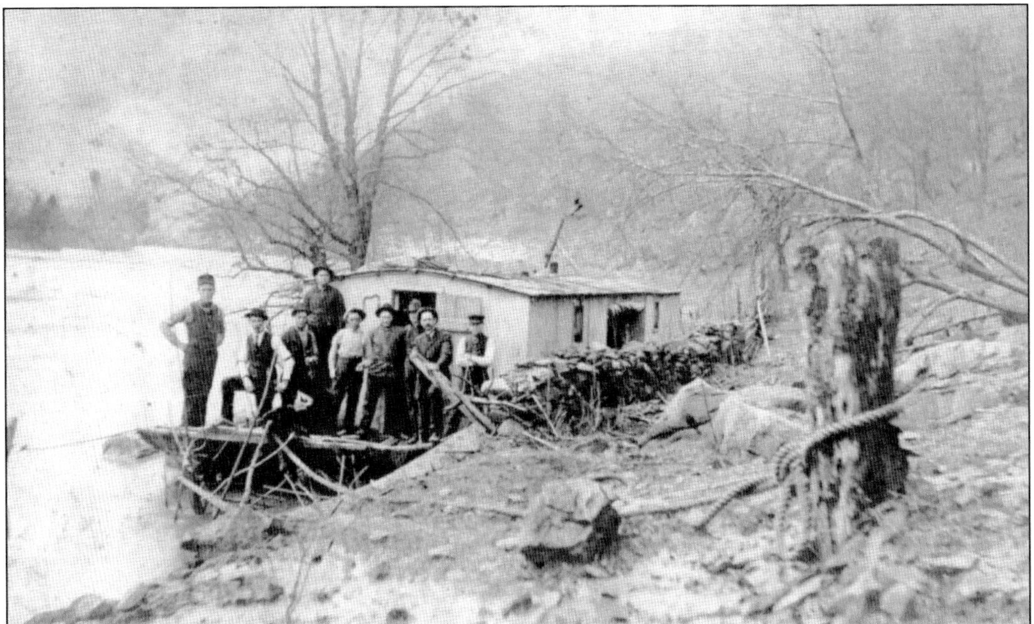

Push boats, or flatboats, were one type of craft that once plied the Guyandotte River. They were just that—flat-bottomed boats that were pushed along the river using poles. With nothing but muddy ruts for roads during this time, it was far easier to move heavy goods on water than to fight loaded wagons across Lincoln County's hilly terrain. (Courtesy of F. Keith Davis.)

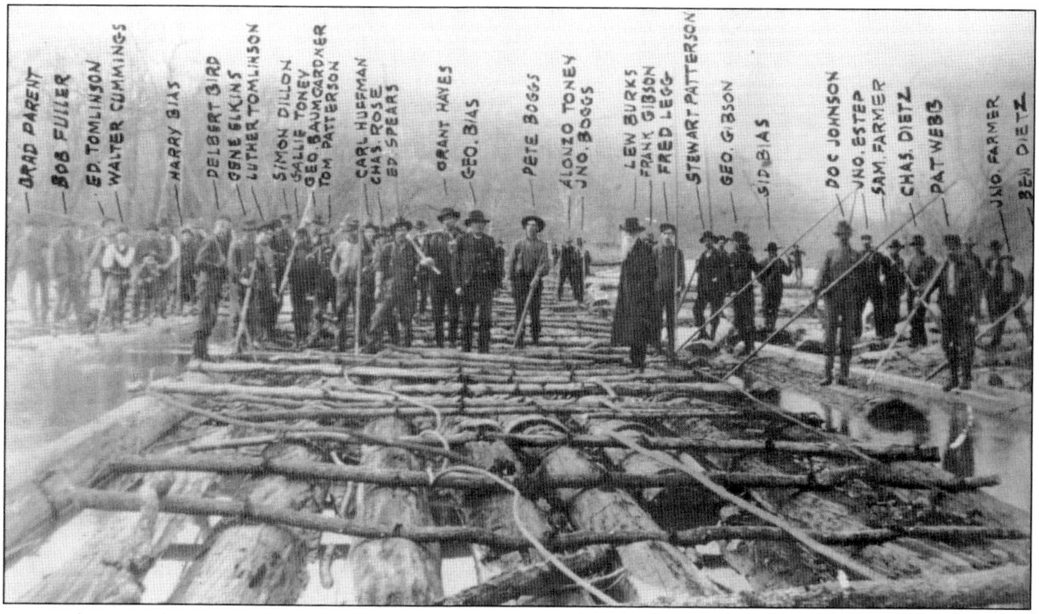

Log rafts were lashed together by an intricate network of rope and wooden cross bracing, clearly illustrated in this photograph. Such rafts were floated down to the Ohio River at Guyandotte, where these raftsmen pose aboard their craft. Names such as Cummings, Estep, and Toney indicate that at least some of this crew was from up Harts Creek way. (MU-Lambert.)

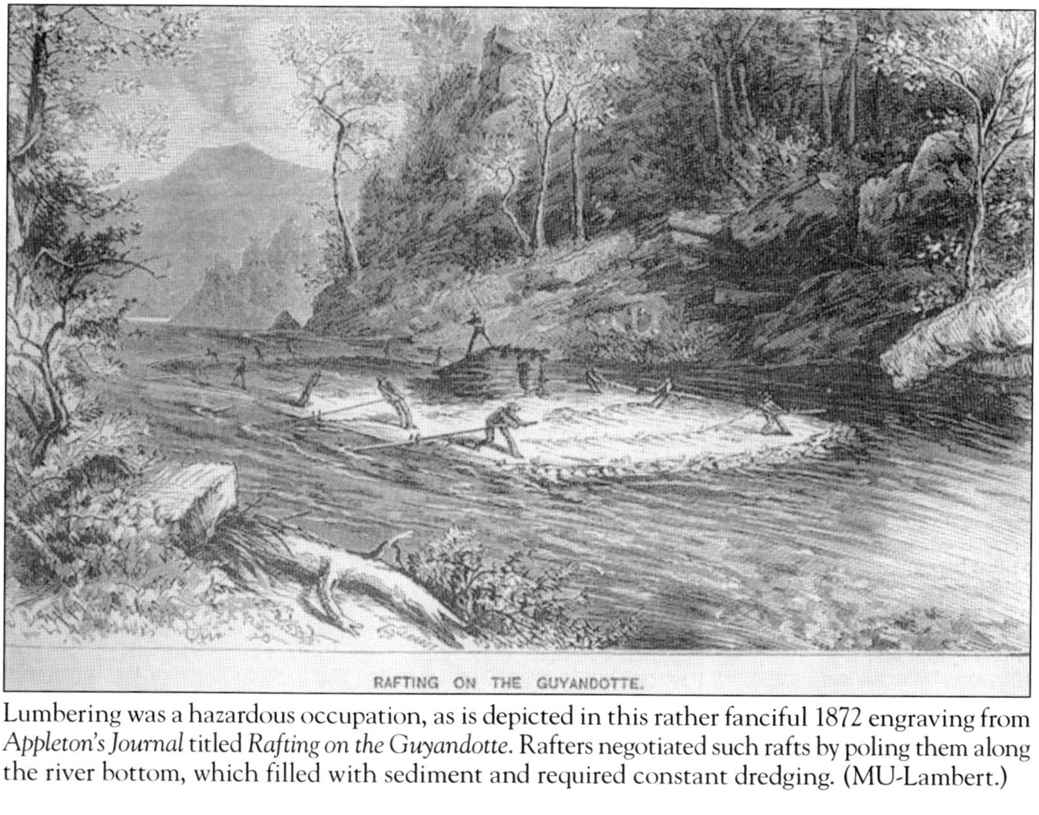

RAFTING ON THE GUYANDOTTE.

Lumbering was a hazardous occupation, as is depicted in this rather fanciful 1872 engraving from *Appleton's Journal* titled *Rafting on the Guyandotte*. Rafters negotiated such rafts by poling them along the river bottom, which filled with sediment and required constant dredging. (MU-Lambert.)

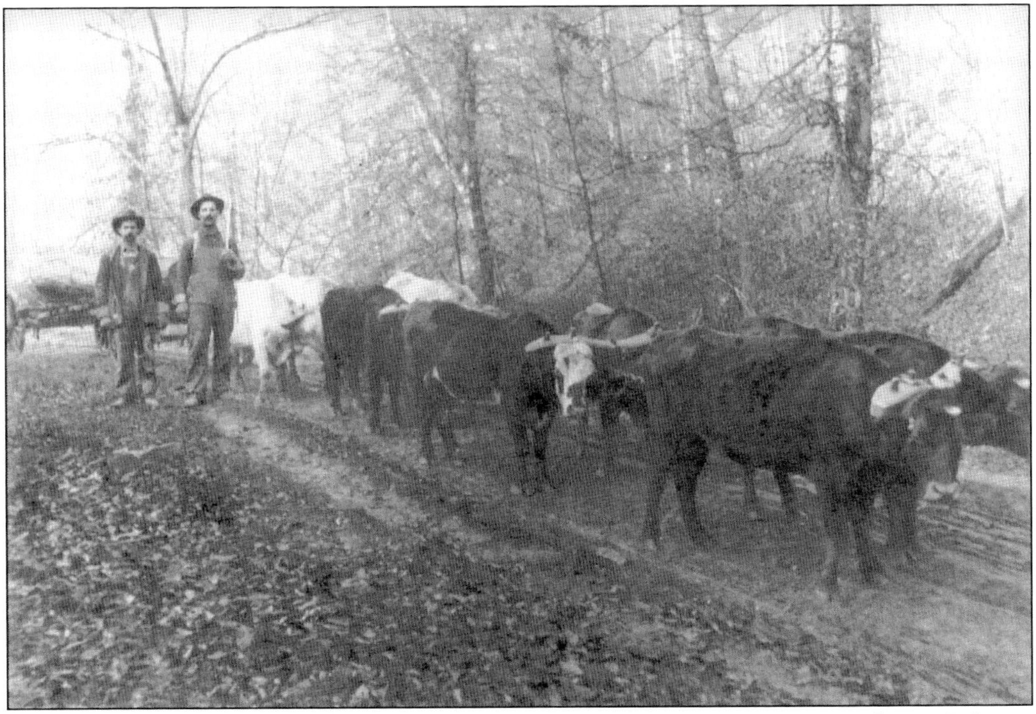

Getting huge logs from the forest to the river was no easy feat. Here, a team of oxen helps to accomplish the task. When lumber was later shipped by rail, getting it onto trains was also a tricky proposition. Incline ramps were built along the riverbank to achieve the transfer. (Courtesy of Walter Midkiff.)

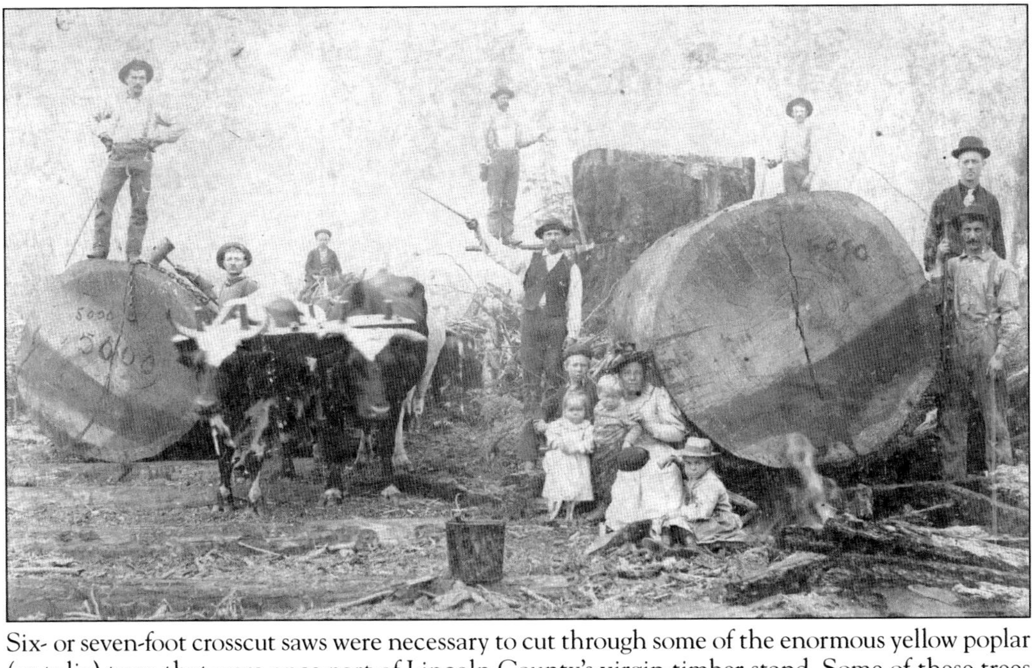

Six- or seven-foot crosscut saws were necessary to cut through some of the enormous yellow poplar (or tulip) trees that were once part of Lincoln County's virgin timber stand. Some of these trees reached nearly 200 feet in height. (MU-Lambert.)

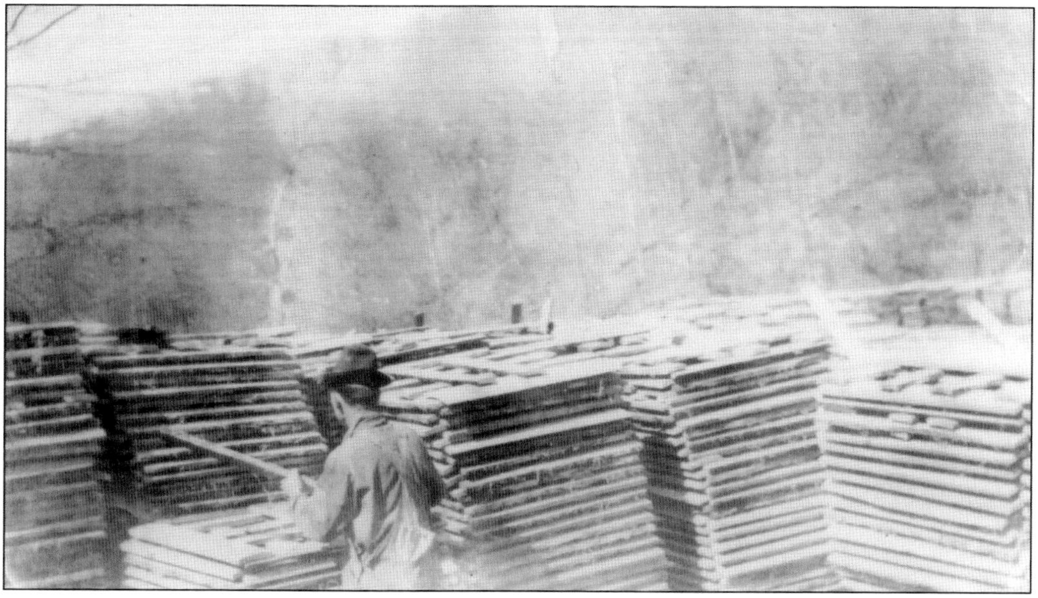

Much of Harts Creek's raw timber was processed locally, and area sawmills were busy converting it to finished product that was used for building materials, railroad ties, and mineshaft bracing. Pictured is a stave mill that was located on Francis Creek at the head of Little Harts. (Courtesy of Odell Dingess.)

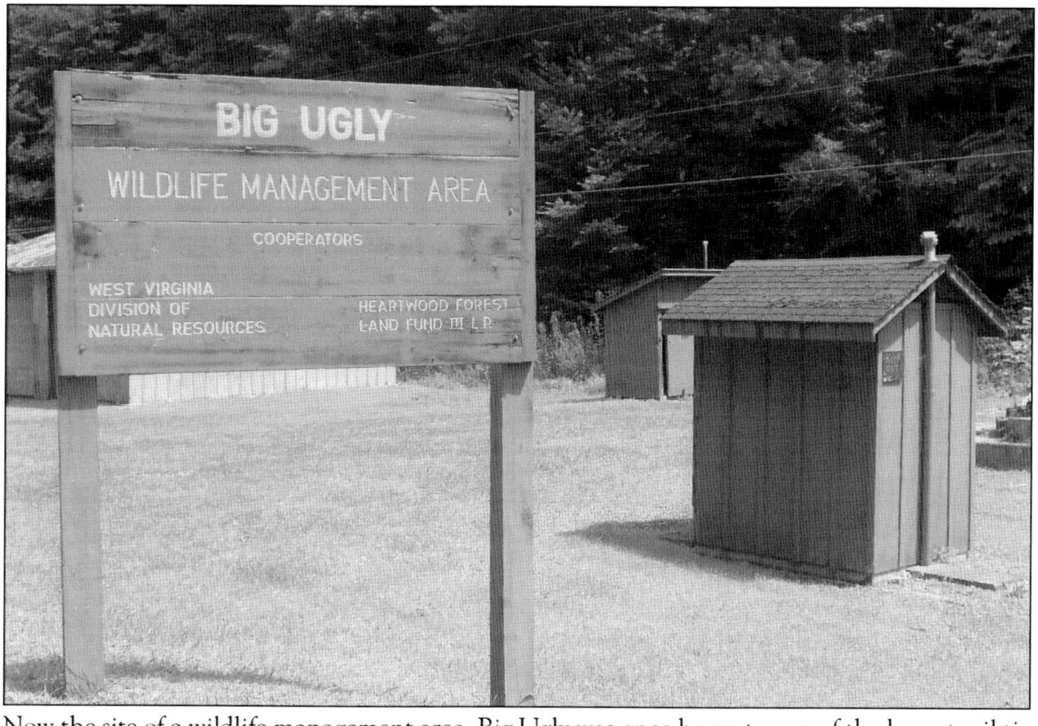

Now the site of a wildlife management area, Big Ugly was once home to one of the largest rail tie and lumber companies in America: Johnson and Son, run by Indiana native Benjamin Johnson. He constructed a narrow-gauge or dinky railroad from his Stringtown lumber camp to Gill on the Guyandotte River. The line was sold to the Huntington Development Company in 1917. (AC.)

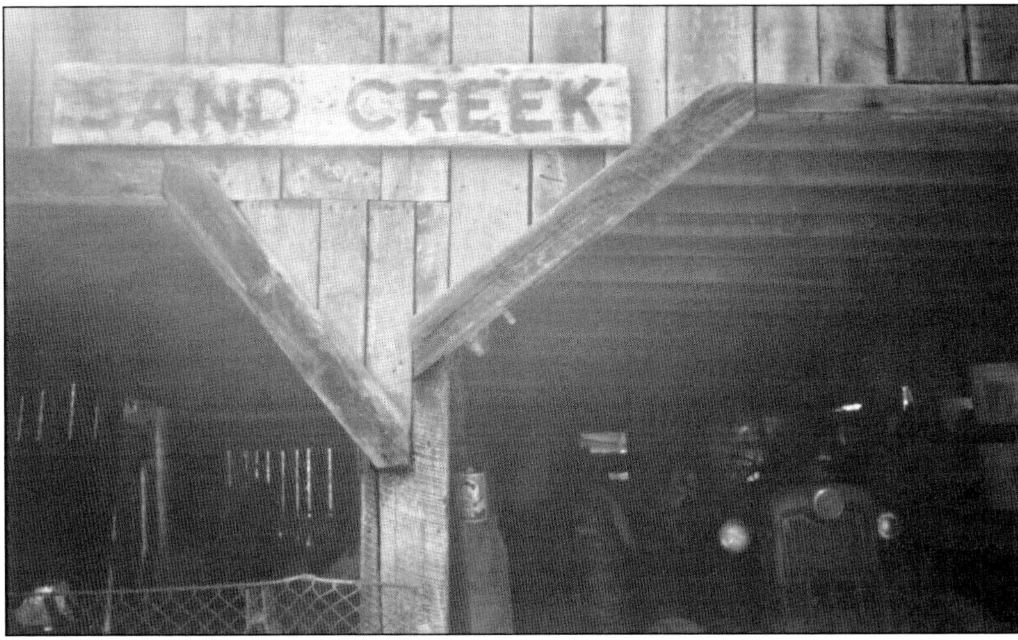

Sand Creek (its depot functioning as a tractor barn in later years), was a whistle-stop on the C&O Railroad. Nearby were the Eden Park coal mines, which operated for only a short time around 1906. Eden Park gained a notorious reputation for the murder of Rochester coal entrepreneur J.X. Hill. Like Rochester, Eden Park is now another Lincoln County ghost town. (Courtesy of Billy Adkins.)

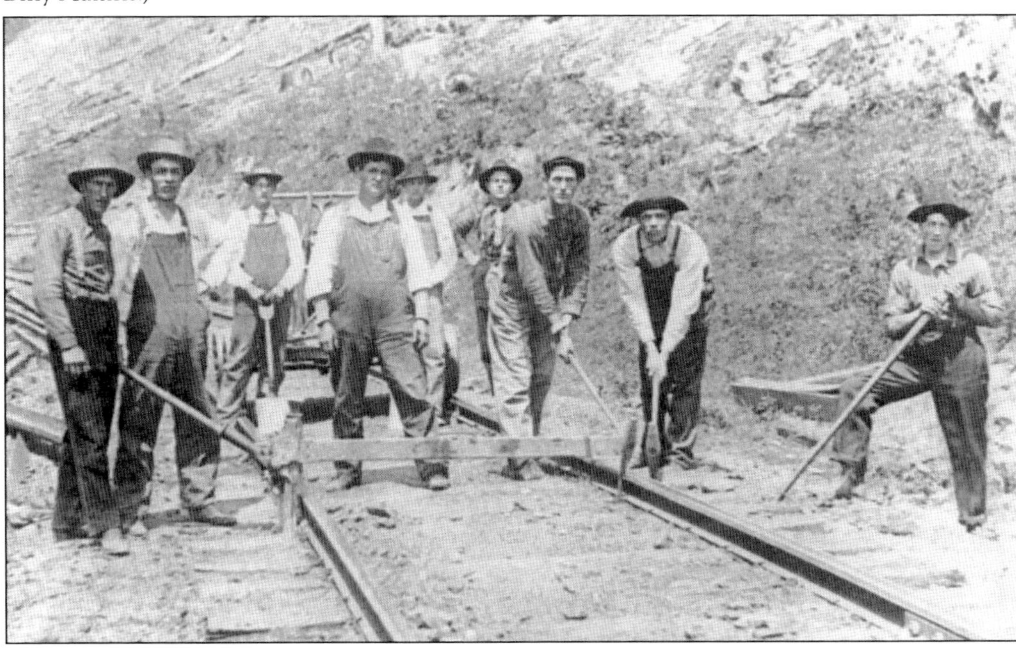

This work crew laid a section of track for the C&O Railroad between Harts and Ferrellsburg in 1904. Pictured from left to right are Tolbert Caldwell, Harry Powers, Howard Bowles, Emzie Petrie (foreman), Mack Adkins, Wilburn Adkins, Cleve Fry, Bob Powers, and Frank Davis. (Courtesy of Billy Adkins.)

Immediately replacing the river as a better way to move people and goods, the railroad enjoyed a near transportation monopoly from 1904 until approximately 1925, when Route 10 was opened to Harts. This C&O Railroad worker is using a one-wheel dolly to inspect the quality of the rails. (Courtesy of Lucian Isaacs.)

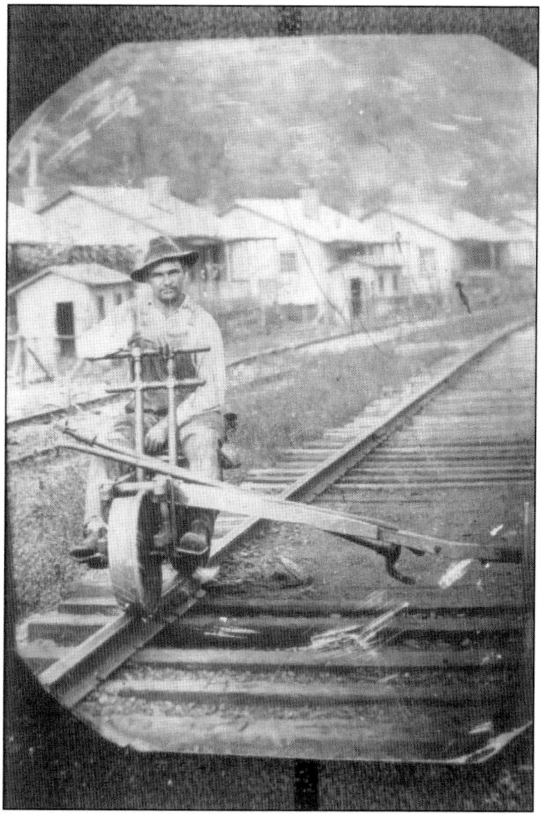

Trains carrying coal from Logan and Mingo Counties to Huntington remain a fixture here. This northbound steam engine train waits to cross into Lincoln County, just across the county line at the Big Creek rail depot. Route 10 can be seen at the left, wedged between the railroad and a rock cliff. (Courtesy of Billy Adkins.)

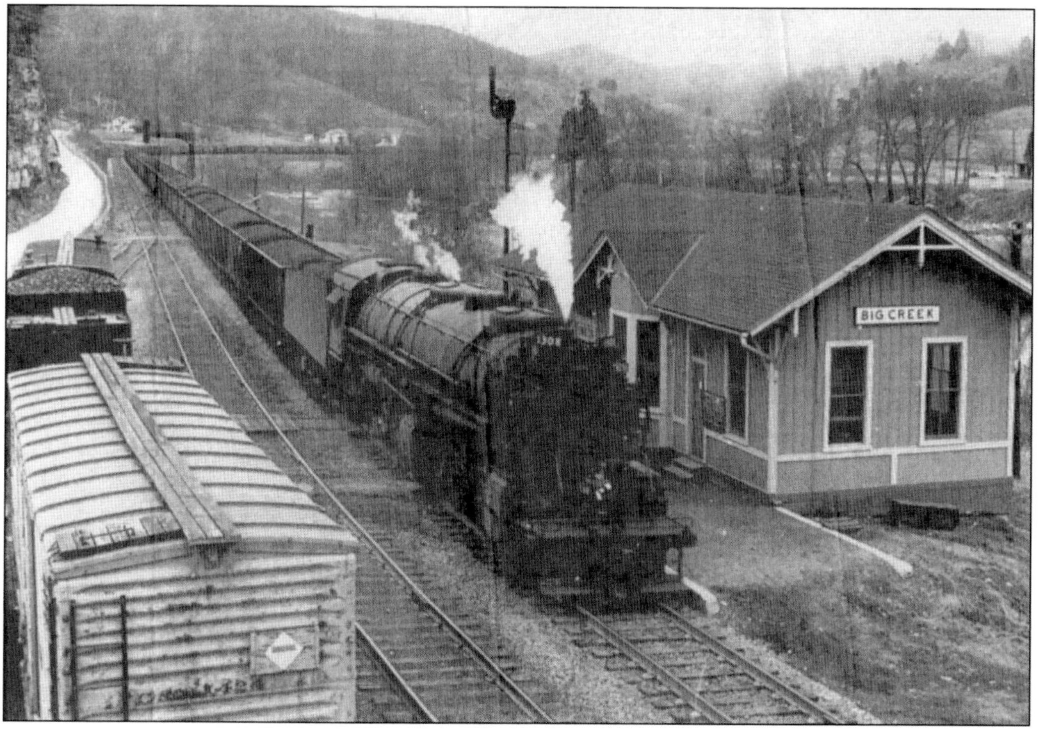

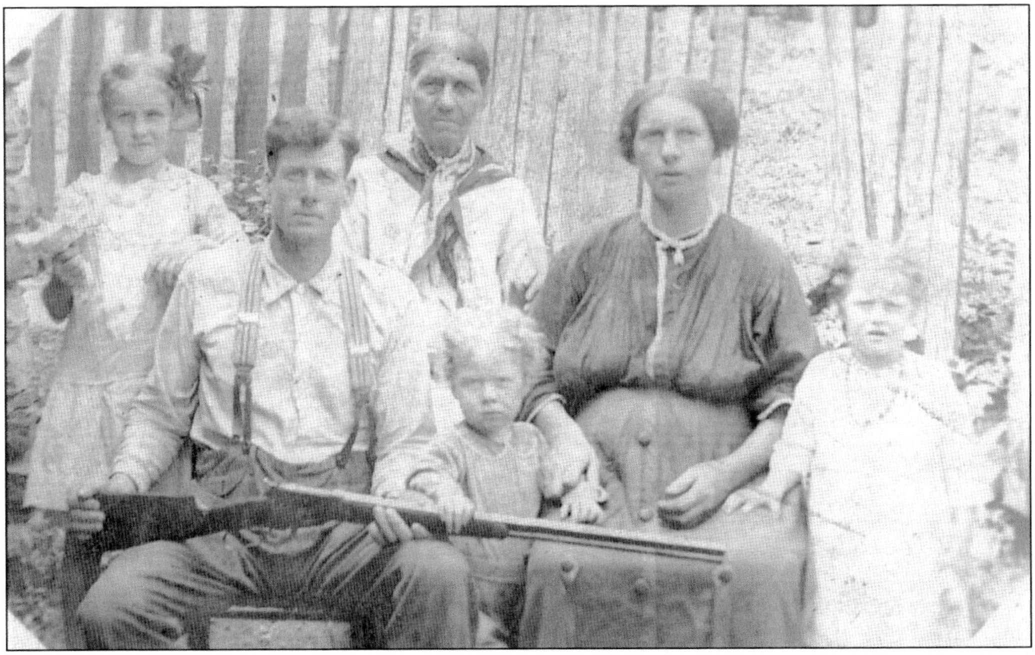

The Dalton family of Big Branch of Harts Creek exemplifies the hardscrabble lifestyle of rural Appalachia a century ago. Guns were essential for hunting game. "Young 'uns" growing up in such rural areas often learned how to shoot not long after mastering the skill of walking. (Courtesy of Ray Bias.)

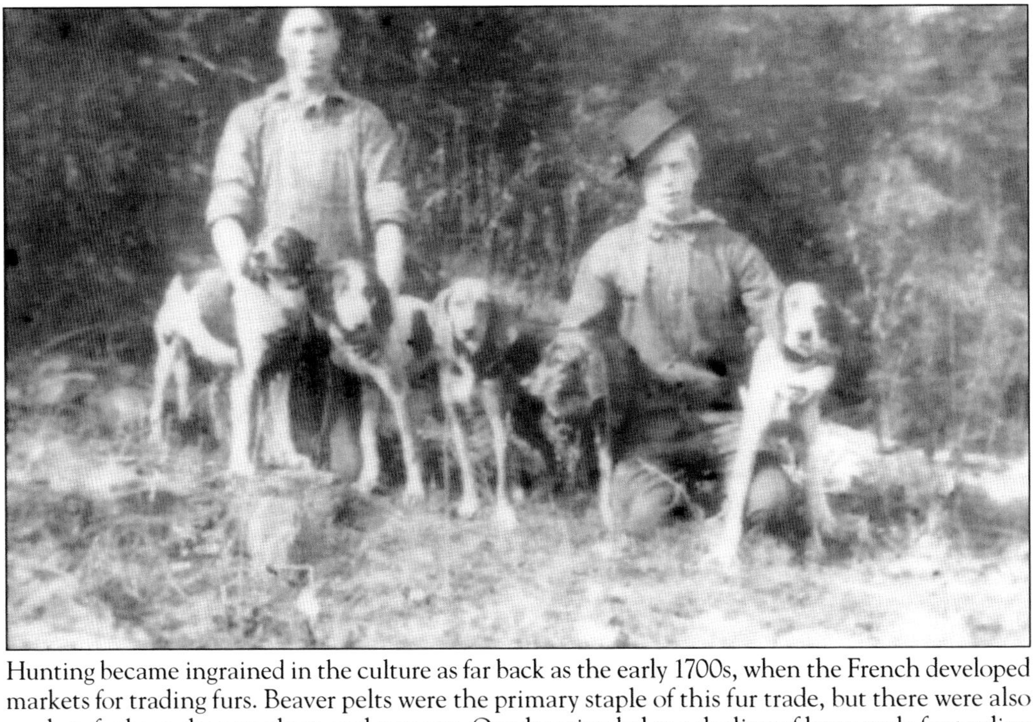

Hunting became ingrained in the culture as far back as the early 1700s, when the French developed markets for trading furs. Beaver pelts were the primary staple of this fur trade, but there were also markets for bear, deer, muskrat, and raccoon. Overhunting led to a decline of large-scale fur trading by the 1840s, but coonskins are still collected on a local level. (Courtesy of Odell Dingess.)

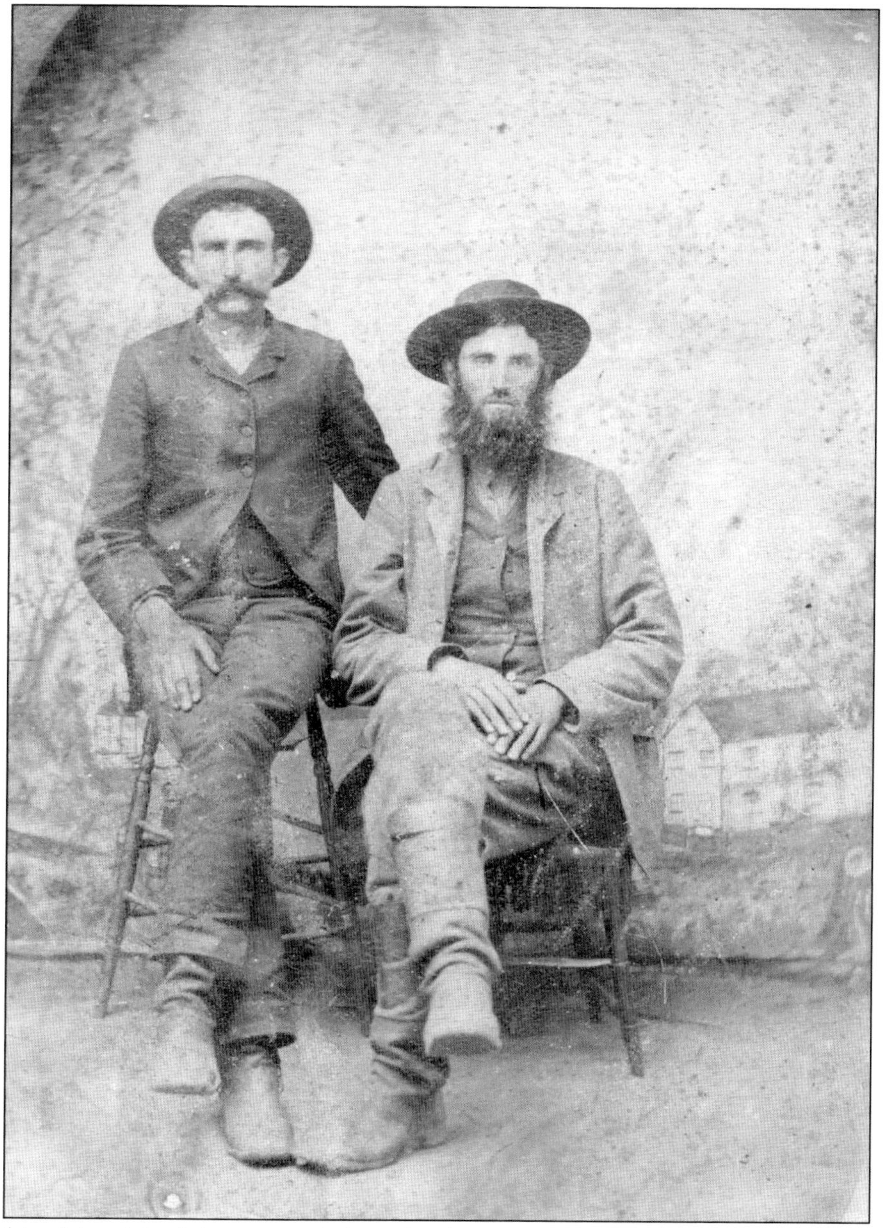

Pictured in this original tintype are believed to be participants in the famed "Lincoln County Feud" of 1889–1890. Al Brumfield, a prosperous Harts merchant who made his fortune running timber and whiskey, was a central figure in this dispute. The Brumfield family had been gaining enemies since 1884 when Al's father killed Boney Lucas. Chief among their rivals were Cain Adkins and John Runyon, who hired two gunmen to murder Al. Events came to a head on September 22, 1889, when Al and his wife were shot (though neither fatally) by Milt Haley and Green McCoy. In retaliation for the ambush, Al led a posse into Kentucky to bring the hired gunmen to justice. After confessing, Haley and McCoy were executed (either brained, hanged, knifed, or shot) and buried in a single grave on the West Fork of Harts Creek. The feud ended when Adkins fled to Wayne County and Runyon sold his business interests to Al. Modern-day archaeologists continue to search for the Haley/McCoy gravesite. (MU-Lambert.)

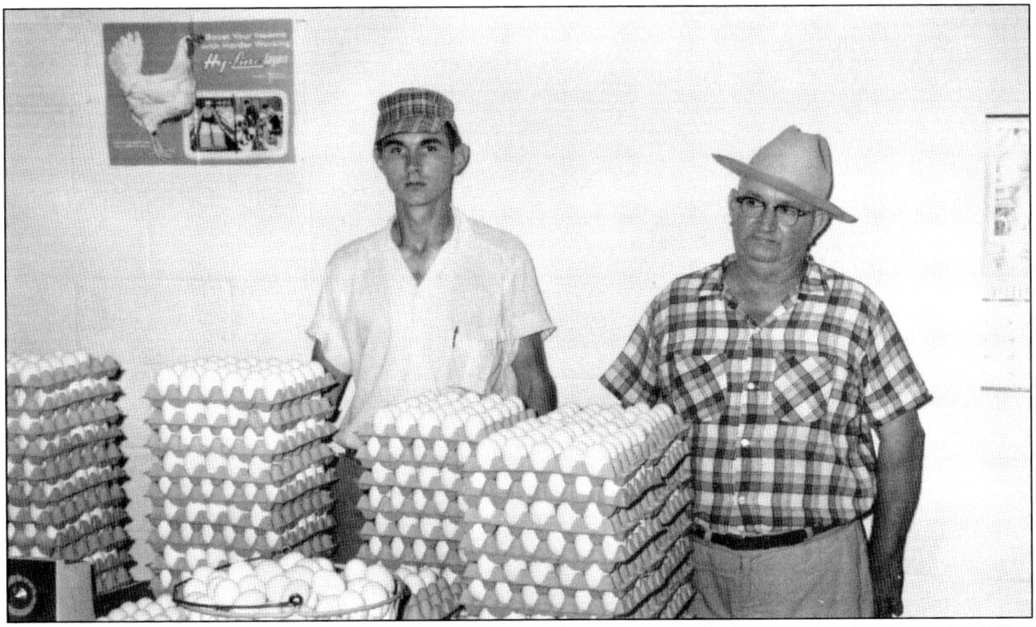

The Atkins and Son poultry farm operated on Little Harts Creek during the 1950s and 1960s. These 30 crates of eggs indicate the scale of the business. Chickens were leghorns, which were shipped from Cincinnati. At the peak of operation, Atkins and Son boasted over 3,000 laying hens. Feed bins for the birds were stocked with laying mash and chopped corn. (Courtesy of Morgan Hoke.)

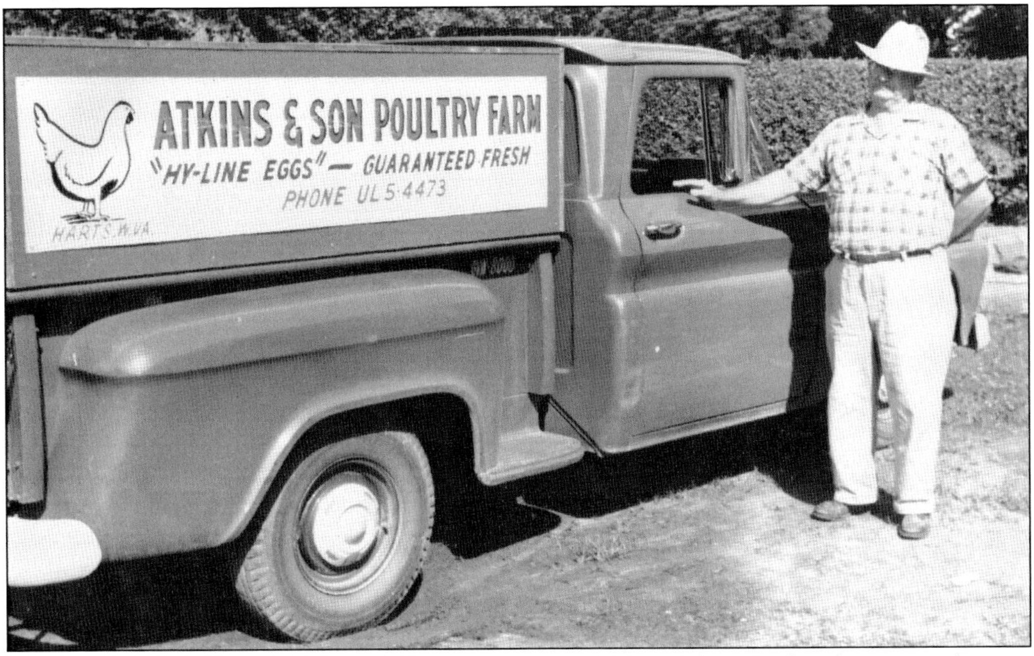

Owner Sidney "Sid" Atkins delivered eggs from his poultry farm to local supermarkets in Chapmanville and Logan, but sometimes the family drove to Ashland, Kentucky, to pick up more eggs if business was brisk. Barns, which served as hatching areas, were heated, and there was also a refrigeration room. Many of the buildings still stand. (Courtesy of Morgan Hoke.)

Positioned at one of the highest points (1,439 feet in elevation) in Lincoln County on Gartin Fork of Little Harts, the fire tower on Manns Knob once afforded a sweeping vista of surrounding forests. It was built in the 1930s by the Civilian Conservation Corps. Here, local aviator Jim Hypes (left) inspects a map with Lincoln County forest ranger Marvin Booth. (AC.)

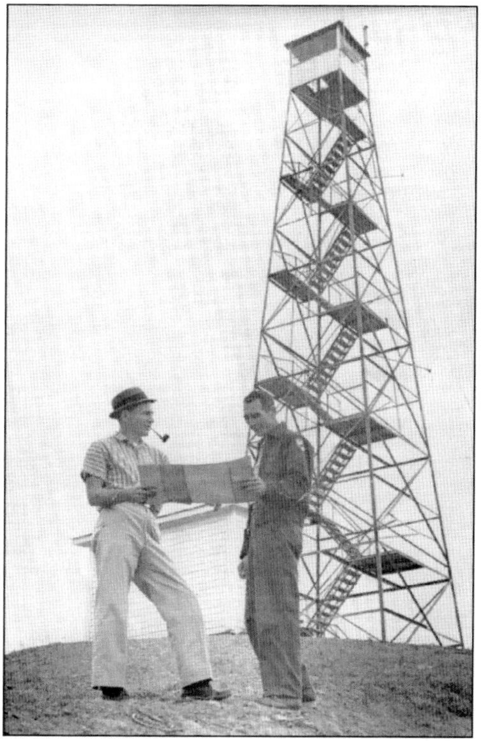

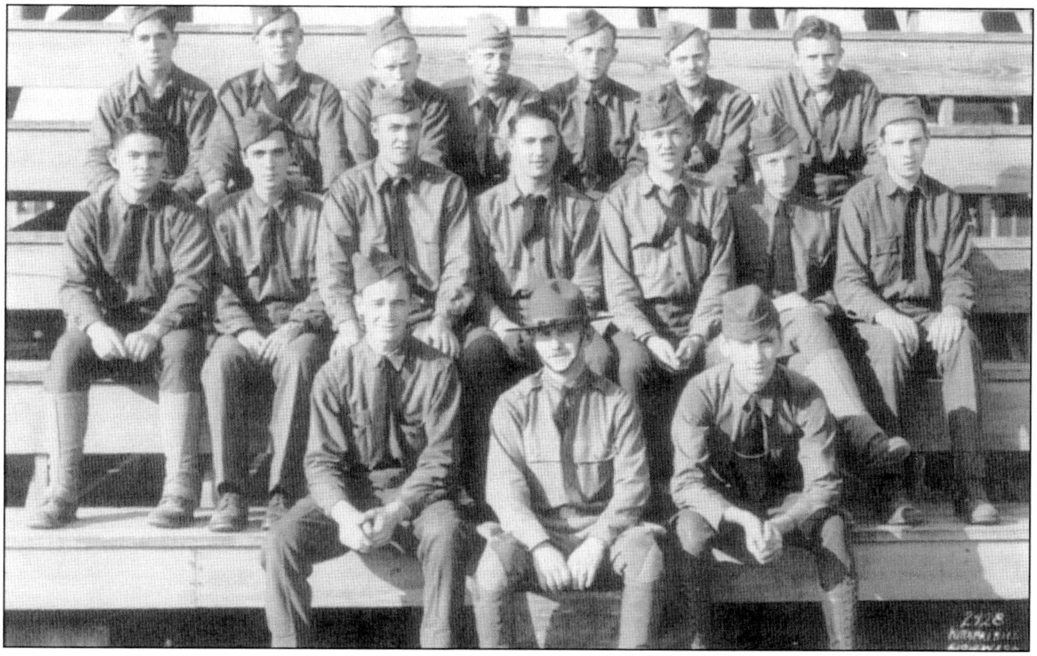

Besides building the fire tower on Manns Knob (and another one on Summit Ridge at Sumerco), the Civilian Conservation Corps was active in Lincoln County during the 1930s. Its most lasting contributions are the cabins and picnic shelters at nearby Cabwaylingo State Forest. The park is named for the four counties it serves: *Cab*ell, *Way*ne, *Lin*coln, and Min*go*. (Courtesy of Lucian Isaacs.)

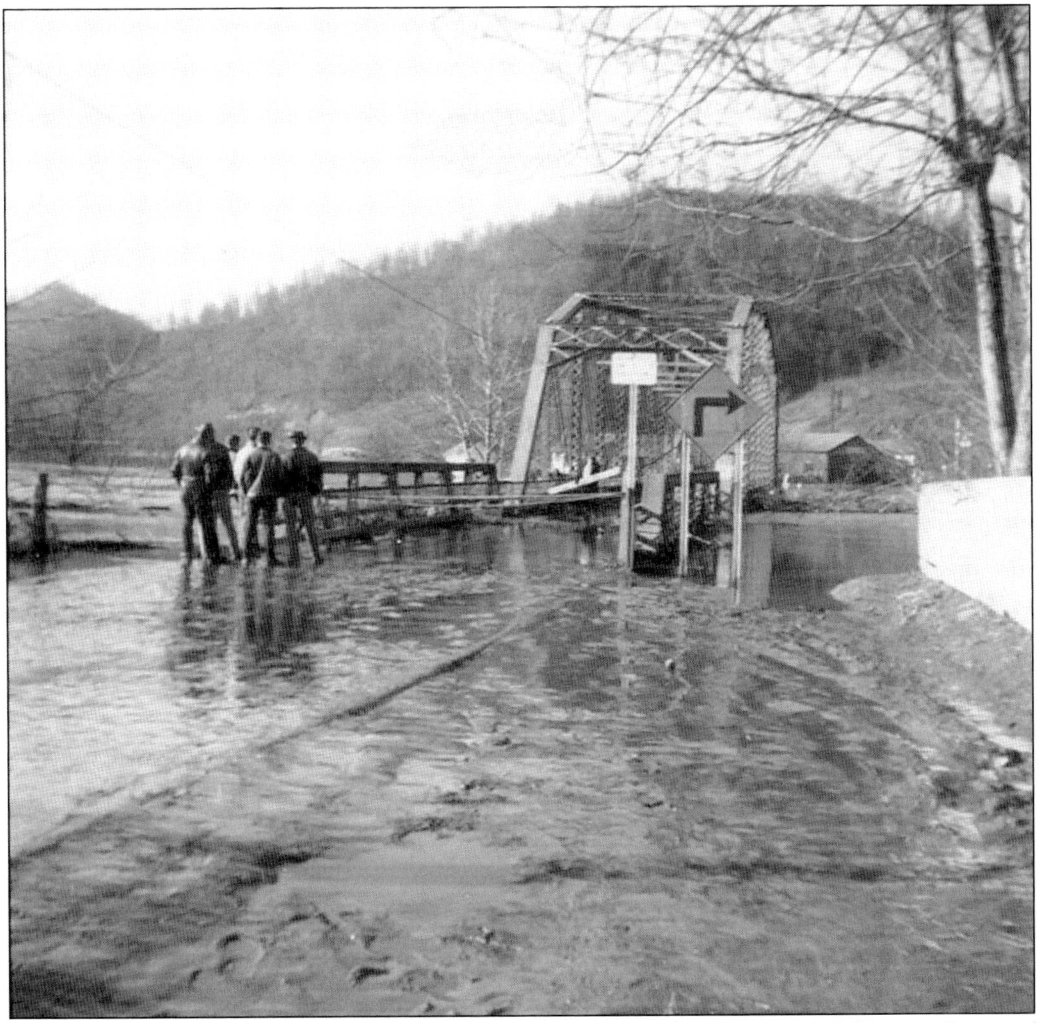

Floods like these were a common occurrence along the Guyandotte River until the completion of the R.D. Bailey Dam in 1985 in Wyoming County. Shown here during the 1963 flood, the Harts Creek Bridge was the southernmost of eight iron truss bridges across the Guyandotte River or its tributaries along Route 10 in Lincoln County. Others were (from north to south) West Hamlin, Branchland, Four Mile, Midkiff, Ten Mile, Ranger, and Atenville. The Harts Creek Bridge, like all the others, is now gone. A large railroad tie yard, where ties were loaded onto boxcars for shipment by rail, was once located in the central business district at the foot of the bridge. Also here was the Adkins-Dial-Fleming store (having since been torn down, this business was associated with Watson Adkins and sat beside the modern post office), the Adkins-McCann-Fleming store (which doubled as the post office and was run for a time by Herb Adkins), the landmark L.T. Jones General Store and Esso station, and the White Shed Inn. (Courtesy of Cori Brumfield.)

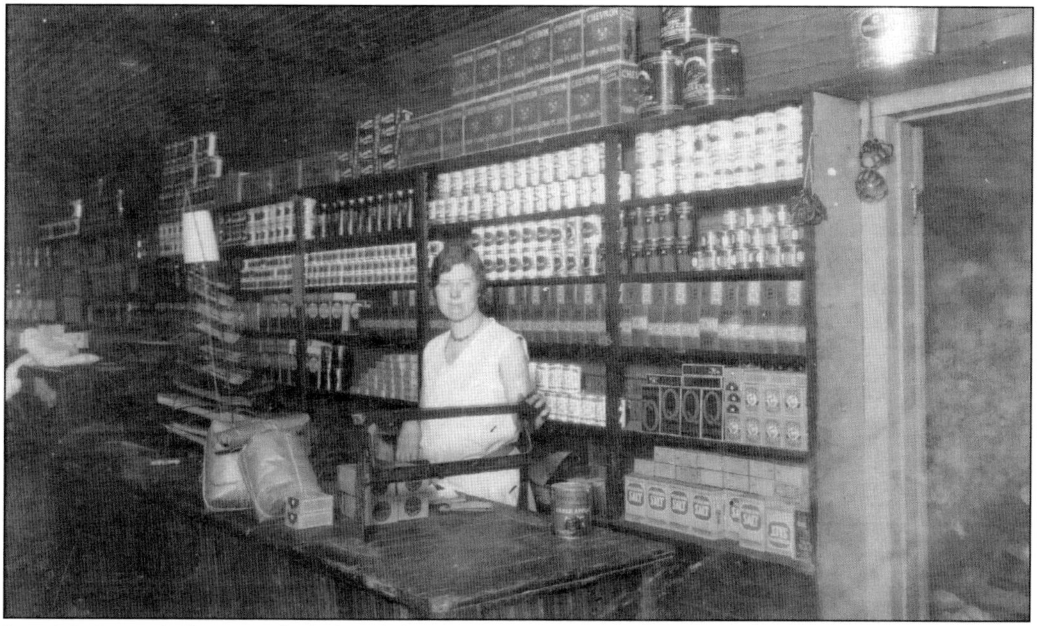

Inez McCann Adkins works behind the counter of Watson Adkins's store, which competed with the Herb Adkins store across the street. The latter establishment was "turned" (meaning that the back door became the front) when Route 10 was opened since fewer customers were arriving by rail. Watson Adkins was a Lincoln County sheriff and lived in the former Al Brumfield residence. (Courtesy of Billy Adkins.)

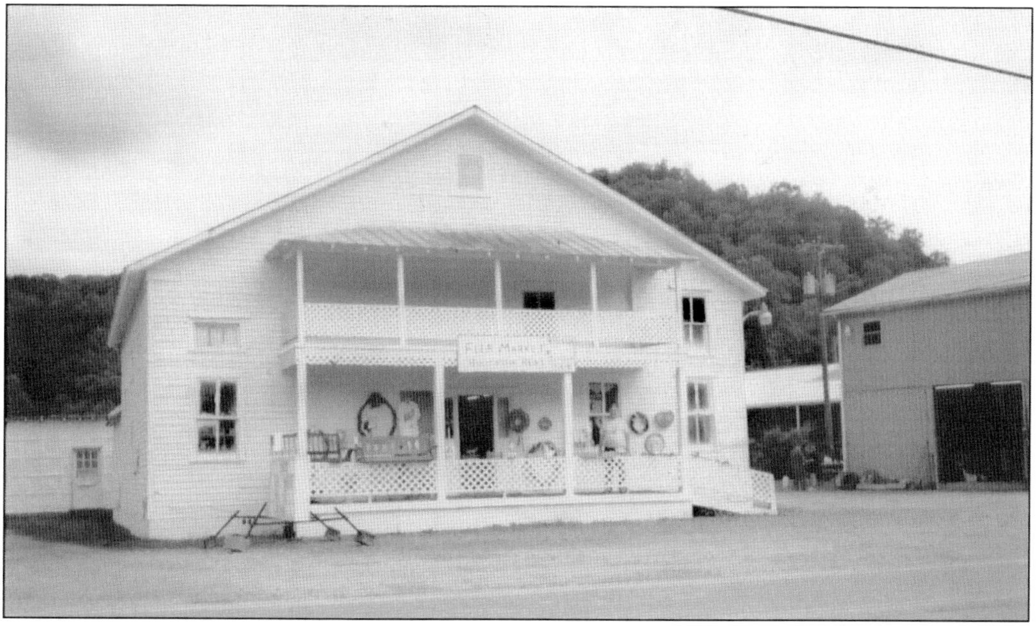

Shown is the exterior of the Adkins-McCann-Fleming grocery store. Established in 1891 and run by three generations of the Adkins family, it also functioned as Harts's post office. A flea market in later years, the historic building was razed in 2006. Besides being "turned," the store was moved multiple times during its 115-year history, ending up where Harts Pharmacy is located today. (Courtesy of Billy Adkins.)

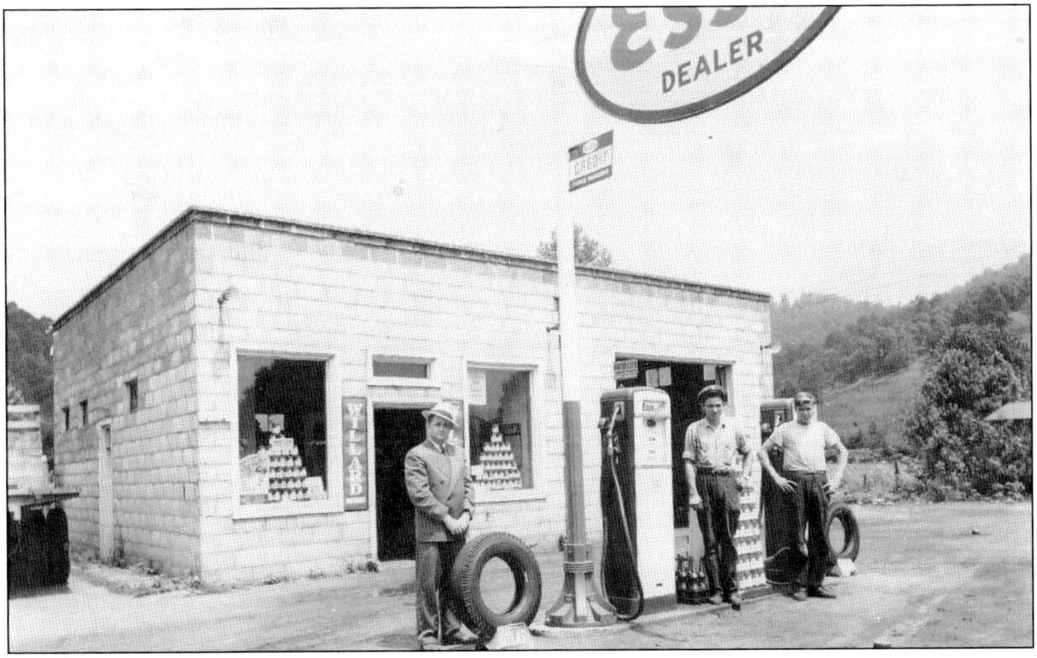

Lucian Taylor Jones (left) operated a gas station, shown here in 1948, and general store at Harts. Established in 1929, it remained in operation as a hardware store into the early 21st century and sold everything from appliances to shoes. During its earliest days, goods were carried out of the store in sacks and thrown across the backs of horses by customers. (Courtesy of Don Jones.)

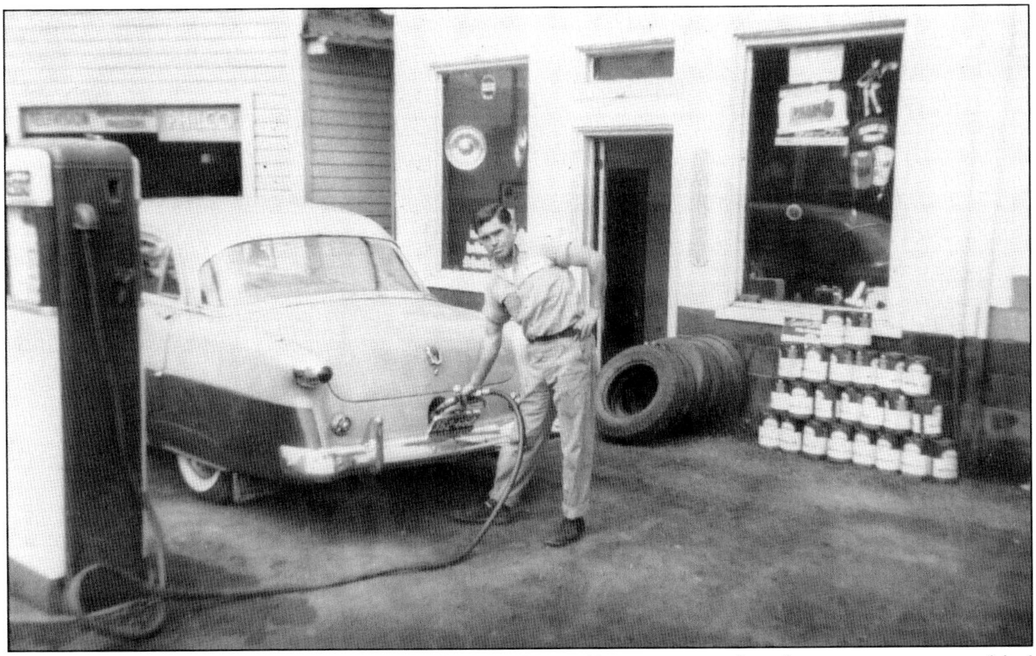

Jimmy Mullins fills up his 1952 Ford at the L.T. Jones Esso station. Gasoline pumps were added some years after the store opened, and tanker trucks parked here were once a common sight. Jones also sponsored a local softball team. Lincoln County once supported as many as 30 recreational league softball teams. (Courtesy of Don Jones.)

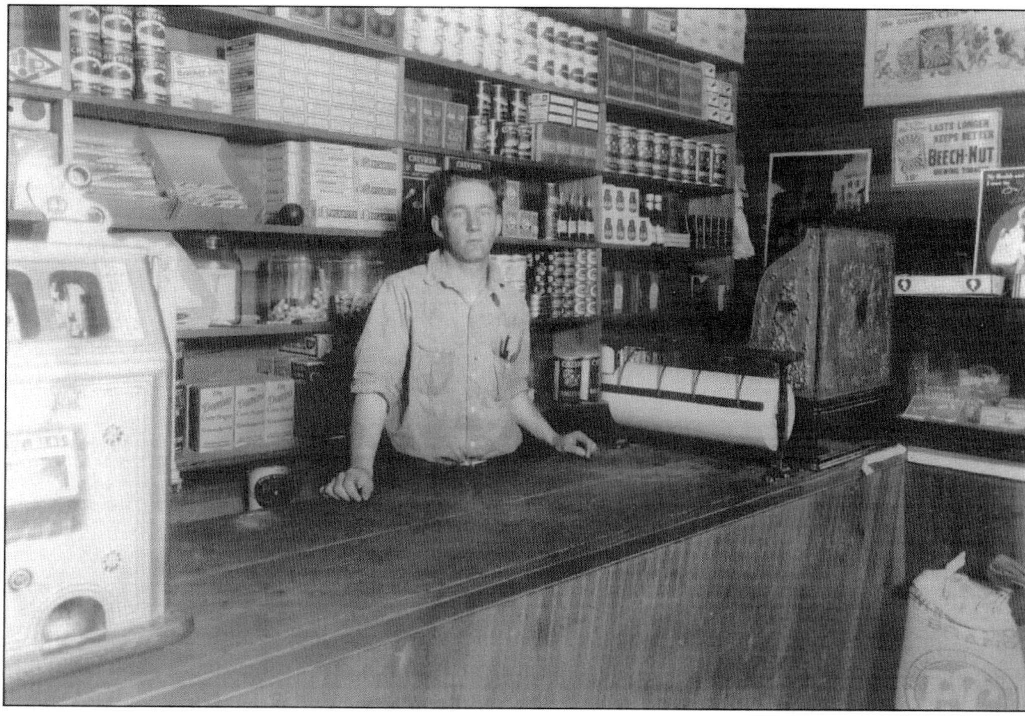

L.T. Jones stands behind the counter of his general store in 1930. From humble beginnings with only a few groceries and a cracker barrel, the store enjoyed a prosperous era during the 1940s and 1950s. Jones also dabbled in the sawmill business, selling railroad ties and mine posts. (Courtesy of Don Jones.)

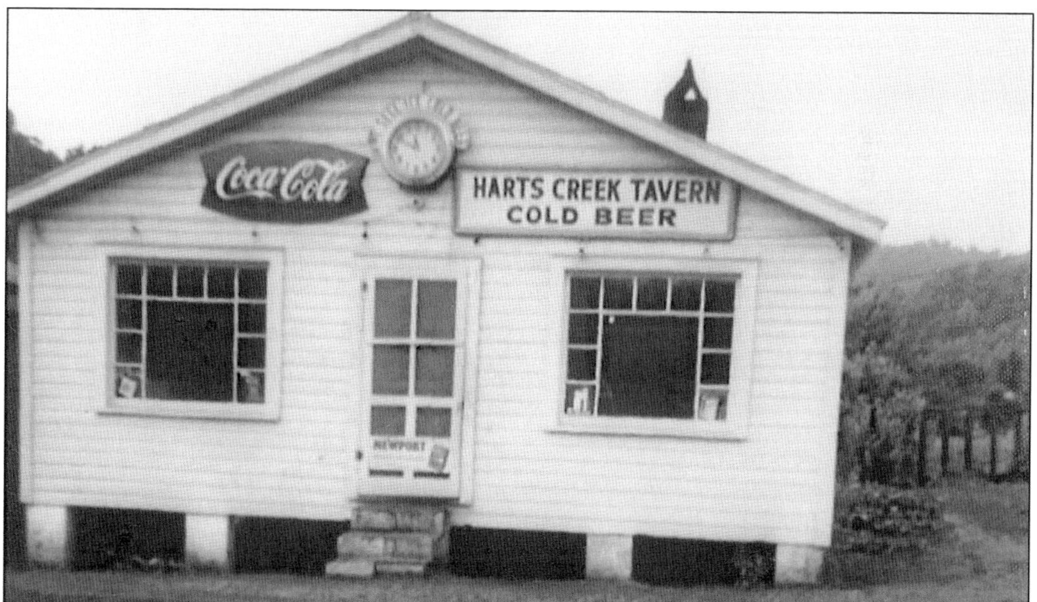

In addition to the enterprises of L.T. Jones, both Adkins' grocery stores, the post office, and the railroad tie yard, another downtown Harts business of bygone days was the White Shed Inn. This beer garden was owned and operated by Taylor Brumfield. (Courtesy of Cori Brumfield.)

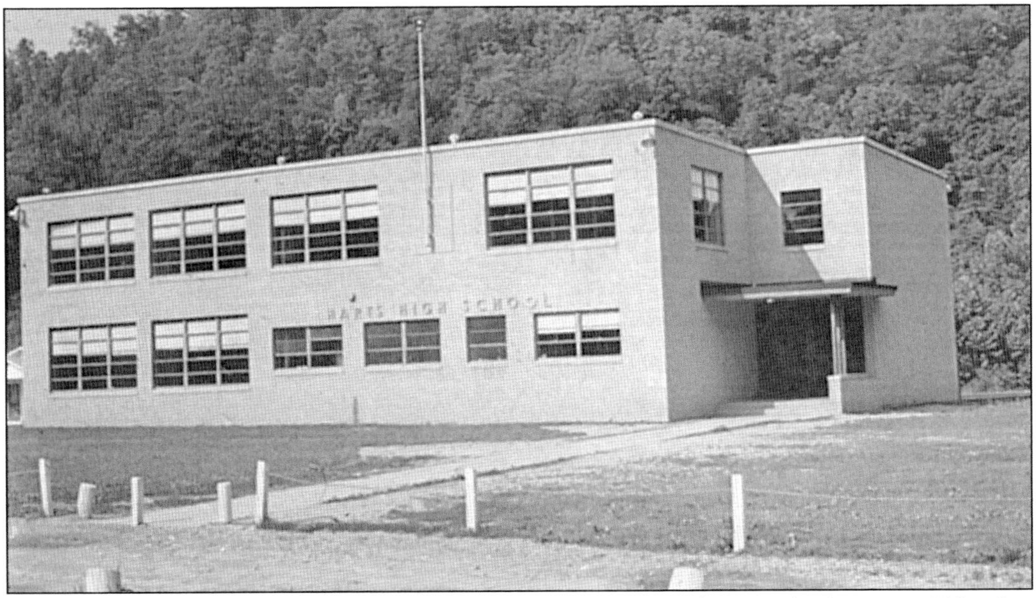

Before Harts High School was built in 1954, students were required to travel a distance of 20 miles, crossing Fourteen Mile Mountain in order to attend Guyan Valley High School at Pleasant View. Avoidance of this long and hazardous bus ride was part of the justification for the addition of the new school. (Harts High School yearbook photograph, courtesy of Odell Dingess.)

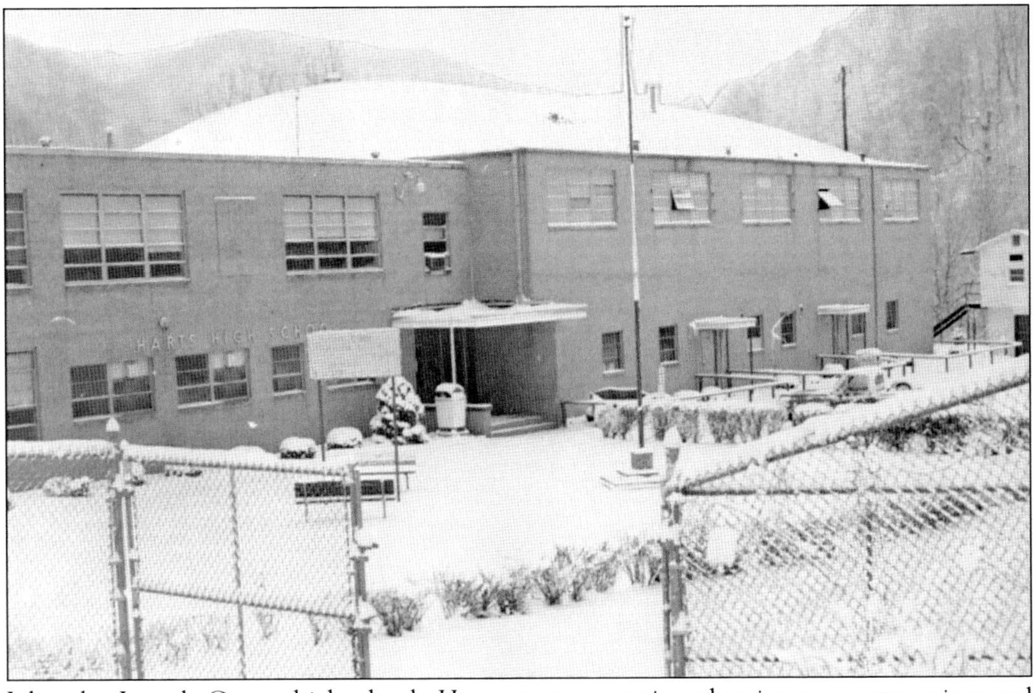

Like other Lincoln County high schools, Harts was no exception when it came to expansions and improvements. This is Harts High School in the mid-1970s after the addition of a gymnasium. The building functioned for a few years as a middle school, but was closed for good when a new Harts PK–8 School was opened in 2011. (Harts High School yearbook photograph, courtesy of Denise Atkins-Hoke.)

The old Harts Grade School building was located at the south end of Harts, across the railroad tracks in a sharp curve where a convenience store is located today. After being closed, it was owned by Herb Adkins, who rented it out to tenants until about 1975. On the porch are, from left to right, Bertha Dempsey, May Dempsey Farley and Winfred Farley, and their dog. (Courtesy of Billy Adkins.)

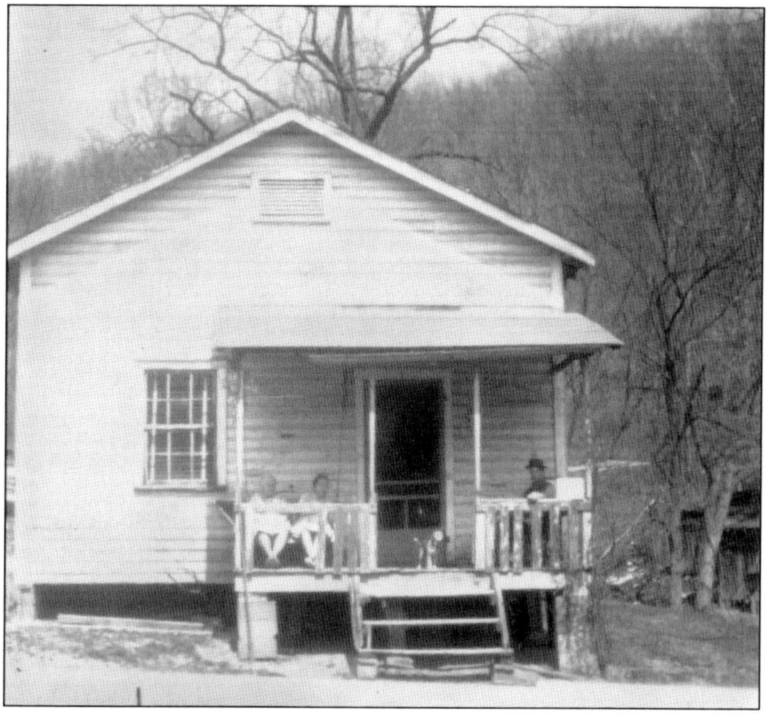

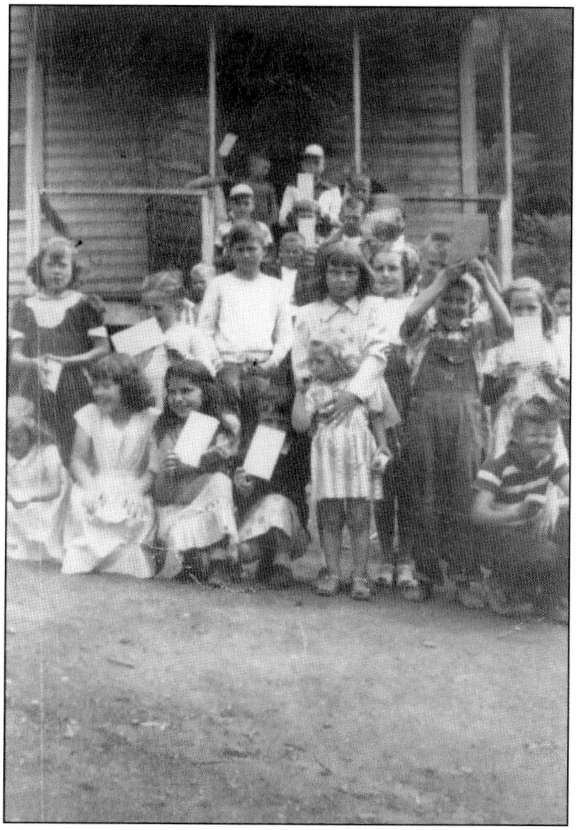

Harts Creek Grade School students appear to be happy about their report cards in this 1952 photograph. Over 100 one-room schoolhouses operated in Lincoln County as late as the end of the 1940s, but most of these were closed during the 1960s. Harts students were sent to a new brick building at Ferrellsburg beginning in 1963. Ferrellsburg Elementary eventually fell victim to further consolidation. (Courtesy of Billy Adkins.)

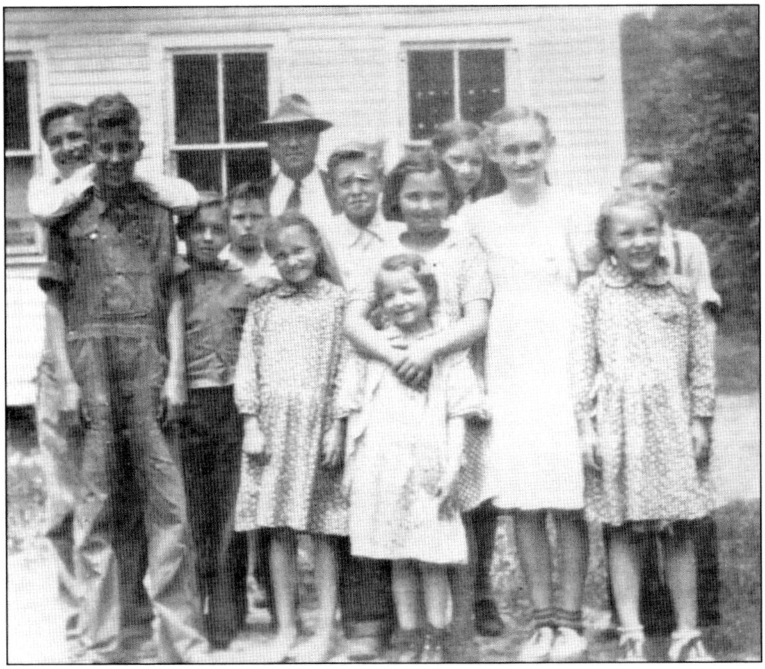

Representative of a typical one-room schoolhouse is the Sand Creek School, seen here behind the students and teacher in 1945. At that time, a total of 28 of these operated in Harts Creek District alone, including Big Branch, Chandler, Dollie, Gill, Green Shoal, Harts, High Top, Laurel Fork, Left Fork, Limestone, Perry, Thompson Branch, and Toney. (Courtesy of Billy Adkins.)

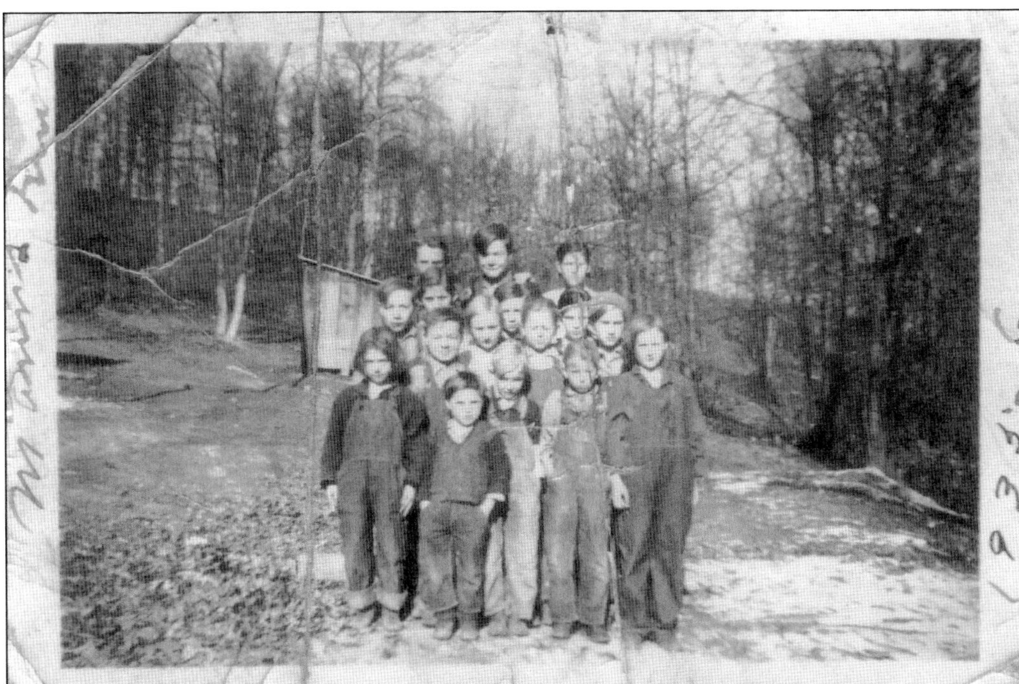

These are students at Manns Knob School on Little Harts in 1933. Pictured behind them is their privy. Completing the list of Harts Creek District schools were Adkins, Atenville, Broad Branch, Cole Branch, Copley Trace, Farley, Ferrellsburg, Fourteen, Francis Creek, Gartin, Lucas, Short Bend, and Union Gap. (Courtesy of Lucian Isaacs.)

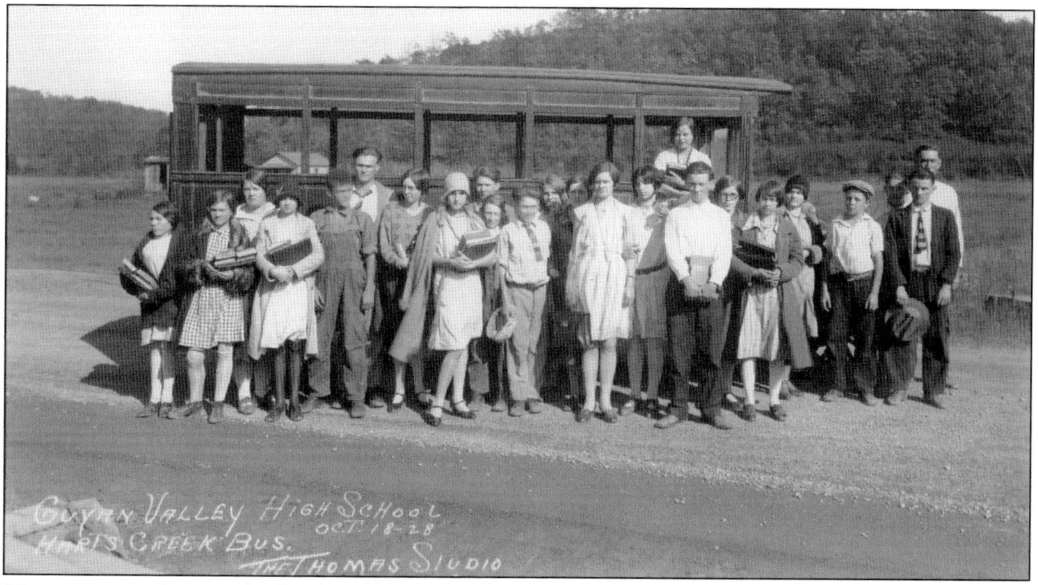

Harts-area students rode this bus to Guyan Valley High when it opened in 1926. Others took the train to the Sheridan depot, crossed the swinging bridge there, and walked the remaining mile to school. Harts residents responded to school consolidation in 2006 by sending their students to Chapmanville Regional High School in Logan County, only 15 minutes away, rather than sending them by bus to Hamlin. (MU-Lambert.)

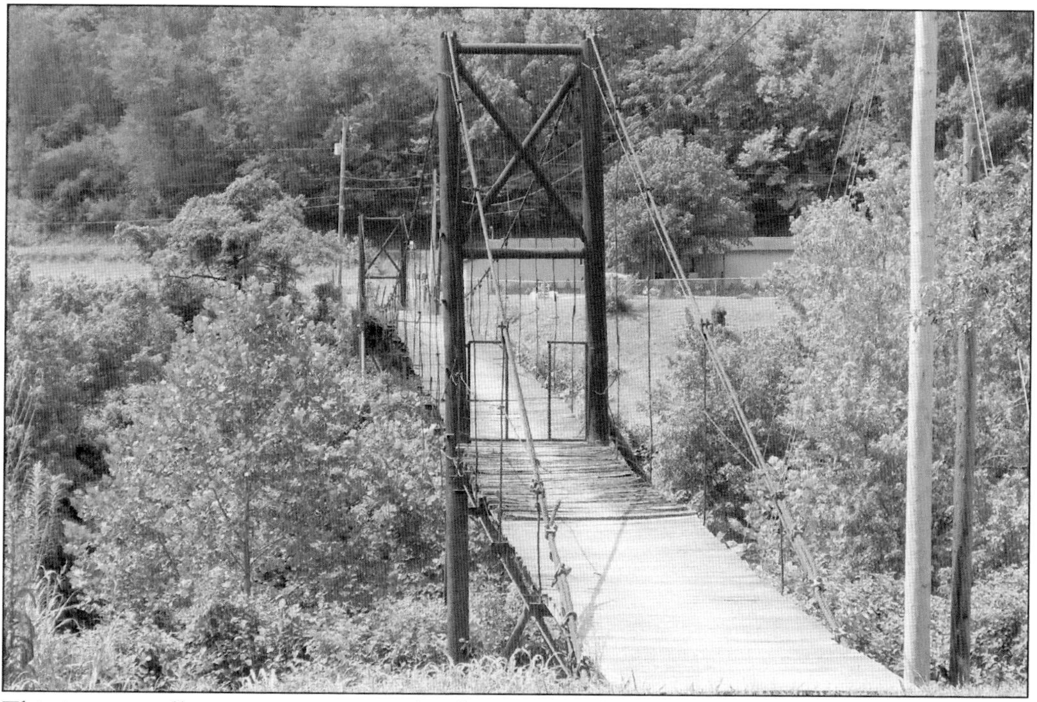

This is an excellent surviving example of a swinging bridge, located at Ferrellsburg near the intersection of Route 10 and Green Shoals Road. Designed for pedestrian traffic, such bridges were used primarily by pupils to travel to and from school. Other such bridges also spanned the Guyandotte River at Sheridan, Hubball, and Atenville. (AC.)

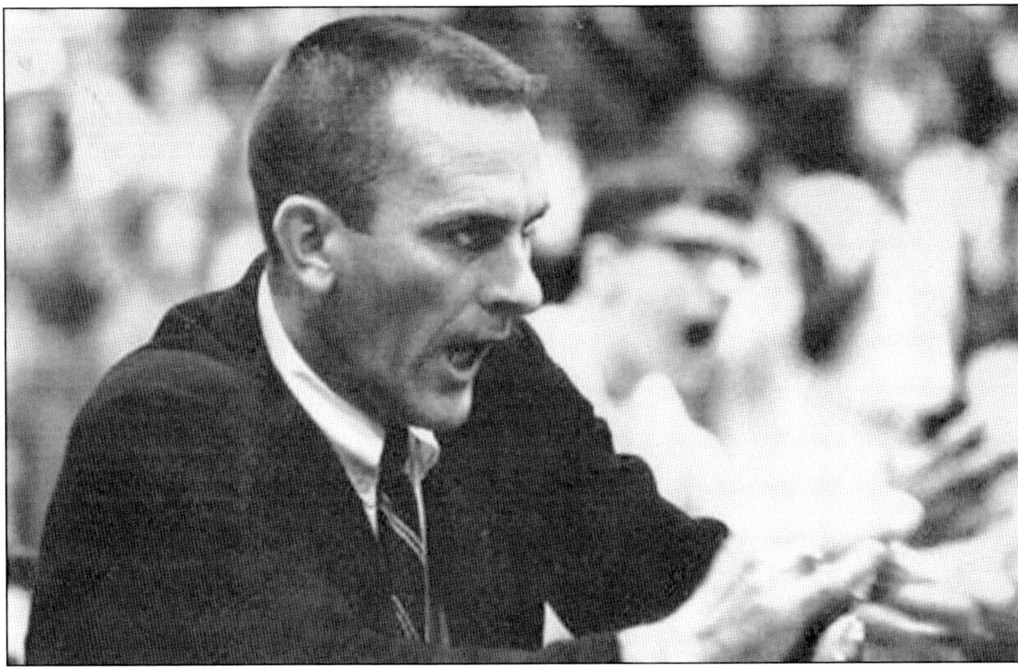

Under the direction of coaches Kyle Garretson (pictured) and Harry Kirk, the Harts High Lions (known for their full-court press and fast-breaking style of play) won West Virginia Class A state basketball championships in 1969, 1978, and 1990. Harts racked up an impressive number of unofficial Lincoln County championships as well. (Courtesy of Ronnie Z. McCann.)

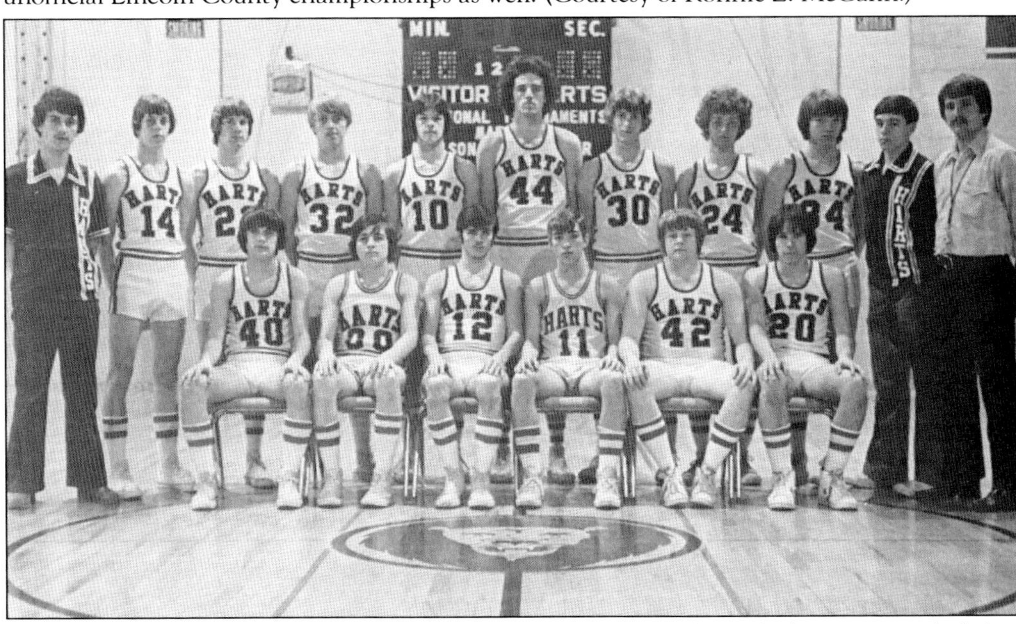

One home-court advantage enjoyed by Harts was a gymnasium where the heat was regularly kept above 90 degrees, causing opposing teams to literally wilt from both the heat and relentless style of play. This 1978 championship squad featured center Scott Frye (No. 44), who went on to have a successful career at Concord College. (Harts High School yearbook photograph, courtesy of Denise Atkins-Hoke.)

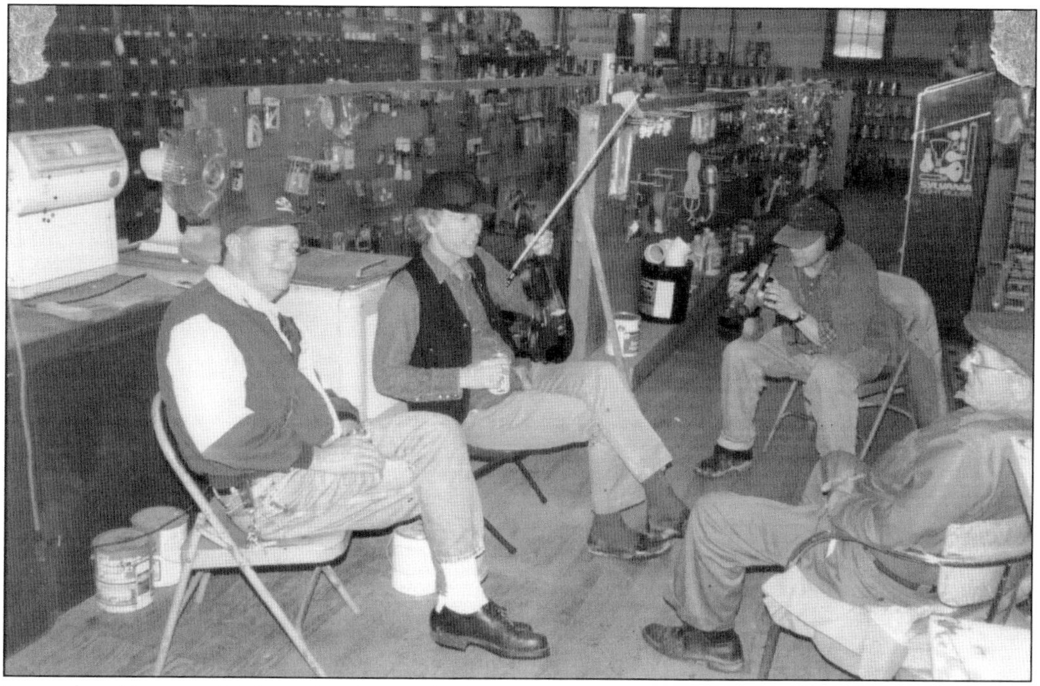

Legendary bluegrass fiddler John Hartford, whose compositions were featured in the motion picture *O Brother, Where Art Thou?*, became deeply interested in the history of Harts Creek through the music of Ed Haley. "Blind Ed" was the son of Milt Haley, who was killed by Al Brumfield's vengeful posse during the "Lincoln County Feud." Hartford is shown here performing at L.T. Jones's store. (Courtesy of Don Jones.)

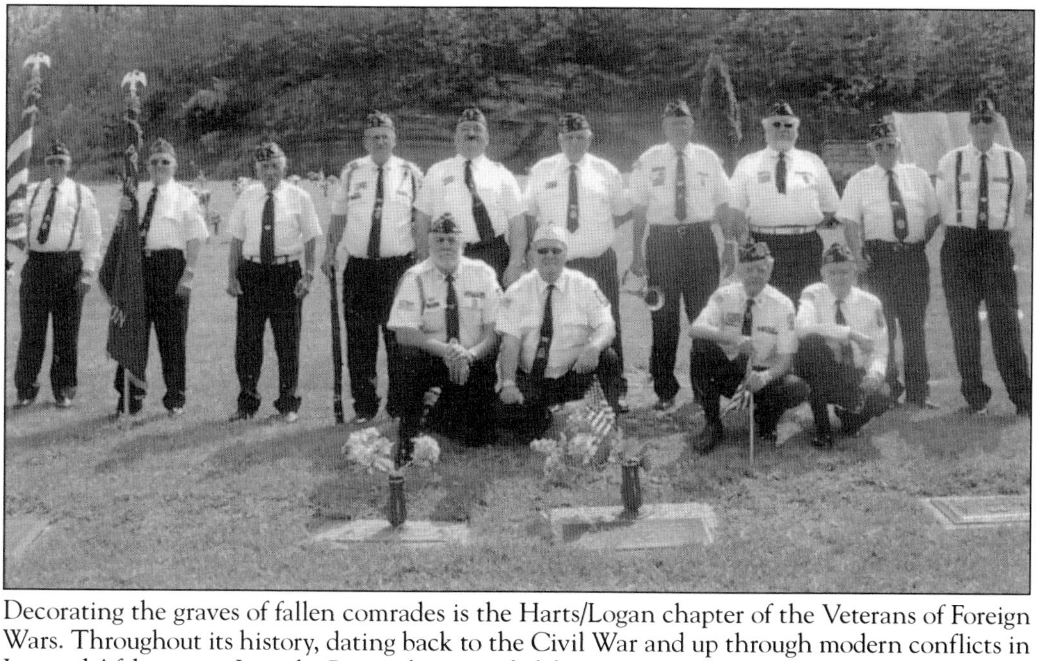

Decorating the graves of fallen comrades is the Harts/Logan chapter of the Veterans of Foreign Wars. Throughout its history, dating back to the Civil War and up through modern conflicts in Iraq and Afghanistan, Lincoln County has provided disproportionately high numbers of servicemen to all branches of the military. (Courtesy of Shorty Frye.)

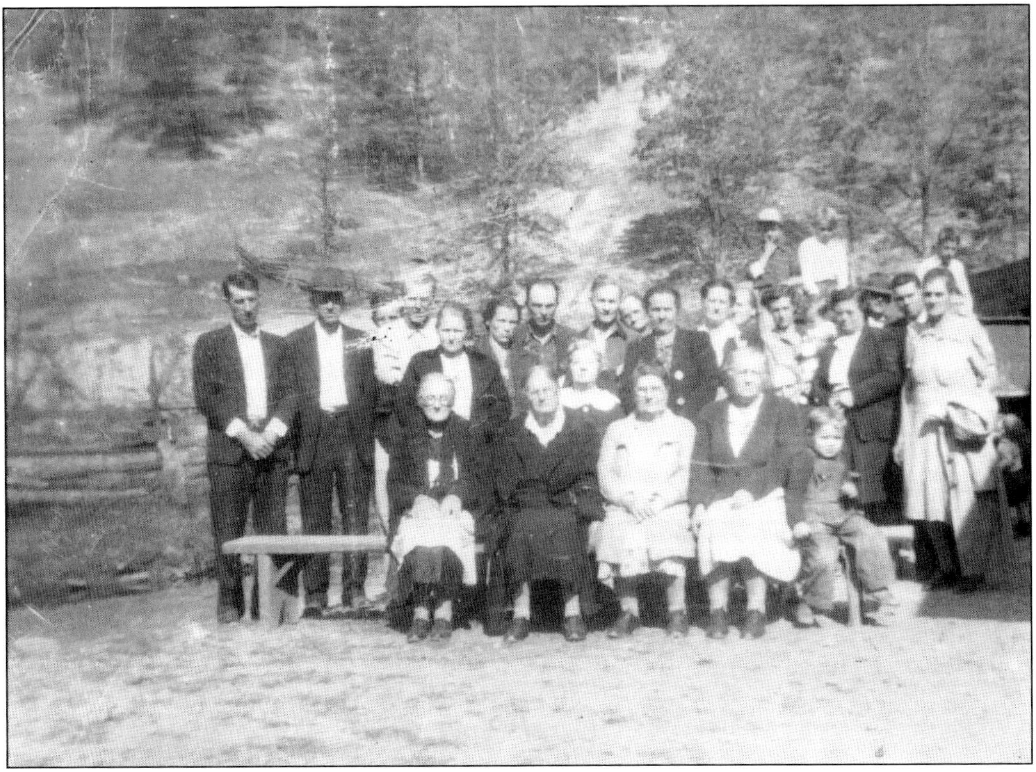

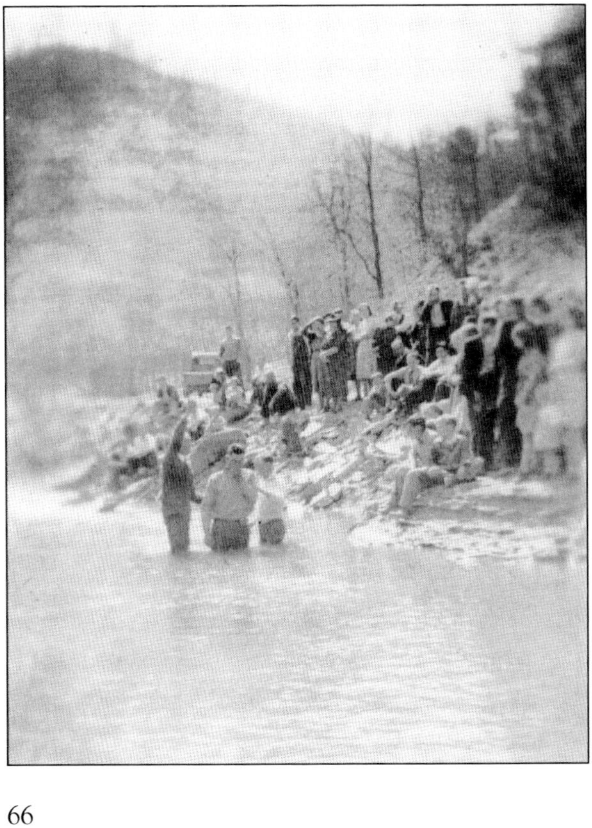

Sitting almost directly astride the Lincoln–Logan county line just off the West Fork of Harts Creek (modern signs identify this by the more directionally-correct label "East Fork," but the stream is actually named after an early settler called West) is the Workman Fork Church. This church gathering dates from around 1940. (Courtesy of Billy Adkins.)

Baptismal ceremonies in local creeks and rivers could sometimes be hazardous due to slippery rocks or swift currents. Pictured here is the 1938 baptism of Scott Fugate in the Guyandotte River. While some Lincoln County churches have installed baptismal wells, riverside ceremonies are sometimes still performed. (Courtesy of Billy Adkins.)

Three

Hamlin on the "Mighty" Mud

Hamlin represents another Lincoln County oddity; it is a rare county seat that is not located on any navigable river or railroad. About all that was here when Lincoln County was organized was Likens's Mill and—so says the legend—a briar patch, although the town might have been mapped out in honor of Leonidas Hamline and recognized by the Virginia General Assembly in 1853. The county jail was the first public building constructed.

Despite its location on the "mighty" Mud, the largest tributary of the Guyandotte River (but hardly deep enough to float a boat), Hamlin has evolved over the years into the commercial and business center of Lincoln County. By 1884, it boasted eight stores, two hotels, two mills, three doctors, and six lawyers. Today, it is home to the county's only high school, newspaper, and library. Two spectacular fires—the courthouse in 1909 and the high school in 1949—are momentous events in the town's history.

The twisting, meandering Mud (Hardesty's history describes it as "torturous") has carved out a broad, flat floodplain that is ripe for tobacco farming. "Devil weed" remains the number one cash crop in Lincoln County. It was in one of these sleepy little Mud River towns tucked in among the tobacco fields that the area's most famous resident was born. That would be Charles Elwood Yeager, who on October 14, 1947, climbed into the cockpit of a rocket-powered Bell X-1 aircraft and became the first human being to ever fly faster than the speed of sound.

Hamlin-area communities located along the "mighty" Mud and its numerous tributaries include Myra (Yeager's birthplace), Palermo, Portersville, Sias, and Sweetland.

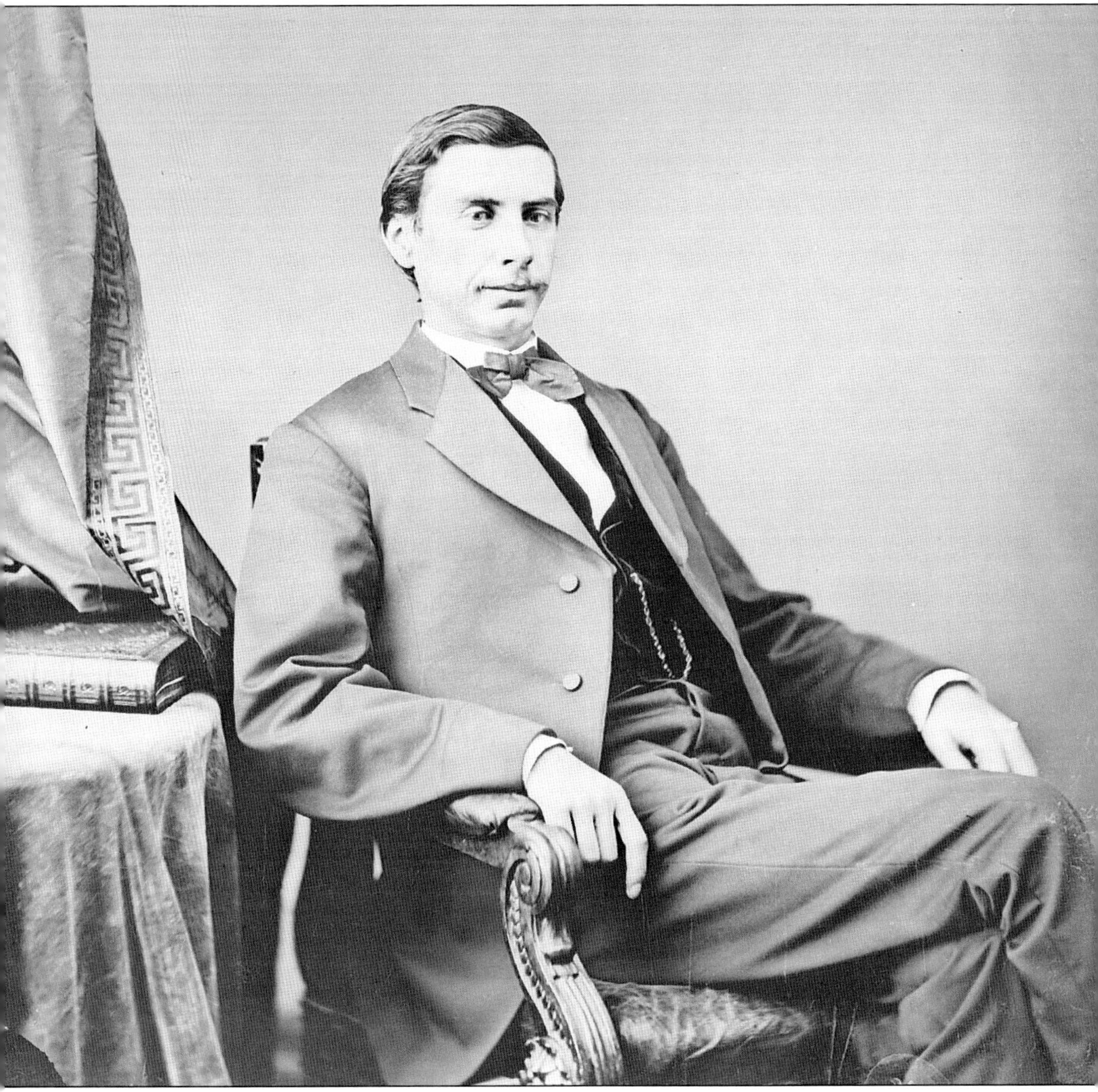

Gen. John Seashoal Witcher (1839–1906) was born in Cabell County, Virginia (now Lincoln County, West Virginia), and attended local public schools. He was elected clerk of the county circuit court in 1861 before enrolling in the 3rd West Virginia Cavalry Regiment as a lieutenant at the onset of the Civil War. His first cousin Vincent Addison Witcher commanded the Confederate 34th Battalion Virginia Cavalry. After rising through the ranks, General Witcher was mustered out of military service as a brevetted brigadier general. After the war, he served in the West Virginia House of Delegates (1865), as West Virginia's secretary of state (1866–1869), and in the US House of Representatives (1869–1871). Defeated for reelection to Congress in 1870, Witcher, a Republican, was appointed collector of internal revenue for West Virginia's Third District (1871–1876) by Pres. Ulysses S. Grant. Witcher later served as US pension agent (1878–1880) and US Army paymaster (1880–1899) before his retirement. He is buried in Arlington National Cemetery. (Photograph by Mathew Brady, courtesy of National Archives.)

Born in Lynchburg, Virginia, William Clifton Mahone (1821–1883) circulated the petition to have Lincoln County named after Abraham Lincoln and was the first president of the county board of supervisors. Mahone was the father-in-law of Gen. John S. Witcher and was married to Nancy Carroll, daughter of James Tillman Carroll. Mahone is buried in Fairview Memory Gardens at Hamlin. (AC.)

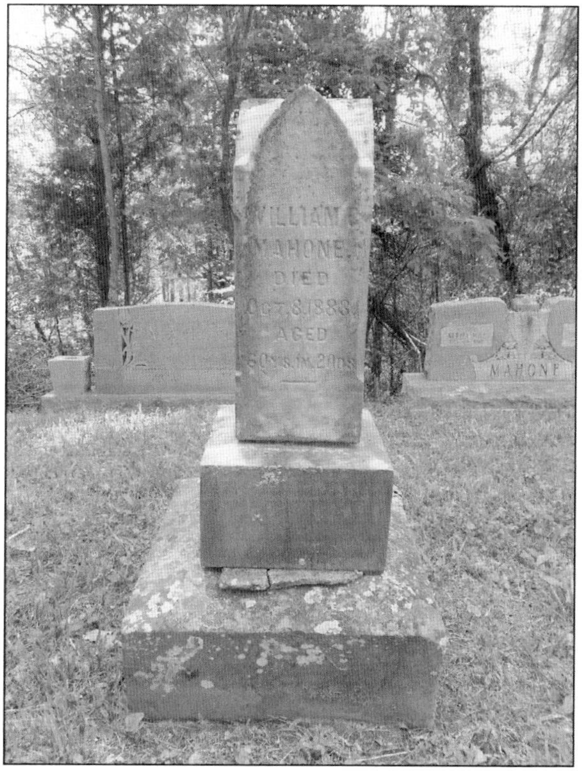

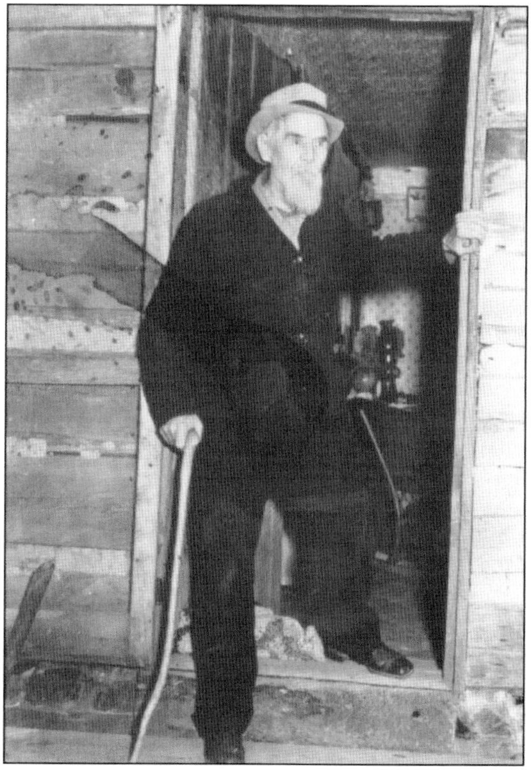

Fought near Hamlin on May 29, 1864, a Civil War skirmish between a company of the 3rd West Virginia Cavalry and scattered Confederate forces commanded by Maj. John Chapman was a Union victory. Fernandez Hager (pictured) was reportedly the only Union veteran attending the 75th anniversary ceremonies at Gettysburg in 1938 who did not need assistance climbing Little Round Top. (Courtesy of Debbie Pennington.)

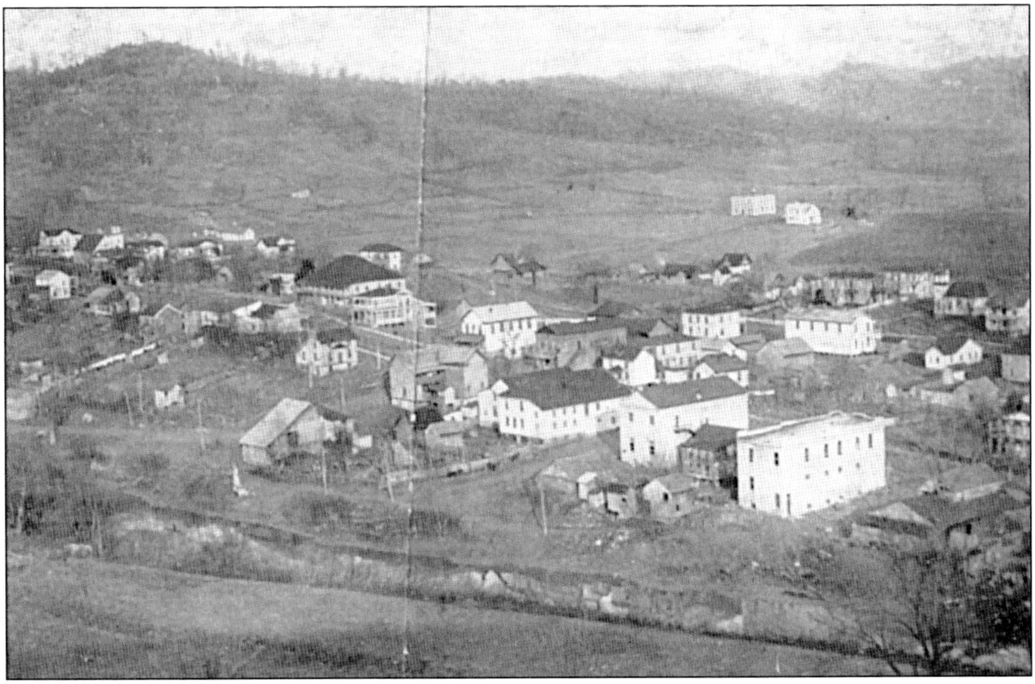

This c. 1910 bird's-eye view of Hamlin looks northeast across Mud River with the courthouse just out of view at the extreme left. The three prominent buildings along Main Street in the foreground are (left to right) Sweetland's General Store, Lincoln National Bank, and the Odd Fellows Hall. A hotel, with its hip roof and wraparound porch, can also be seen. (MU-Lambert.)

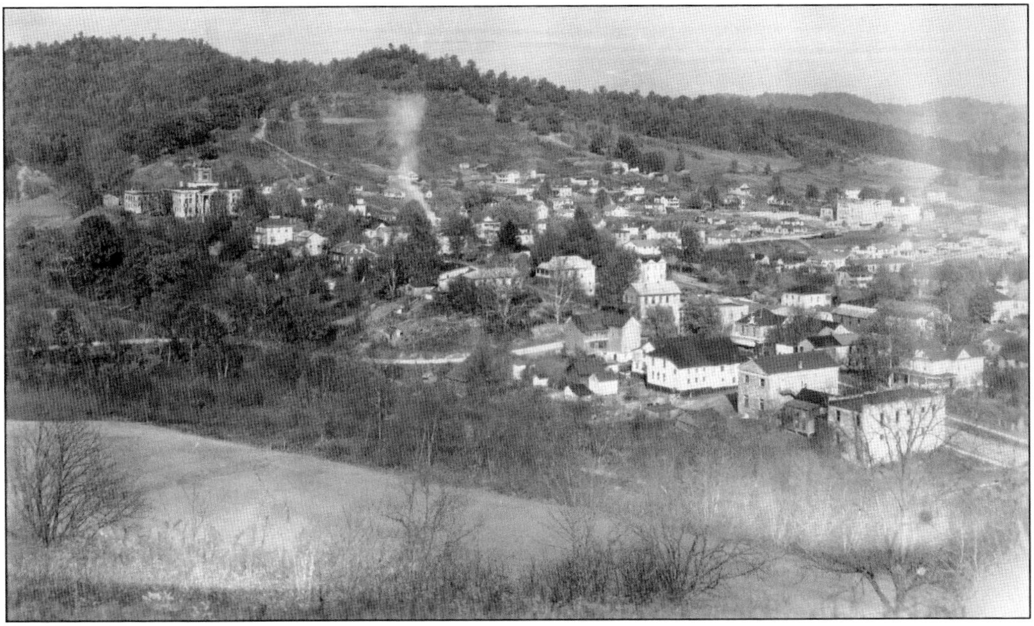

Considerable development had taken place in Hamlin by the time of this c. 1925 photograph, which was taken from approximately the same vantage point as the one shown above. Now visible are the courthouse, sitting at the top of Main Street, as well as Carroll District High School and Hamlin Grade School, the large buildings on the east side of town (back right). (MU-Lambert.)

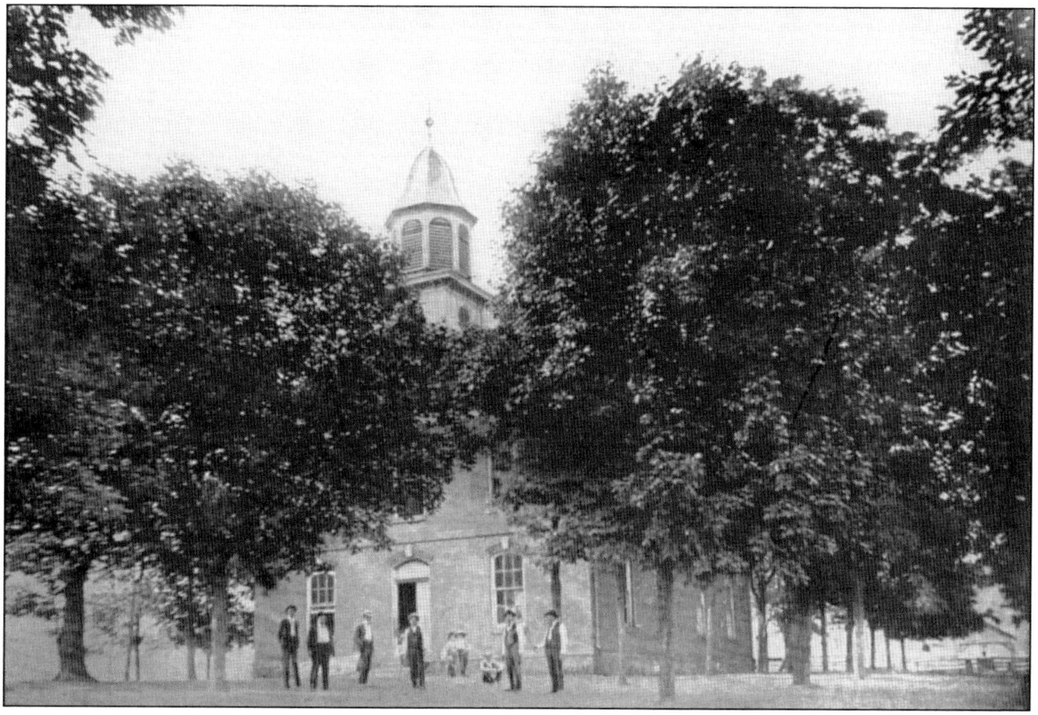

Lincoln County's first board-of-supervisors meeting was held at Hamlin Chapel on the Curry farm on March 11, 1867. Business was then conducted at White Hall (Hamlin Methodist Episcopal Church) until a suitable courthouse building could be constructed. The site that was eventually selected for this new building had previously been a briar patch. (MU-Lambert.)

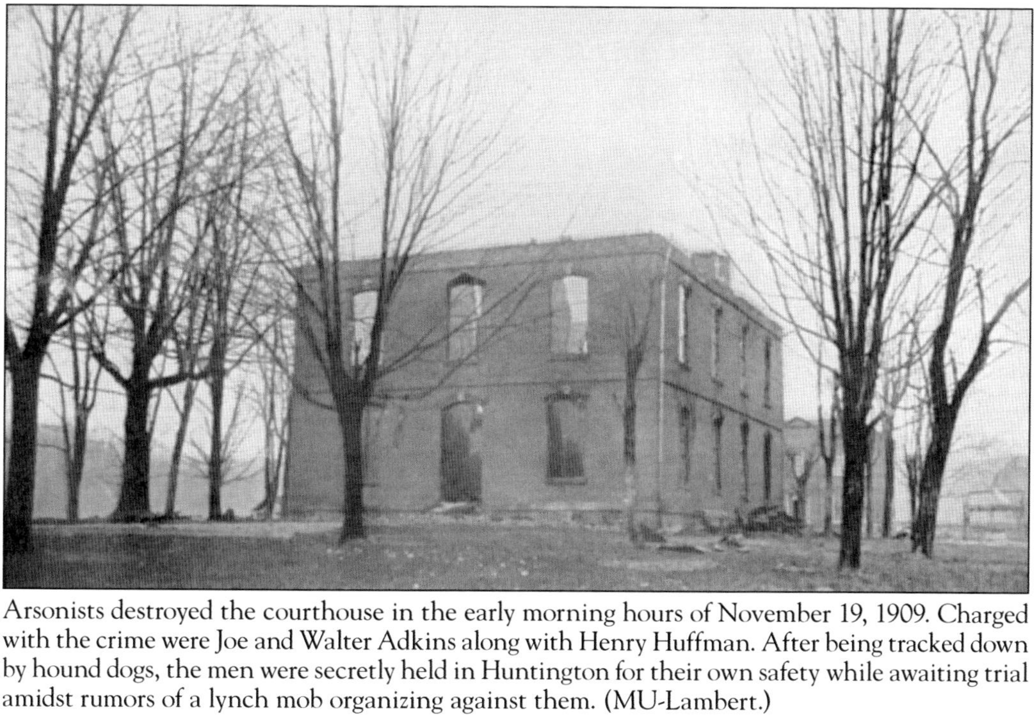

Arsonists destroyed the courthouse in the early morning hours of November 19, 1909. Charged with the crime were Joe and Walter Adkins along with Henry Huffman. After being tracked down by hound dogs, the men were secretly held in Huntington for their own safety while awaiting trial amidst rumors of a lynch mob organizing against them. (MU-Lambert.)

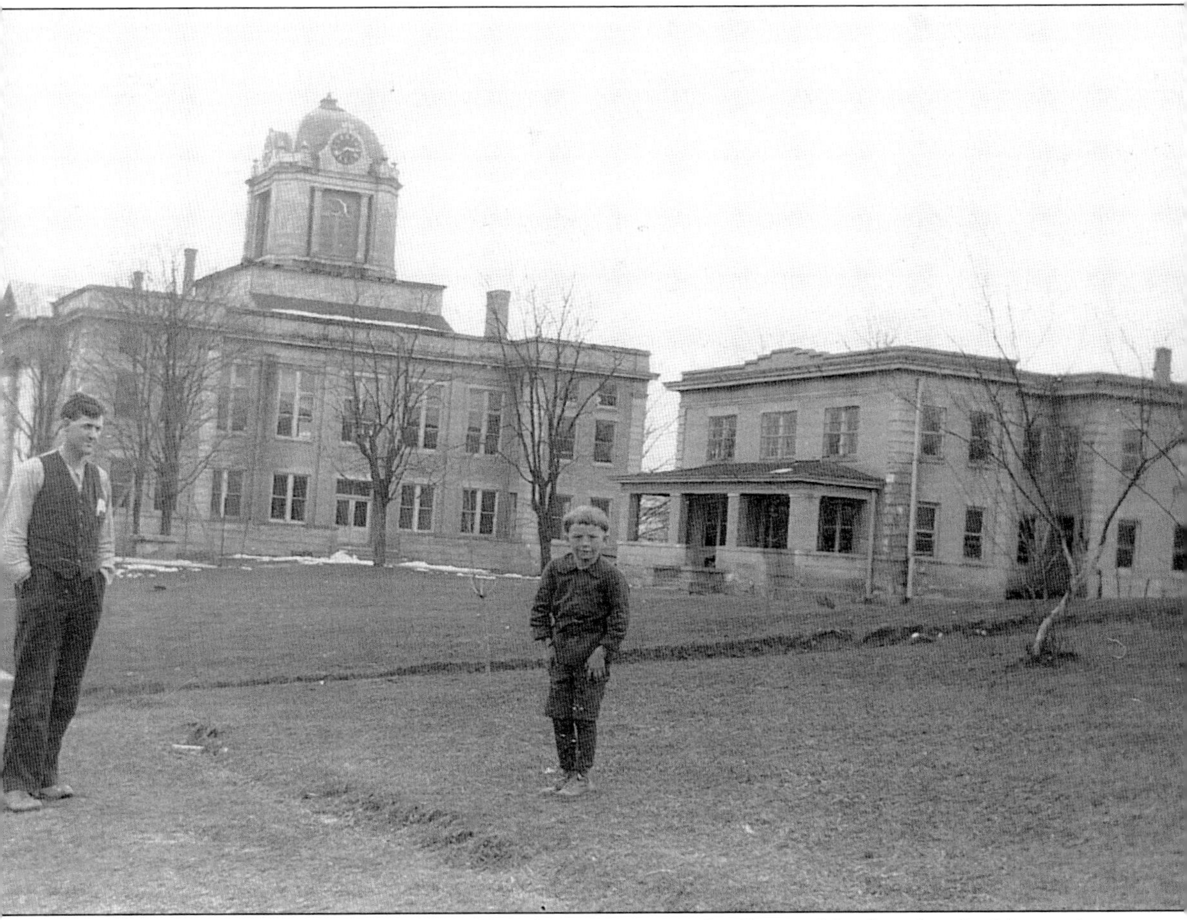

At their preliminary hearing, the alleged arsonists gave the flimsy alibi that they had been playing poker at Elias Stowers's house. But the case was never heard before a grand jury, and there is no surviving evidence of their prosecution. Destruction of property records has long been the suspected motive for the 1909 courthouse fire, which destroyed nearly all land and tax records, as well as birth certificates and marriage licenses. A new courthouse (left) was constructed between 1910 and 1911. Somewhat confusingly known as the "old" courthouse, it served the county faithfully for over half a century. The county jail (right) was Lincoln County's first public building. It was originally a 40-foot-by-40-foot two-story log structure with eight rooms. The jailer lived downstairs. Iron rods bolted to stone window frames in the upstairs prison cells were a deterrent against escape. (Courtesy of Billy Adkins.)

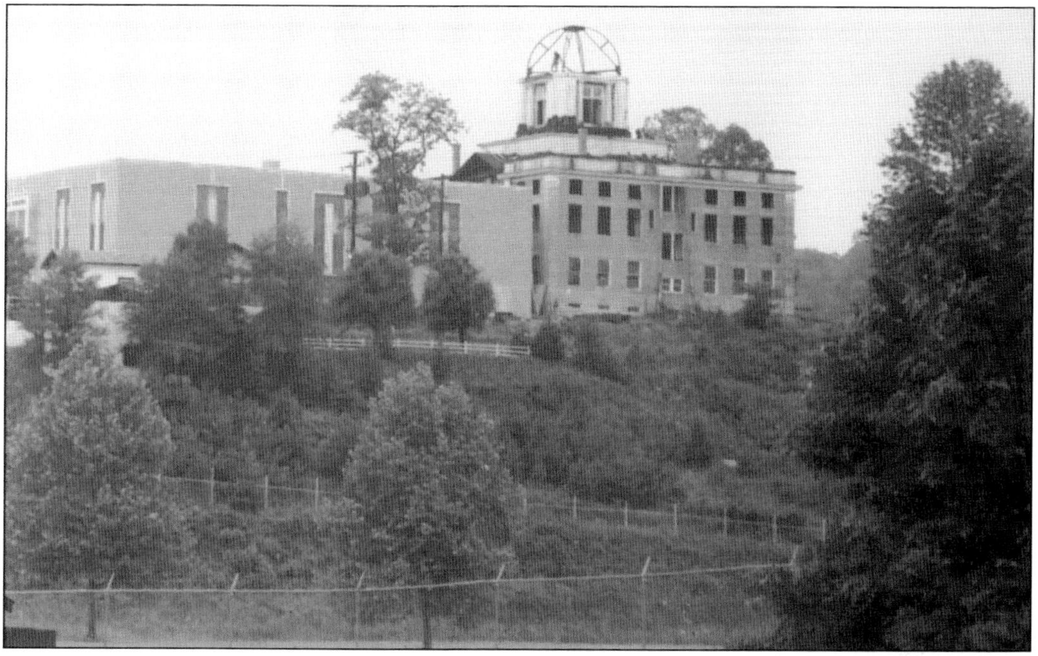

The cupola clock tower on the "old" courthouse comes down in 1964. Viewed from the ball fields along Route 3, the old courthouse sat back behind the new one. It is apparent from this photograph that the modern-style, square building lacks the character of its predecessor. (Photograph by Gene Brewer, courtesy of Lucian Isaacs.)

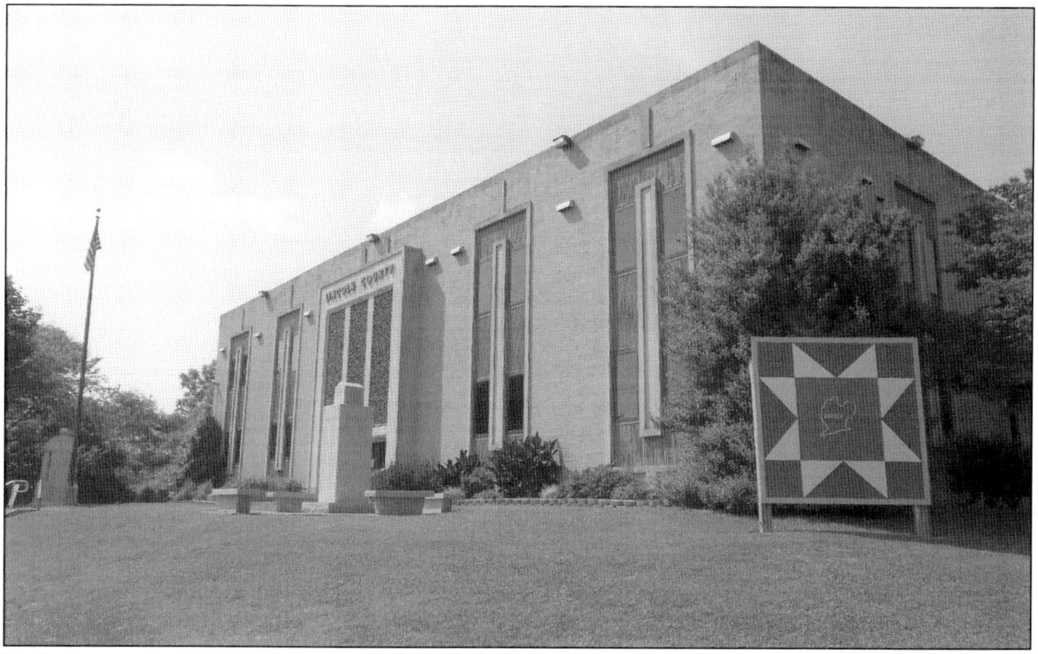

Today's courthouse, with its quilt square and monuments to fallen veterans, is home to the offices of the assessor, circuit clerk, circuit court, county clerk, county commission, family court, magistrate court, probation services, prosecuting attorney, and sheriff. A surviving section of the old jail is in a parking lot behind the building. (AC.)

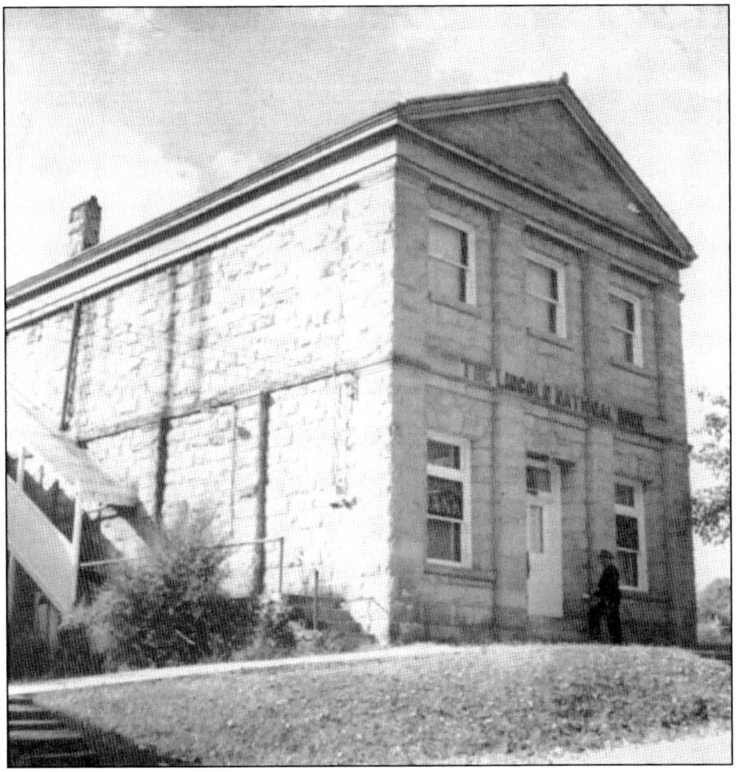

The Lincoln National Bank was founded in 1908 at Griffithsville as the Oil Field Bank and relocated to Hamlin around 1910. Operations were moved to a new facility at the corner of Lynn Avenue (Route 3) and Walnut Street in the early 1960s. It now does business as Community Trust Bank. Today, the old bank building hosts Hamlin Masonic Lodge 79, which was chartered on November 9, 1881. (AC.)

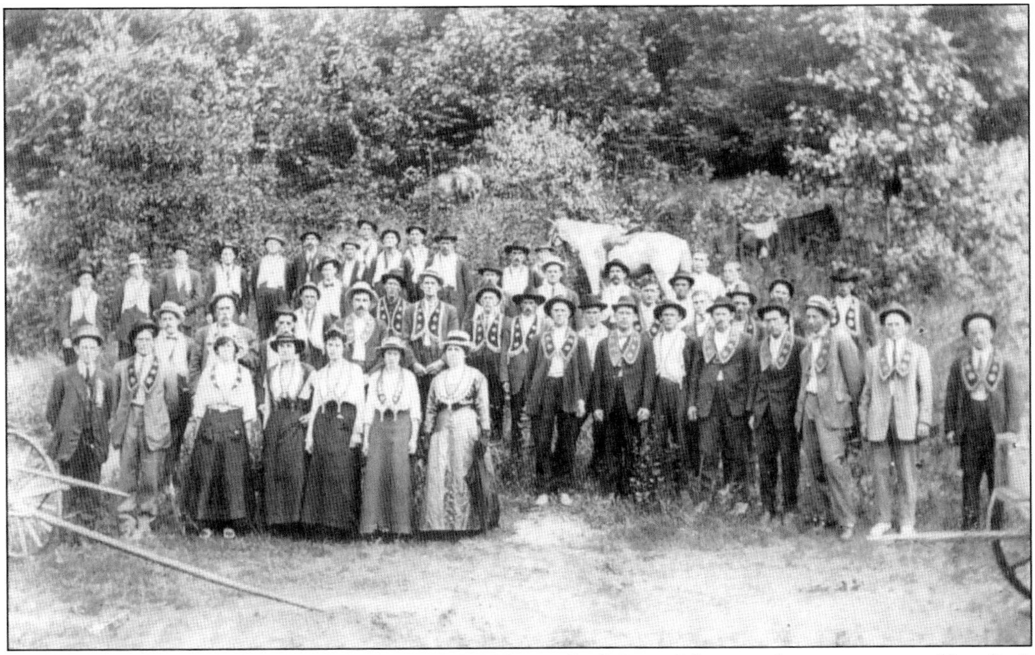

The Independent Order of Odd Fellows (IOOF) is a faith-based fraternal organization. Hamlin's IOOF Hall, where classes were held after the high school burned down in 1949, was located on Main Street beside the Lincoln National Bank. Pictured at this gathering of Odd Fellows are members of the Rebekahs, IOOF's sister organization. (Courtesy of Lottie Midkiff.)

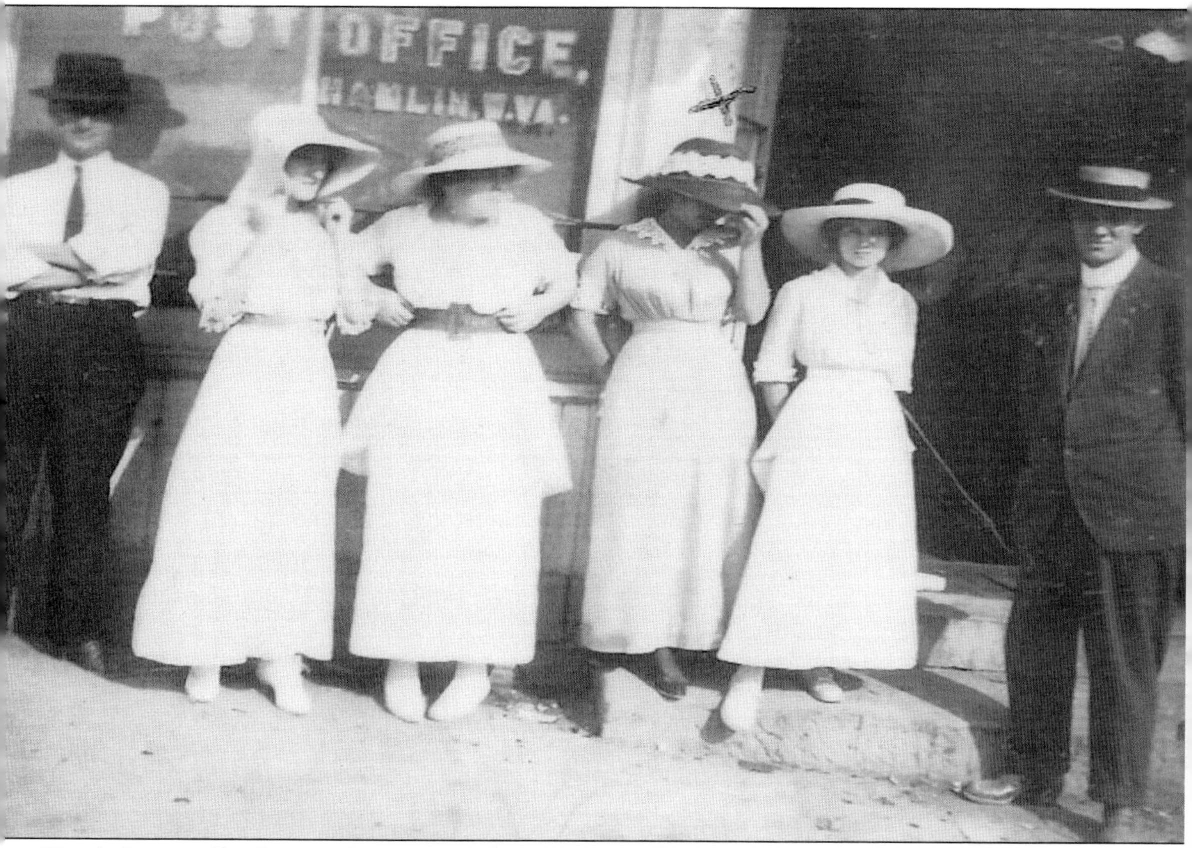

Hamlin's post office has a rather transient history. Originally located at the corner of Main Street and Lynn Avenue opposite Sweetland's Store, it eventually moved a couple of blocks away to Court Avenue. It was housed in the current Lincoln County Friends of the Arts offices for a time until landing in the current brick building across the street beside Route 3. Near the original post office location on Main Street was the Cassandra Hotel. An early boardinghouse, this historic building was also the former home of prominent early citizen John S. Wilkinson. Wilkinson was a judge, sheriff, and legislator whose second wife was the granddaughter of James Tillman Carroll (for whom Carroll District was named). Like most Hamlinite leaders, Wilkinson voted against Virginia's secession ordinance in 1861. (LCFOA.)

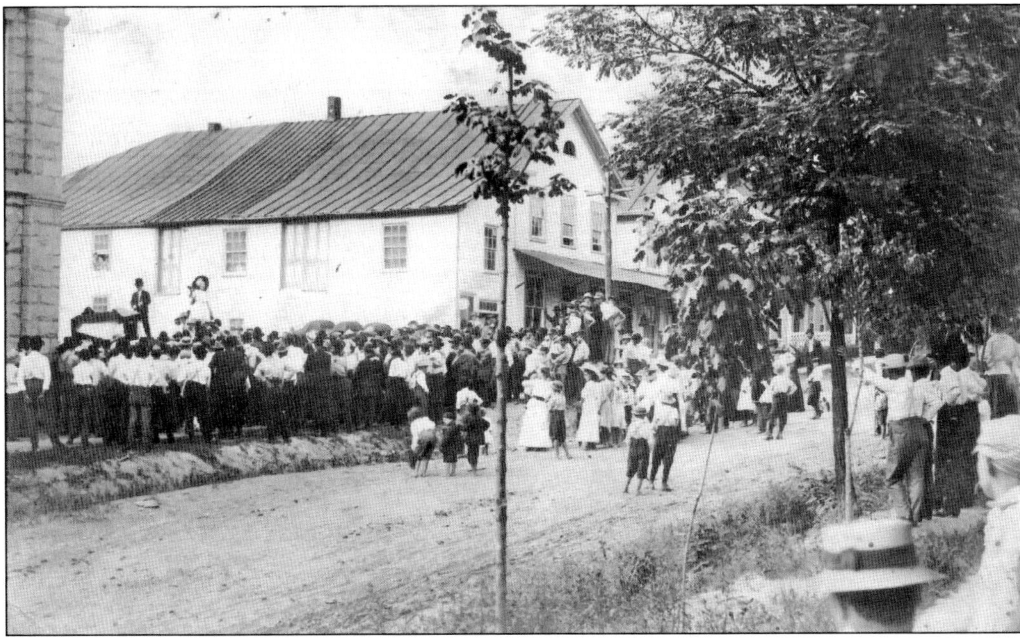

I.V. Sweetland was one of Hamlin's earliest merchants, opening a store here in 1868. His store was located beside the Lincoln National Bank at the intersection of Main Street and Lynn Avenue. This is now the site of the Hamlin-Lincoln County Public Library. The bank may be seen at the extreme left of the photograph. (Courtesy of Gary McClure.)

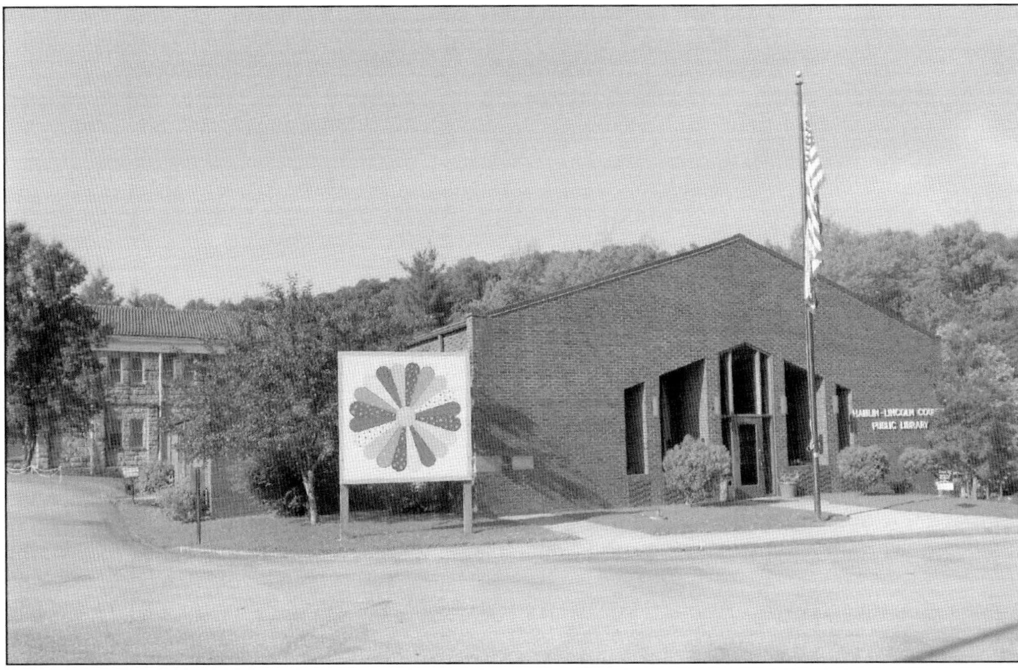

Established in 1972, the collection of the Hamlin-Lincoln County Public Library was housed for years in an unusual octagonal building beside the high school. To accommodate its growing collection, a new facility was eventually constructed on the Sweetland Store site. The old bank building is visible in the background of this modern photograph. (AC.)

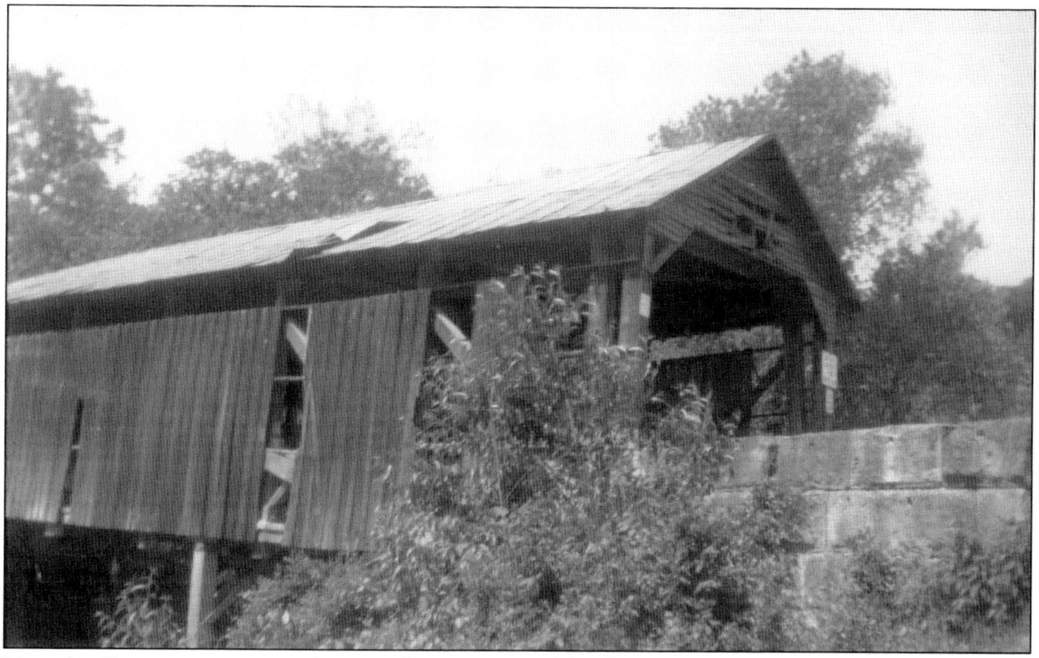

Lincoln County was never known for its covered bridges, since most stream crossings here were achieved by ford or ferry. The Walnut Street covered bridge at Hamlin is an exception. Dating to 1881, it was torn down years ago to make way for a modern structure. (Courtesy of Lucian Isaacs.)

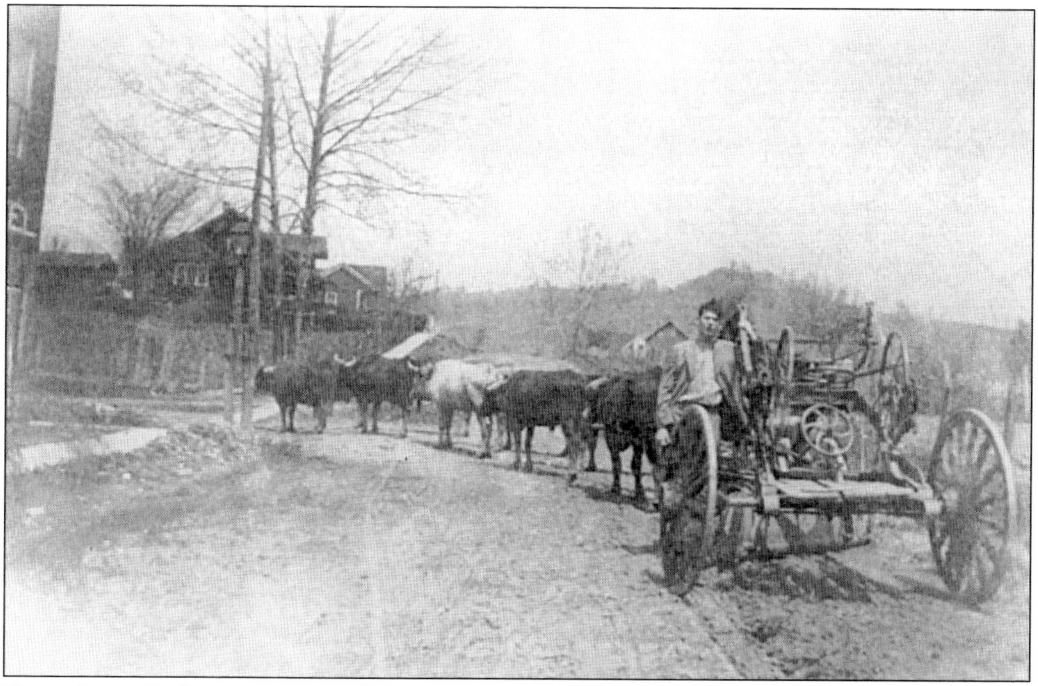

Driver Jason Pridemore poses with his oxen team in this 1916 view along Walnut Street. It was taken from the covered bridge, looking north. Also visible in this photograph is a corner of the Pelfrey Hotel, which was located at Vine Avenue. (HLCPL.)

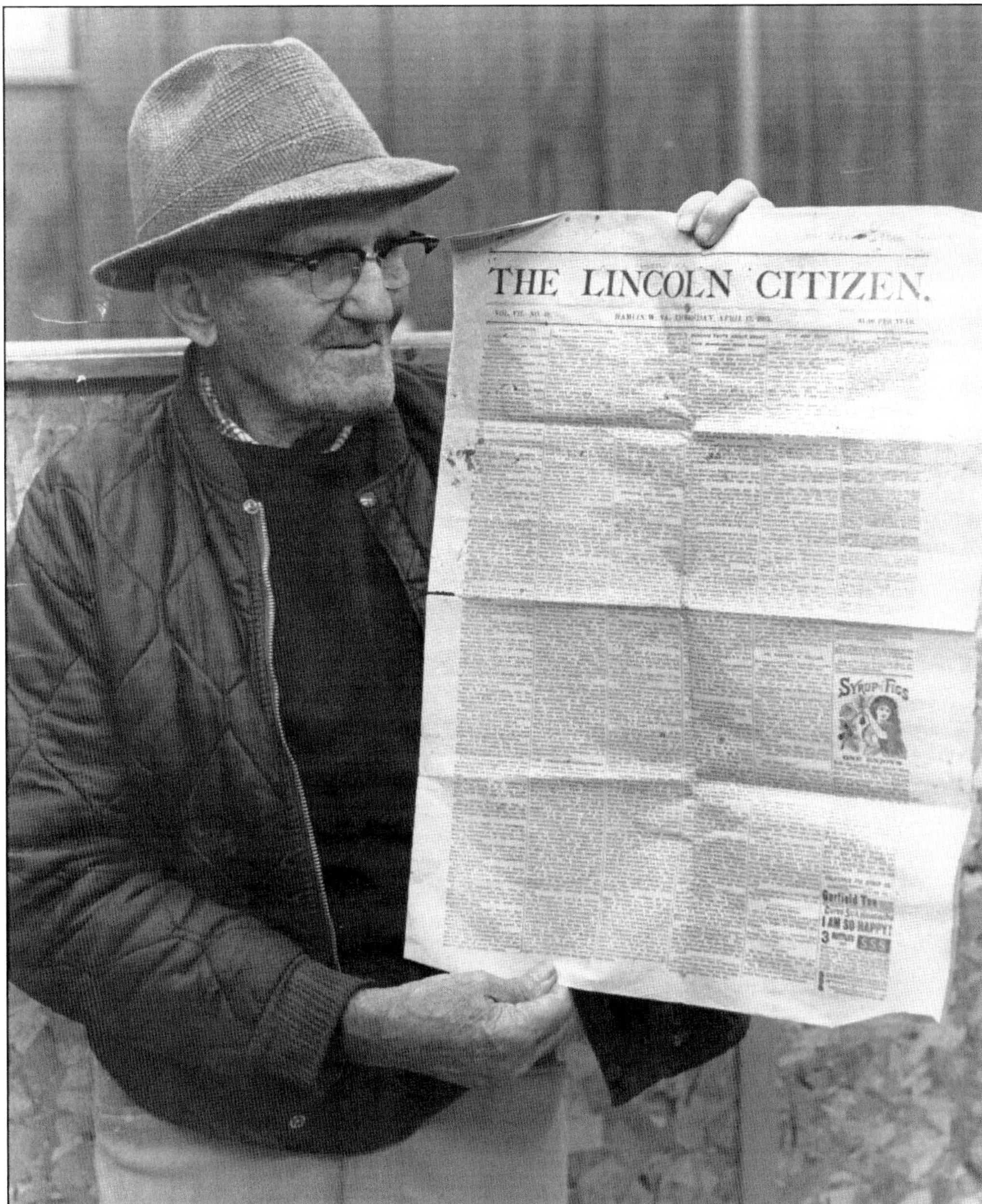

The county's first newspaper was the *Lincoln Clipper*, which went to press on September 15, 1881. Here, a local citizen displays a copy of another early newspaper, the *Lincoln Citizen*. For many years, the *Democrat* and the *Republican* were rival Hamlin newspapers. The *Democrat* eventually became the *Lincoln News-Sentinel* while the *Republican* evolved into the *Lincoln Journal*. With printing presses at 328 Walnut Street, the *Lincoln Journal* is the only operating newspaper in the county today. In bygone days, towns and villages all over Lincoln County published local community newspapers. (Courtesy of *Lincoln Journal*.)

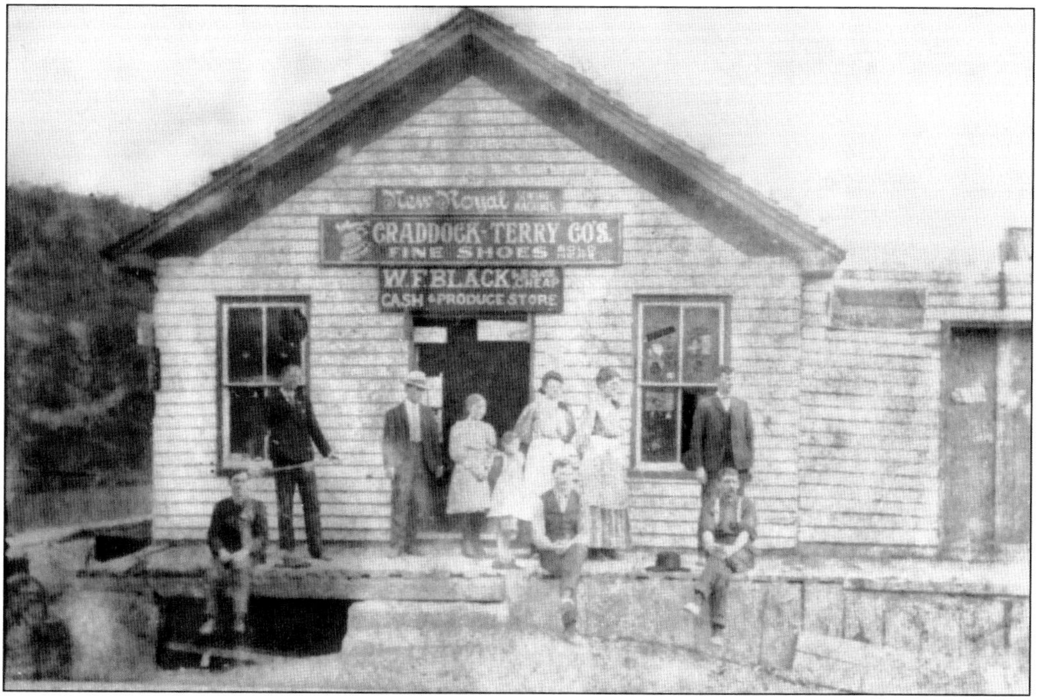

W.F. Black and Sons operated this mercantile store at Myra, selling everything from buggies to caskets. Since Black's store doubled as the Myra Post Office and had the area's only telephone, the building was a community focal point. A vintage 1926 plow from the Black farm now resides at the intersection of Upper Mud River Road and Route 3. (HLCPL.)

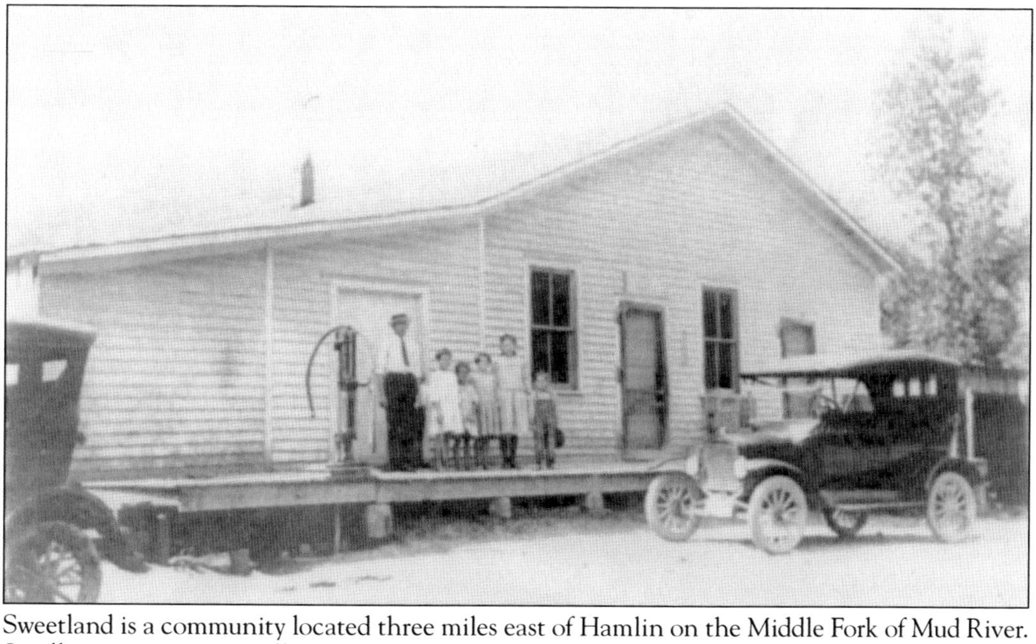

Sweetland is a community located three miles east of Hamlin on the Middle Fork of Mud River. Small community post offices along the "mighty" Mud are a vanishing species. The Sweetland Post Office was closed years ago, and others were shut down in 1994, at Palermo; in 1997, at Sias; and in 2011, at Myra. (LCFOA photograph, courtesy of Olive Hager.)

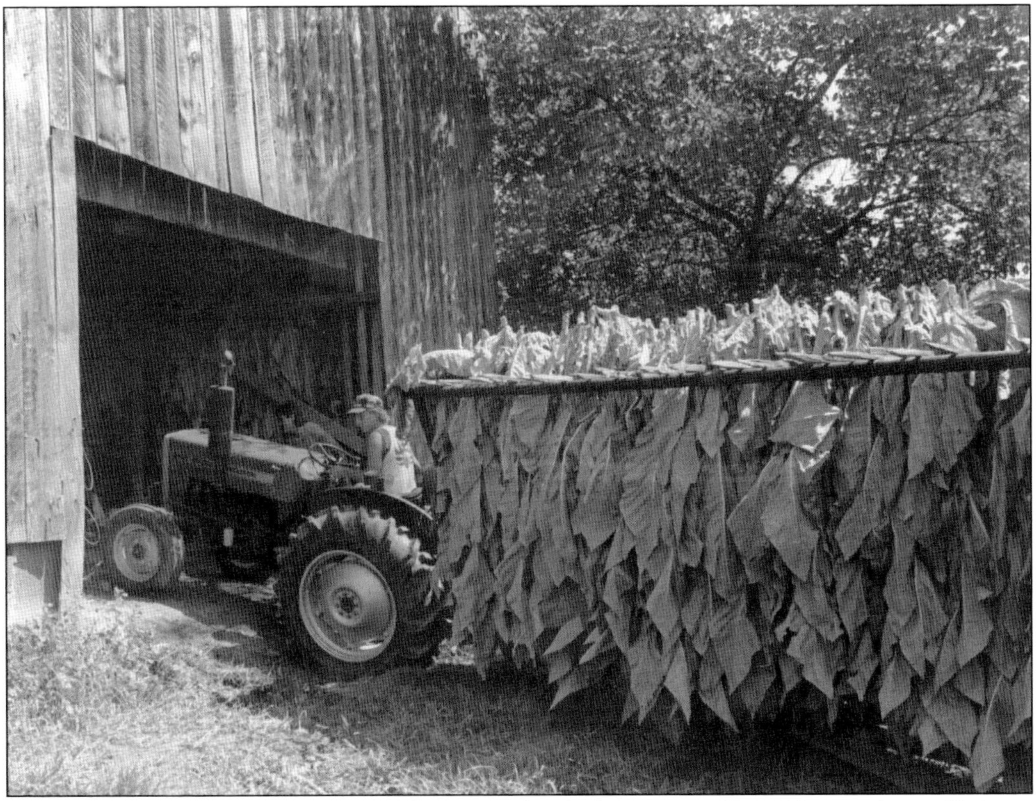

Lincoln County produced over 1.4 million pounds of tobacco in 1953 and has traditionally been West Virginia's leading grower of the crop. Tobacco seedbeds are planted in March, transplanted to the fields in May or June, and harvested in September. The plant is then cut, hung, dried in barns for six to eight weeks, stripped, and sold to market. (Courtesy of *Lincoln Journal*.)

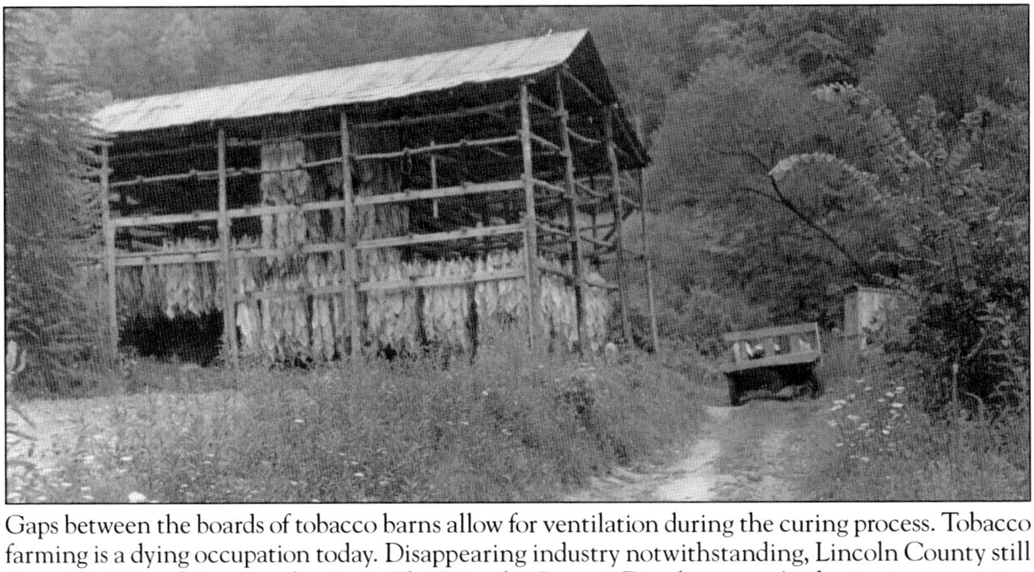

Gaps between the boards of tobacco barns allow for ventilation during the curing process. Tobacco farming is a dying occupation today. Disappearing industry notwithstanding, Lincoln County still draws Mail Pouch barn enthusiasts. The Lincoln County Development Authority is attempting to convert Route 3 into a tobacco barn scenic byway. (Courtesy of *Lincoln Journal*.)

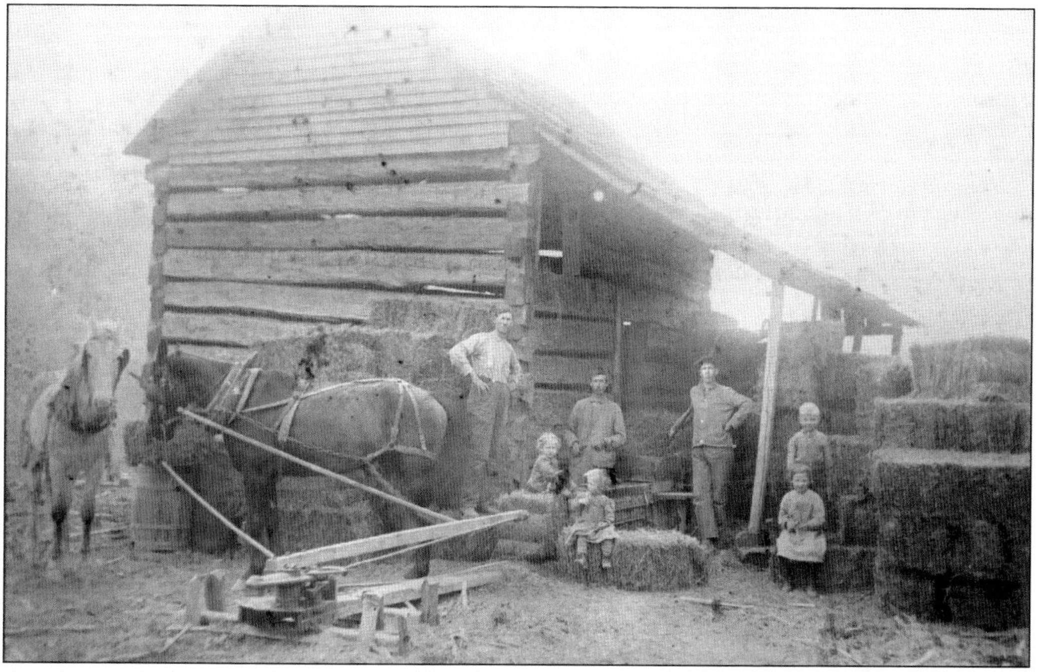

Another agricultural endeavor from olden days still practiced in Lincoln County is baling hay. Hay is cut into neat rows, bound into squares with baling twine (an alternate method is to roll it into large rolls), then stored in barns to dry. Livestock feed is its primary use. (MU-Lambert.)

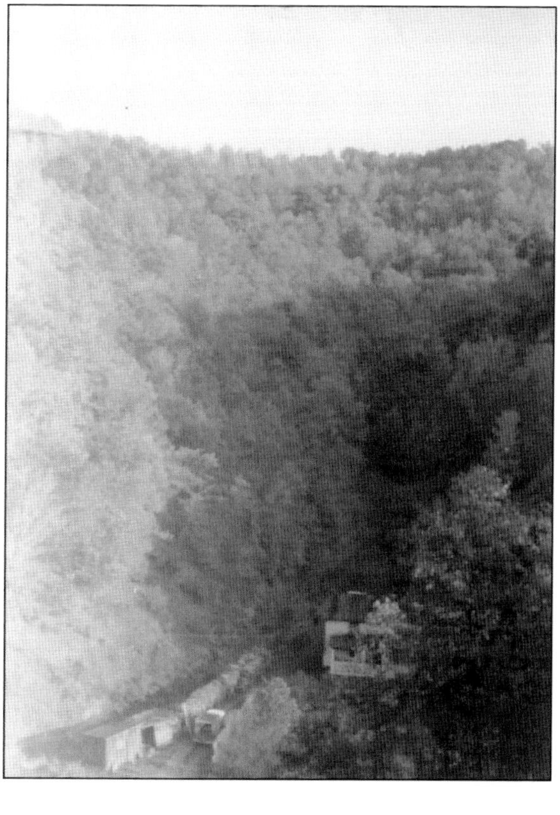

Scenes such as this inspired the national "Back-to-the-Land" Movement of the early 1970s. Lincoln County was at the epicenter of the movement, which locals remember as the time "when the hippies came." Lured by cheap land, natural beauty, and a simpler lifestyle, a commune was even established a few miles from Hamlin. The movement stalled, however, and most of the hippies left. (Elba Davidson collection.)

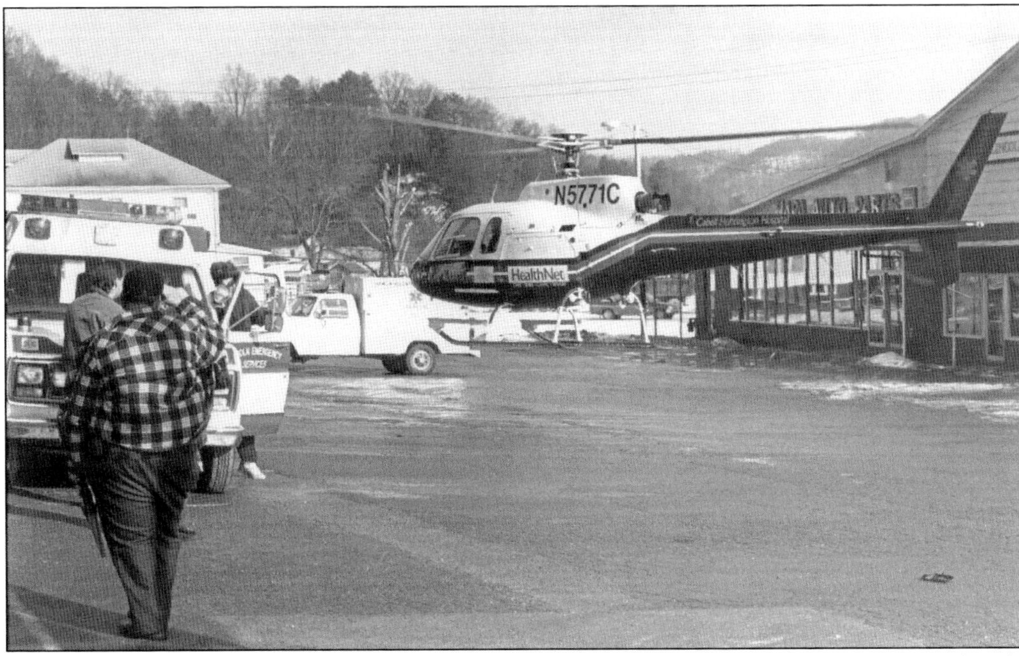

Lost in the excitement of this helicopter rescue is the inconspicuous building at the far right, the first-ever health care facility in the United States to be operated under the federally designated Rural Health Clinics Act (PL 95-210). The Lincoln Primary Care center was established in 1975, with care being conducted in a renovated storefront. (Courtesy of *Lincoln Journal*.)

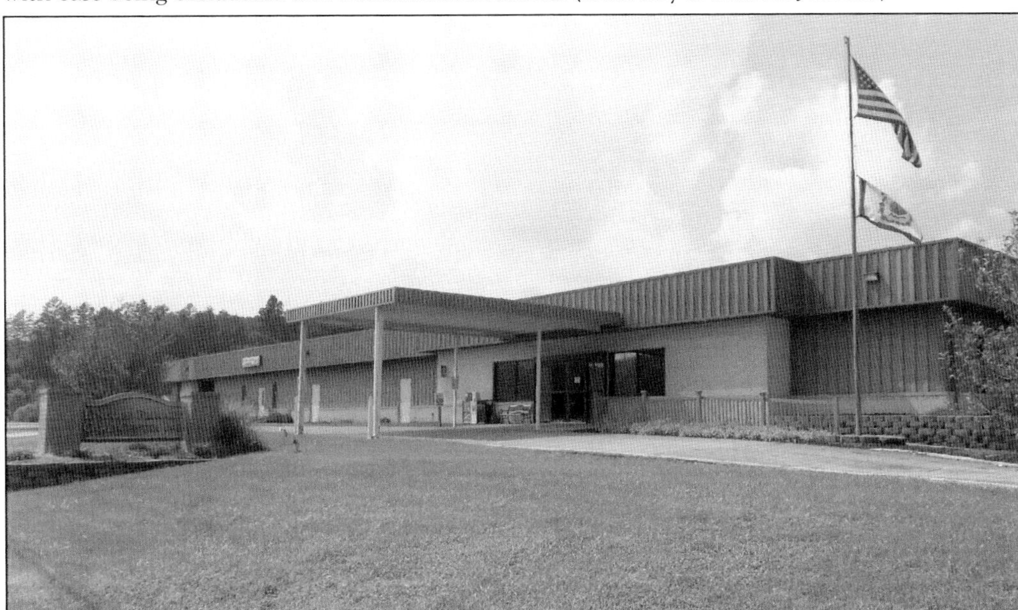

Recognized as a model rural health care provider and honored as the nation's outstanding rural health care practice by the National Rural Health Association, the Lincoln Primary Care Center moved across town into a new state-of-the-art building in 1990. It serves a six-county area and still provides patient transport services via the Health Net helicopter. Emphasis has been placed on family care since its beginning. (AC.)

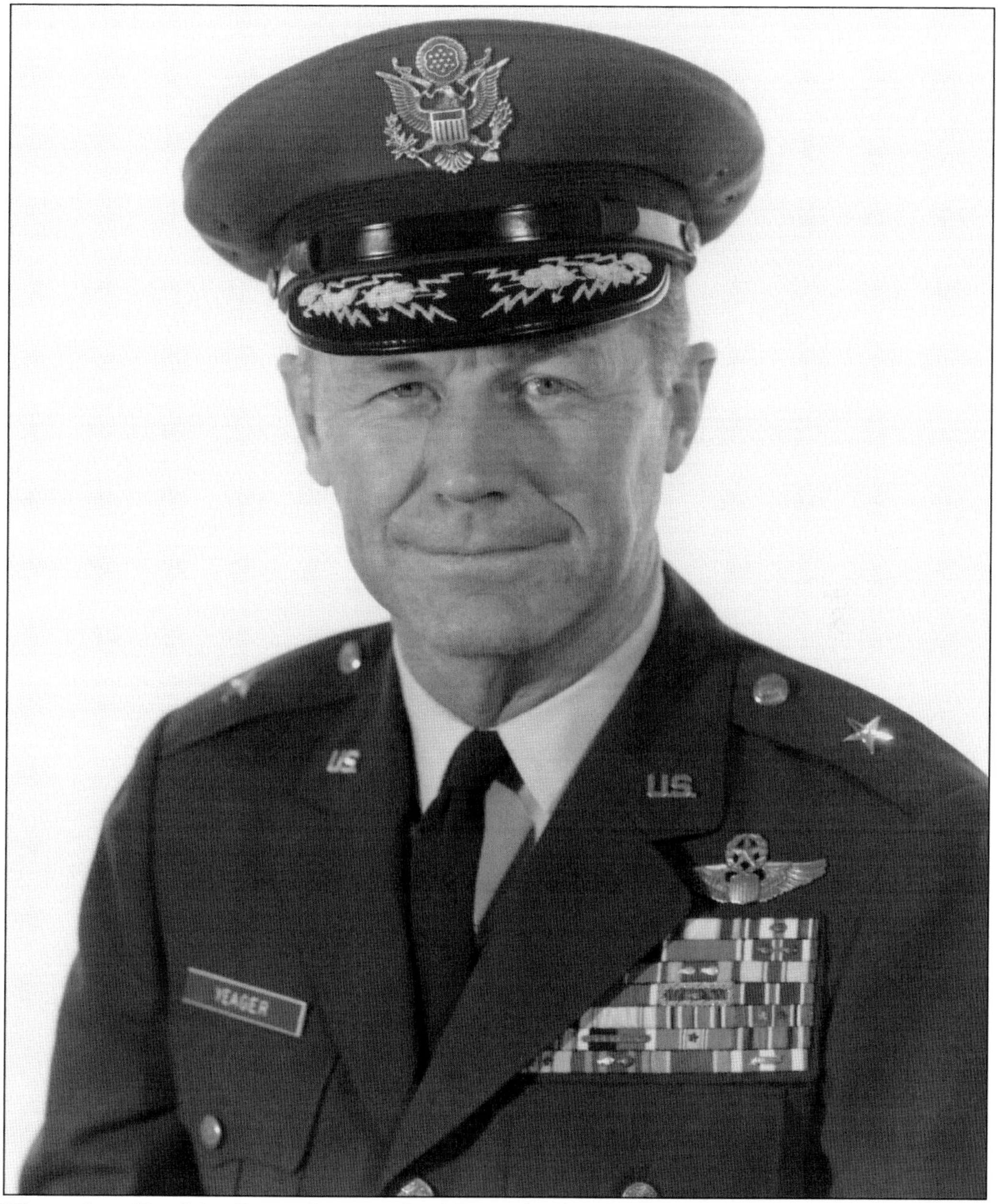

This is the official Air Force photograph of Gen. Charles Elwood "Chuck" Yeager, who was born in a farmhouse at Myra on February 13, 1923. When Yeager's father, Albert Hal, secured a job with the railroad in approximately 1926, the family moved to Hubball, and then relocated to Hamlin when the boy was five. It was while Hal ran a drilling business that young Yeager developed an affinity for anything with an engine in it. He graduated from Hamlin High in 1941. After serving during World War II and breaking the sound barrier in 1947, Yeager logged more combat flight hours during the Vietnam War when he was promoted to brigadier. Noted for his willingness to fly almost anything with wings, he even once piloted a captured Soviet MiG fighter. West Virginia's largest airport, located in Charleston, is named for him. So is the Yeager Scholarship program, the highest academic honor at Marshall University. (Courtesy of US Air Force.)

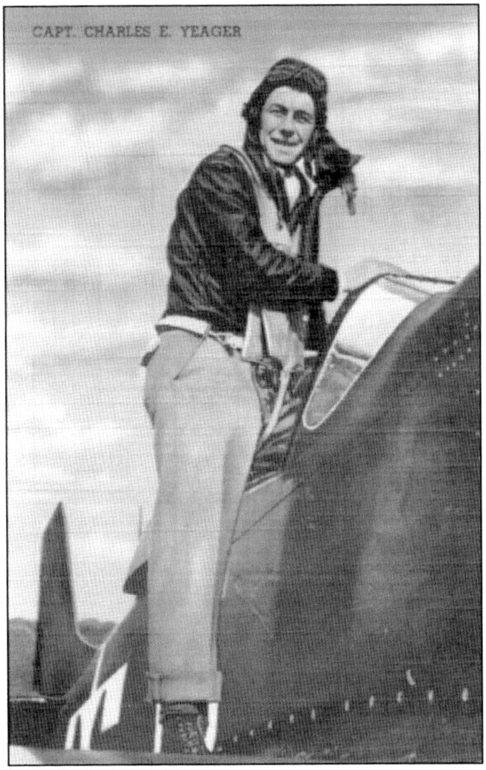

Joining the US Army Air Corps two months before Pearl Harbor as an airplane mechanic, Yeager flew 64 combat missions during World War II. So that he could be closer to his wife Glennis, who was expecting back in Hamlin, he transferred to Wright-Patterson Air Force Base in Dayton, Ohio. Yeager sometimes performed low-altitude "buzz" flights over his hometown during this immediate postwar period. (HLCPL.)

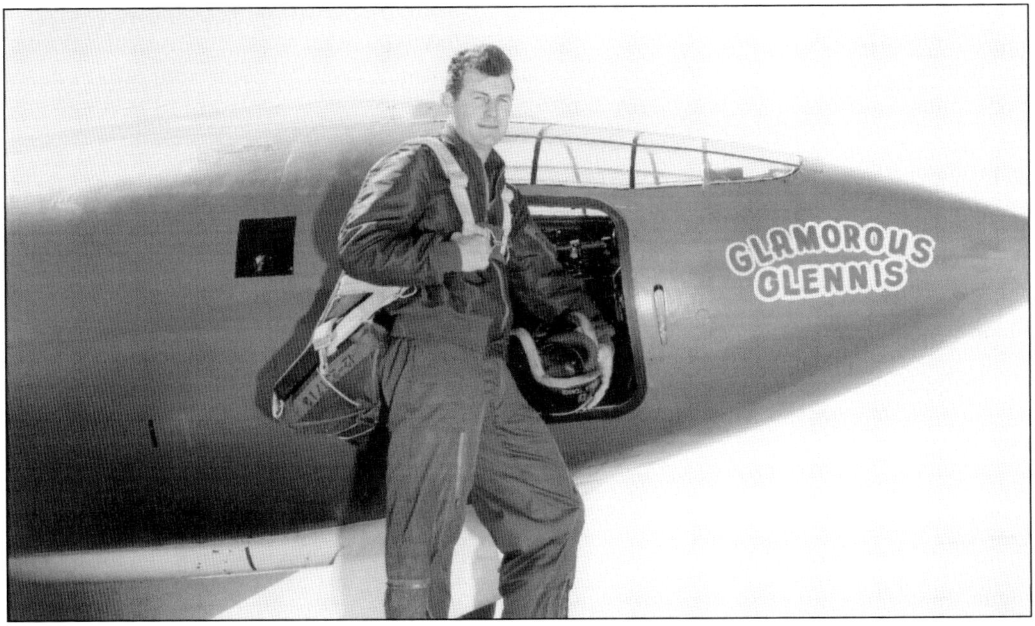

Hand-selected by Col. Albert Boyd (director of the Flight Test Division) as the best instinctive pilot he had ever seen, Yeager was recruited to pilot experimental aircraft at Muroc Army Air Field (now Edwards Air Force Base) in California. He became the "Fastest Man Alive" when he broke the sound barrier on October 14, 1947, in the cockpit of *Glamorous Glennis*, his rocket-powered Bell X-1 aircraft. (Courtesy of National Archives.)

Riding a renewed wave of popularity from the Tom Wolfe novel and motion picture *The Right Stuff* (in which Yeager had a bit part) and his own best-selling autobiography, retired Air Force general and international celebrity Chuck Yeager made a grand homecoming in 1985 for the dedication of this statue in his honor on the lawn of Hamlin High School. (HLCPL.)

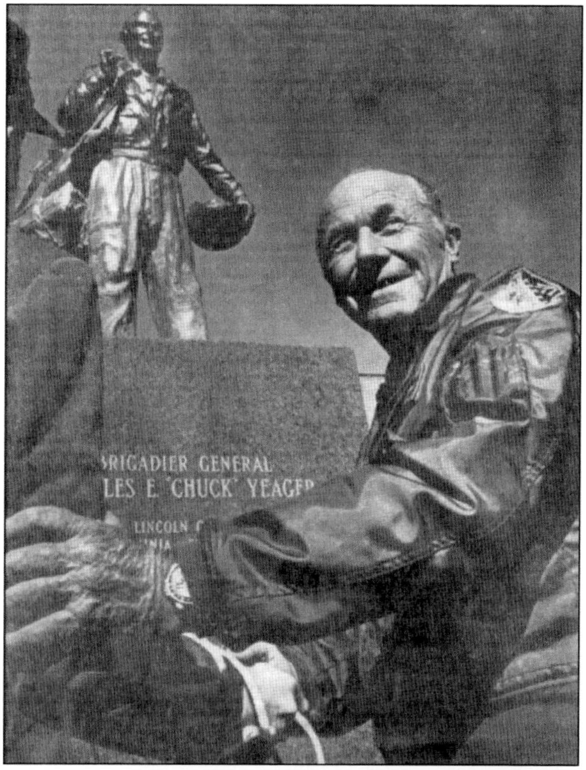

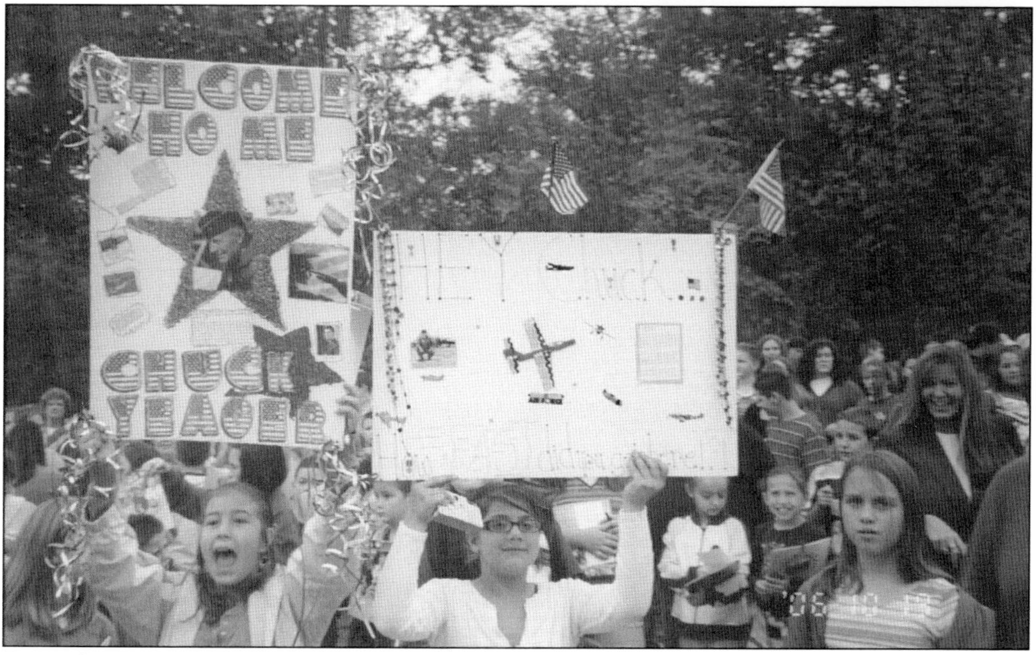

Yeager homecoming events are always celebrated in grand style. Adoring crowds are large and enthusiastic, welcoming their most famous native son with open arms. The general still fondly recalls "swiping watermelons" and "shooting the heads off of squirrels" from his boyhood days growing up on the "mighty" Mud River. (Courtesy of Jim Ryan.)

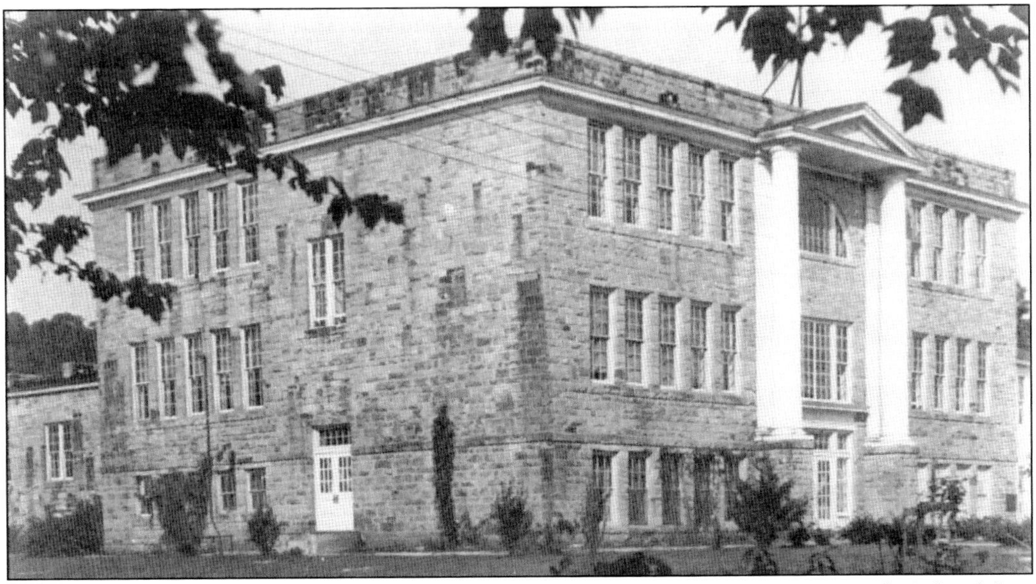

Hamlin's first public school classes were held at White Hall. Carroll District High School first opened in 1919, the new stone building was completed in 1922, and it became Hamlin High School in 1934. Smoke was noticed coming from the building at 1:15 a.m. on February 21, 1949. The ensuing blaze, which started in the furnace room, left nothing but burned-out walls. (Hamlin High School yearbook photograph, courtesy of LCFOA.)

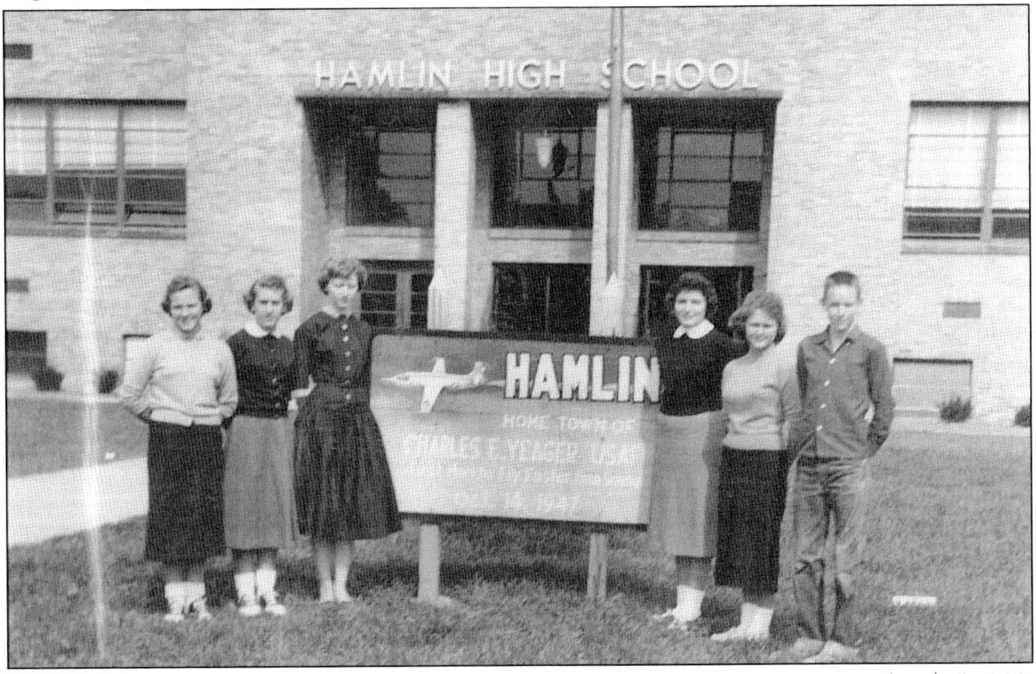

Damage from the fire, which resulted in a total loss of the building, was estimated at $250,000. About 350 Hamlin senior and junior high students were temporarily relocated to four area churches, the Masonic lodge, Odd Fellows hall, courthouse, and the board of education offices. The new building (pictured) was ready by the 1951–1952 school year. (Hamlin High School yearbook photograph, courtesy of LCFOA.)

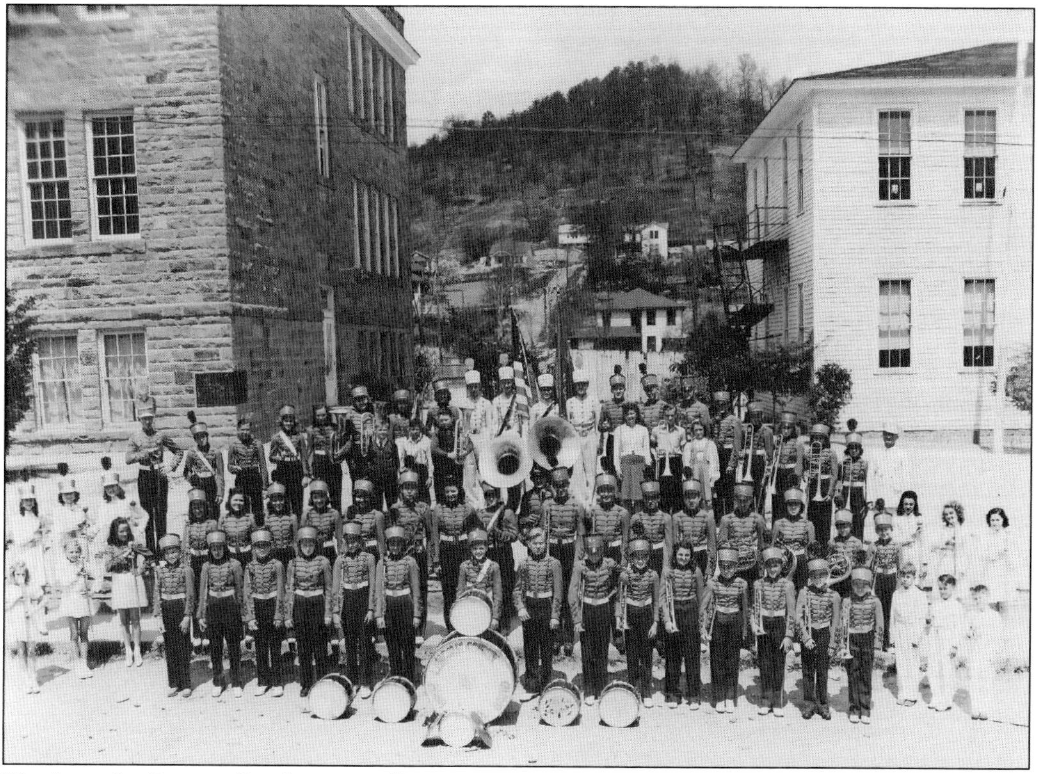

The Lincoln County Band was an all-star assemblage that performed at regional band festivals. It is pictured here about 1940 between the old Hamlin High (left) and Hamlin Grade Schools. All band and athletic equipment was lost in the 1949 fire, as was the new gymnasium. (Courtesy of Lucille Tipton Roy.)

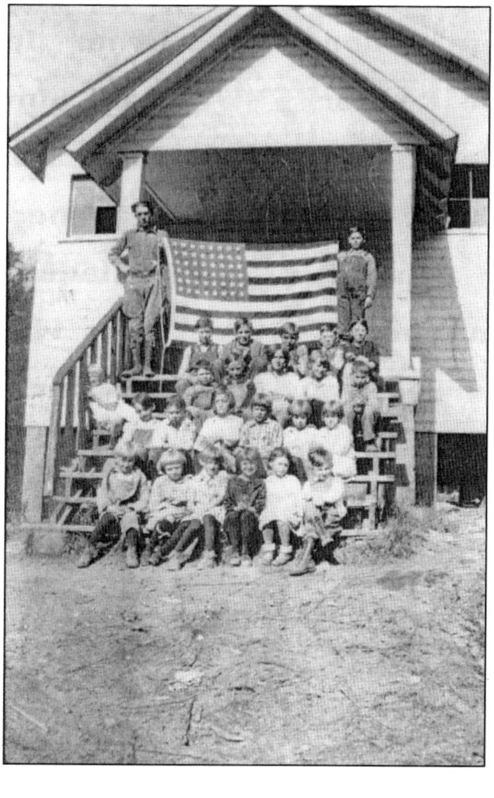

These students include children of the Curry, Elkins, Linville, and Lovejoy families. Harold Ray Smith's 1948–1949 Lincoln County school year census includes 30 elementary schools in Carroll District. Some of these are Cowhide, Curry Chapel on Straight Fork, Dan Bias, Fez, Harvey Creek, Lower and Upper Coon Creek, Maul Fork, Nye Valley, Palermo, Portersville, Ray Knob, Scary, Slash Branch, Sycamore, Trace Creek, and Webb. (HLCPL.)

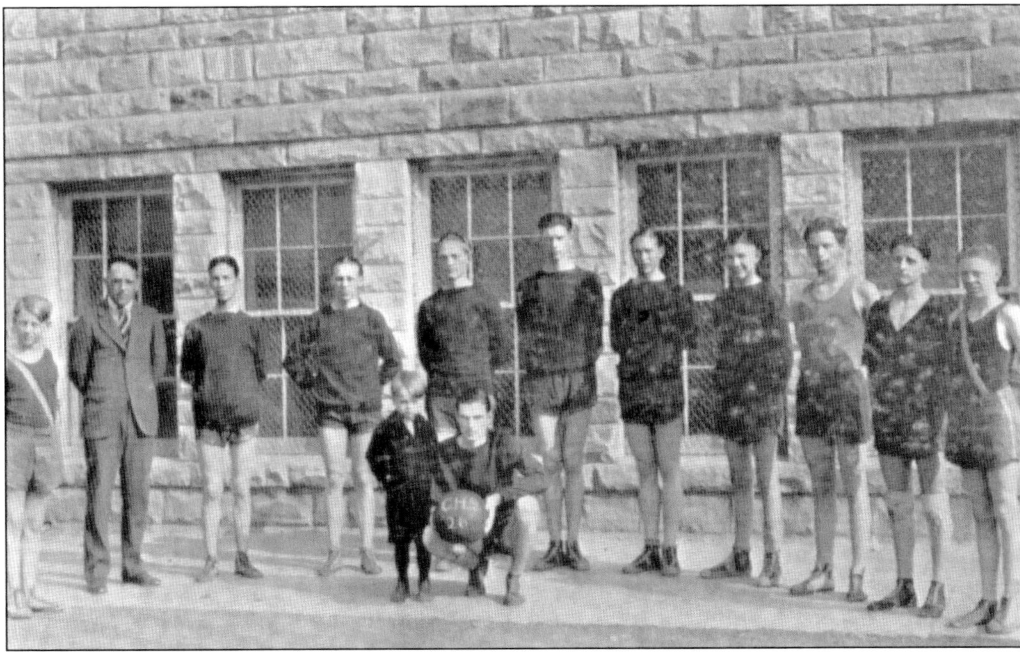

Hamlin High School's Bobcats boasted a long and proud athletic tradition. As indicated by the "C.H.S. '26" basketball, these hoopsters wear the blue and gold for Carroll High School in 1926. Hamlin generally fielded strong squads in both basketball and football. (MU-Lambert.)

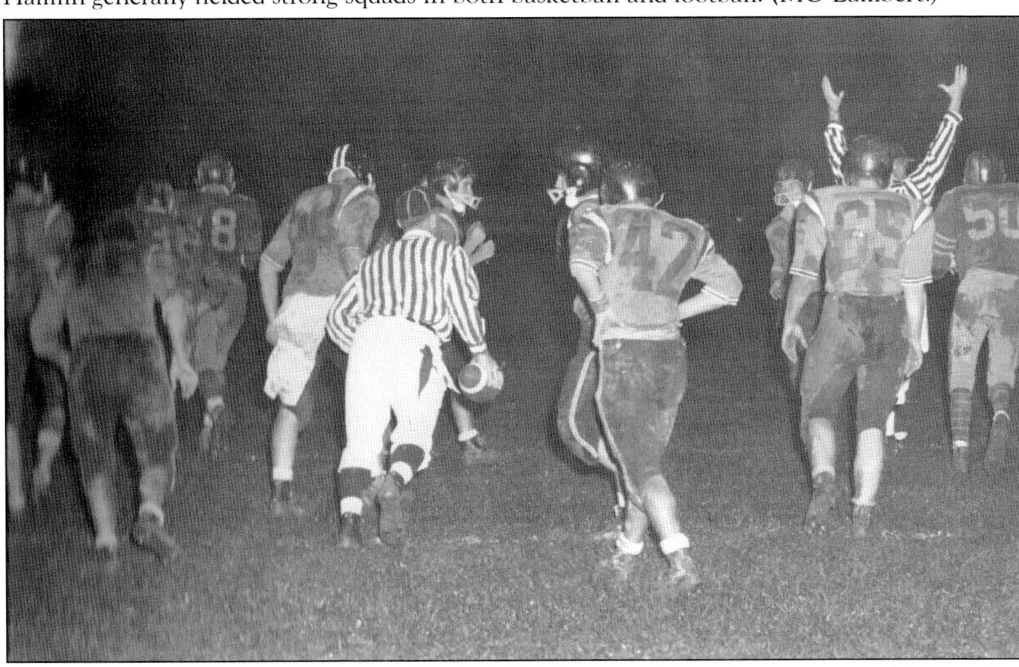

Touchdown, Bobcats! Hamlin was the only county high school to never capture a state championship, but the Bobcats did reach title games in basketball and football, an accomplishment that no other county high school could match. These appearances came in 1971 and 1988 in basketball (losses to Bramwell both times) and in 1974 in football (an 8-0 defeat by Musselman). (Hamlin High School yearbook photograph, courtesy of LCFOA.)

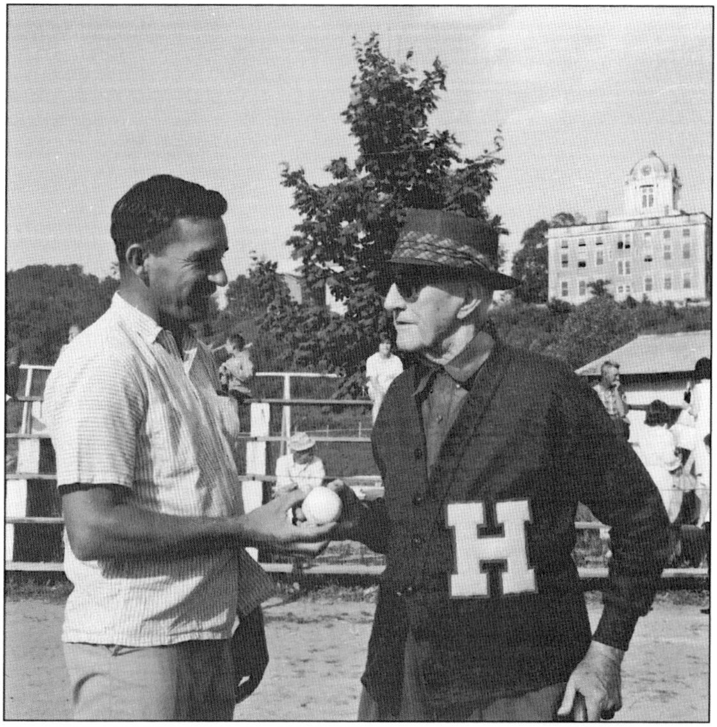

Down through the years, Hamlin Lions Club Field has been considered the "Yankee Stadium" of Lincoln County, where championship games in everything from Little League to Recreational League softball tournaments to July 4th all-star games have always been played. The "old" courthouse looms in the background. (Photograph by Gene Brewer, courtesy of Lucian Isaacs.)

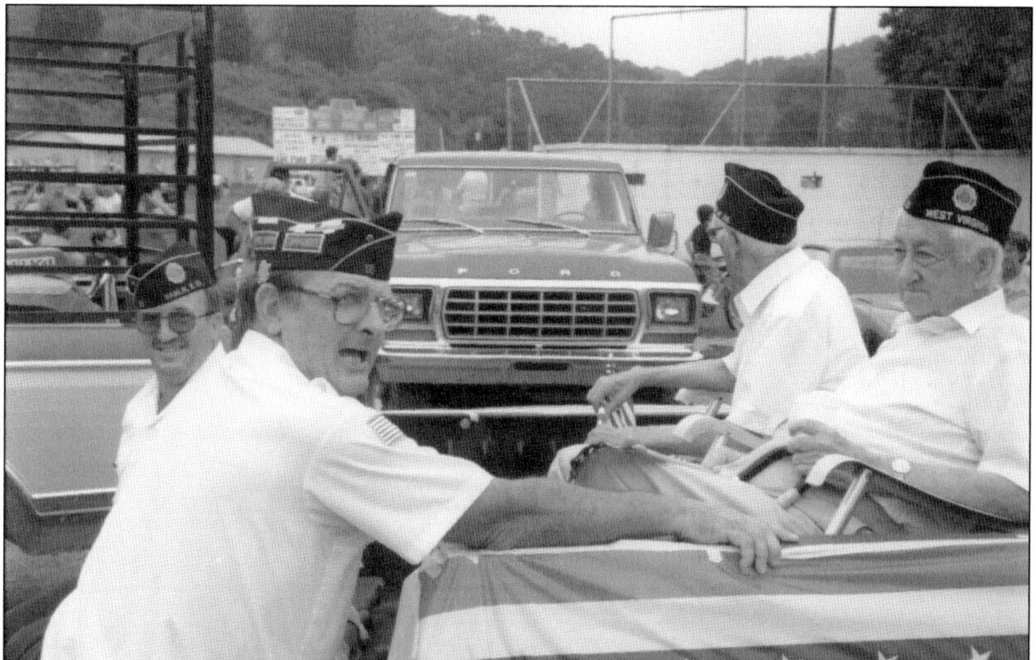

American Legion Post 111 members wait at Hamlin Lions Club Field after riding in the Independence Day parade. The Lincoln County Tobacco Fair was also held here. This festival had all the elements of a typical county fair, such as beauty queens, livestock, tractor pulls, and outdoor concerts. But it also featured some not-so-traditional events, like a tobacco-spitting contest. (AC.)

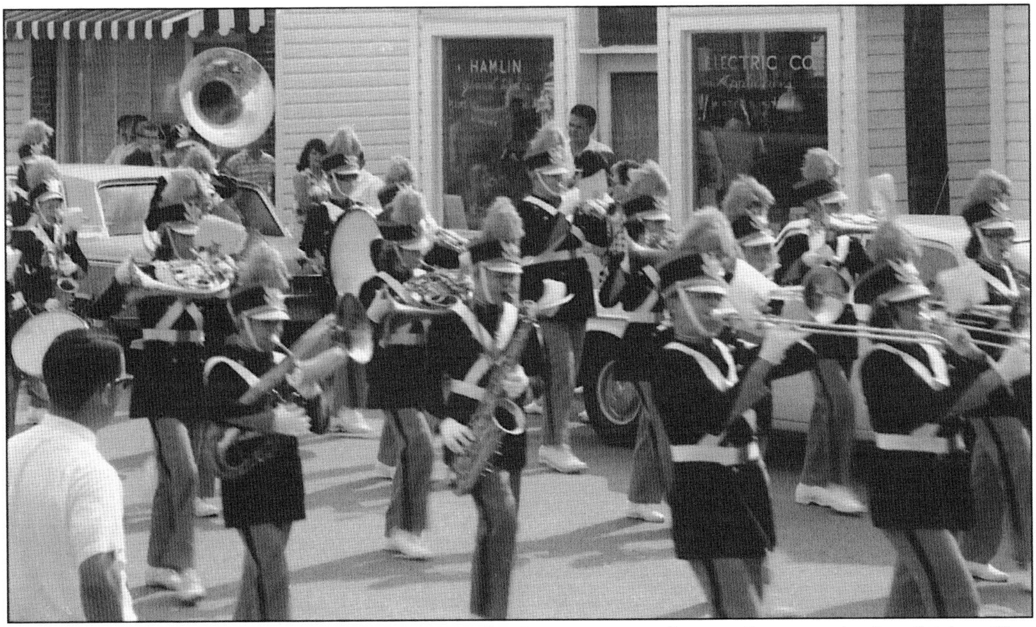

The main Fourth of July celebration in Lincoln County, complete with a parade that kicks off at 10:00 a.m. and fireworks that start at 10:00 p.m., occurs in Hamlin. The parade lines up at Hamlin PK–8 School and marches down Route 3 to the Lions Club Field. Small-town, Americana-type activities—such as arts and crafts, ball games, and concerts—highlight the all-day gathering. (Photograph by Gene Brewer, courtesy of Lucian Isaacs.)

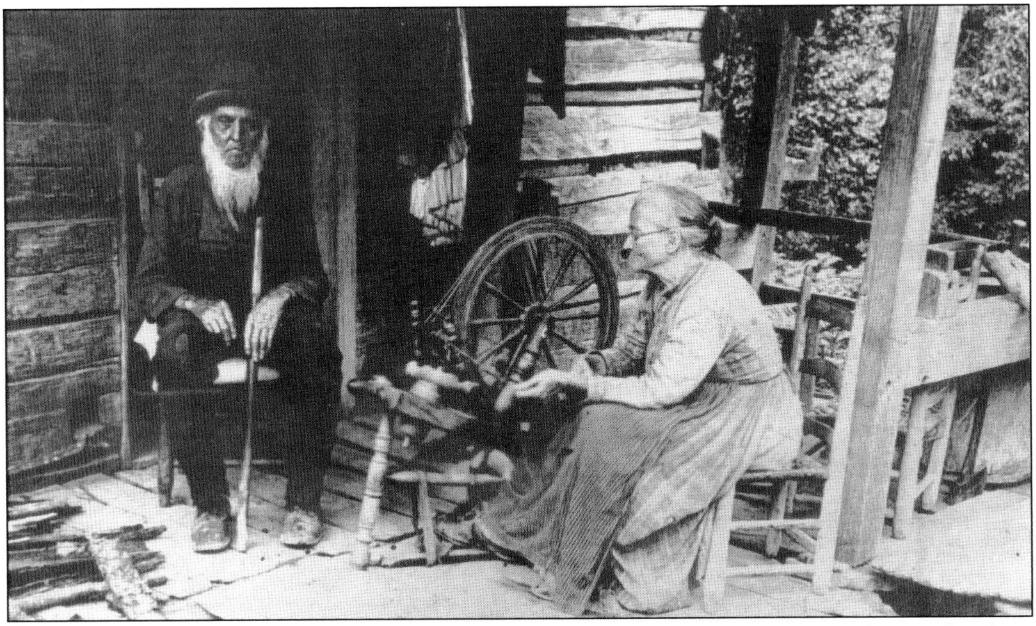

Sewing and quilting are timeless Appalachian traditions, passed along from mother to daughter since the earliest pioneer days, although the spinning wheel is rarely used anymore. It is a common practice for a mother to stitch a quilt for each of her children. Some quilts are done patchwork-style, with individual squares from different individuals sewn together to represent a family, church, or community. (MU-Lambert.)

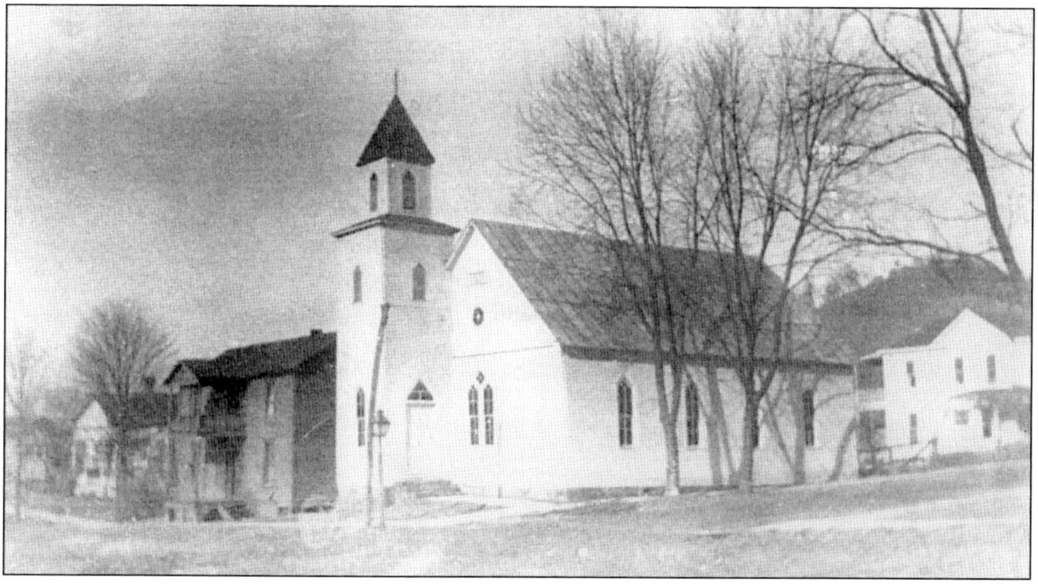

Founded in 1846, the Trinity Methodist Episcopal Church, or White Hall, counted William C. Mahone among its members. It was used occasionally as Lincoln County's first courthouse, by the Ohio Zouaves infantry unit, and as a public school. Leonidas Hamline was an archbishop in the Methodist Episcopal Church, which qualifies as circumstantial evidence that the town may be named for him instead of Hannibal Hamlin. (LCFOA.)

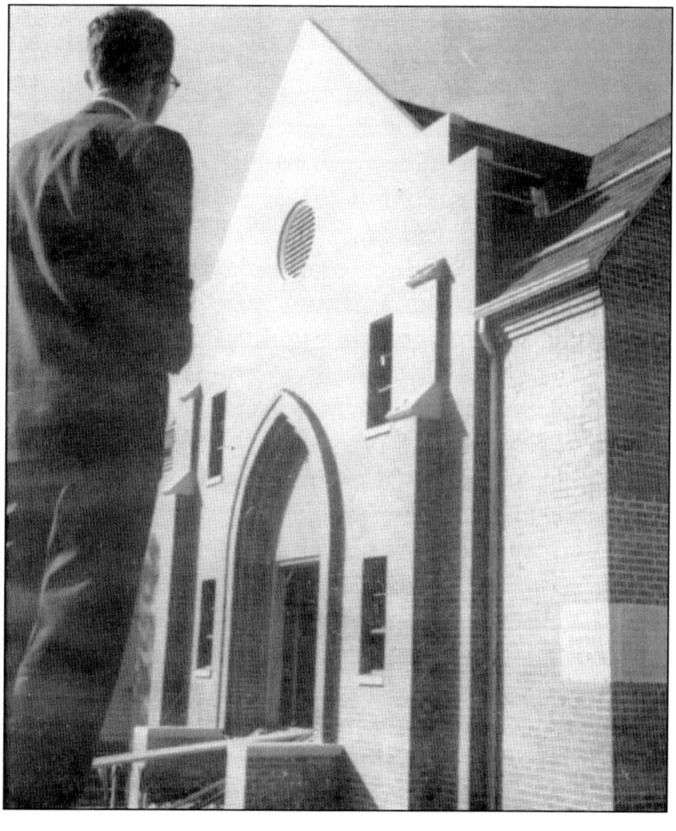

Rev. Rex J. Sandifer views construction of the new Hamlin Baptist Church building in 1953. The church on Sycamore Avenue was established in 1920 at a meeting held in the home of J.H. Nanny. The church is a member of the Southern Baptist Convention. (AC.)

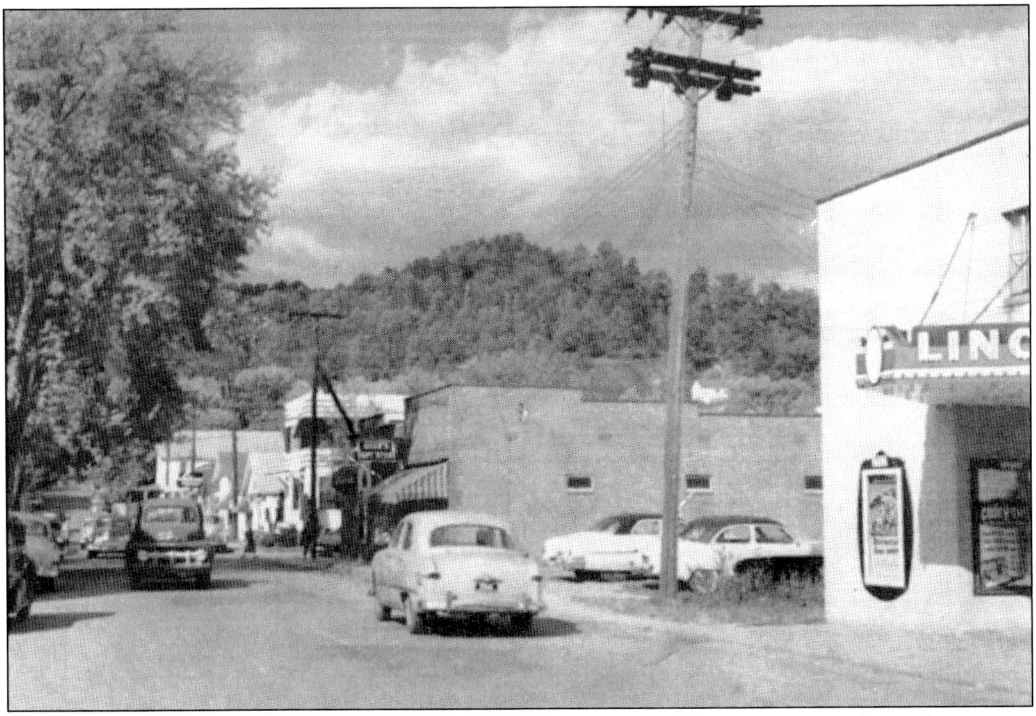

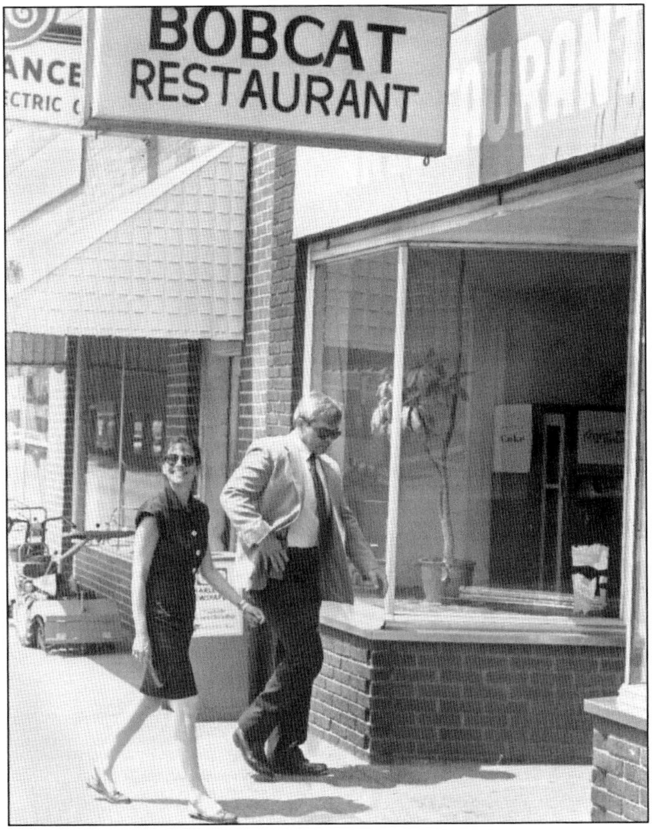

The entrance to Lincoln Theater is captured in this early-1950s view of Walnut Street, looking north. It sat beside the current Koontz Funeral home. There were once several theaters scattered across the county, most notably a drive-in along Route 10 at Pleasant View, but there is no place to catch a motion picture in the county today. (AC.)

The Bobcat Restaurant was once a popular hangout spot for Hamlin High School students and is named after the school's mascot. Along with the old Lincoln Theater and the offices of the *Lincoln Journal*, it is also located on Walnut Street. This central business district was once populated by appliance and furniture stores. (Courtesy of *Lincoln Journal*.)

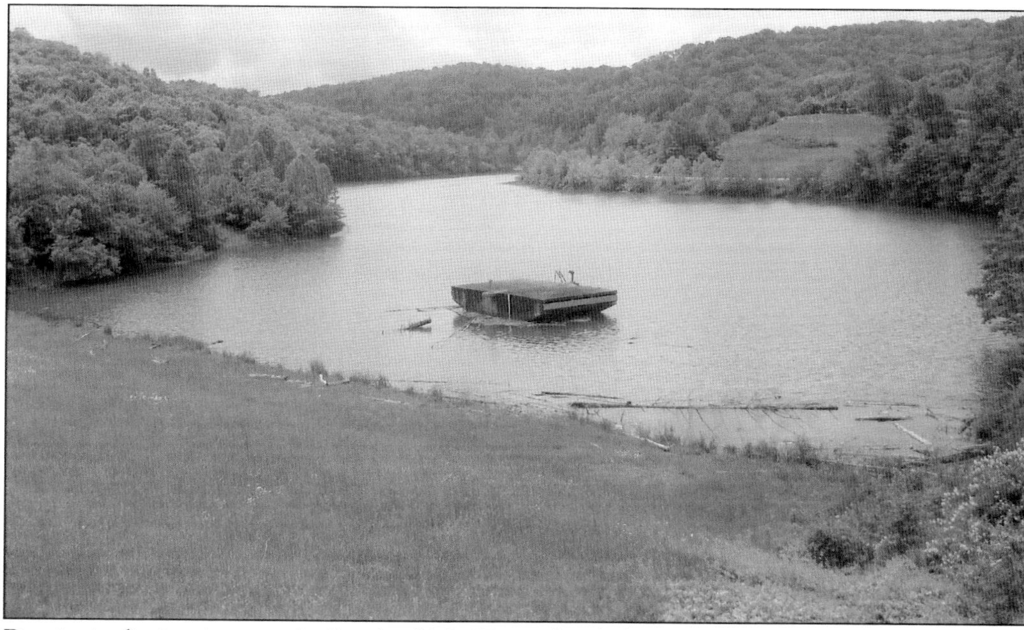

Despite its diminutive size, the "mighty" Mud River flooded every spring in Hamlin. Construction of this dam near Palermo greatly alleviated the flooding problem. Upper Mud River Lake and Wildlife Area was another benefit of this project. A recreational hub, it offers areas for fishing, hunting, and swimming, as well as ball fields, picnic spots, and other amenities. (Courtesy of Guyan Soil Conservation District.)

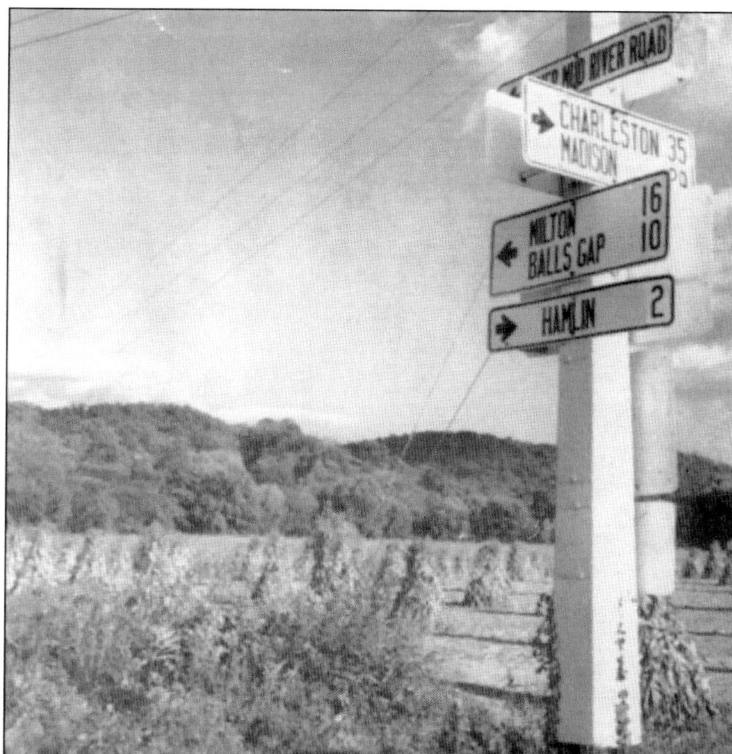

This sign at the intersection of Lower Mud River Road and Route 3 east of Hamlin points the way to area communities. Portersville, not listed on the sign, was the site of an early Lincoln County gristmill. A similar sign reading "Myra 4, Sias 9, Palermo 13" once stood alongside Route 3 at Upper Mud River Road. (AC.)

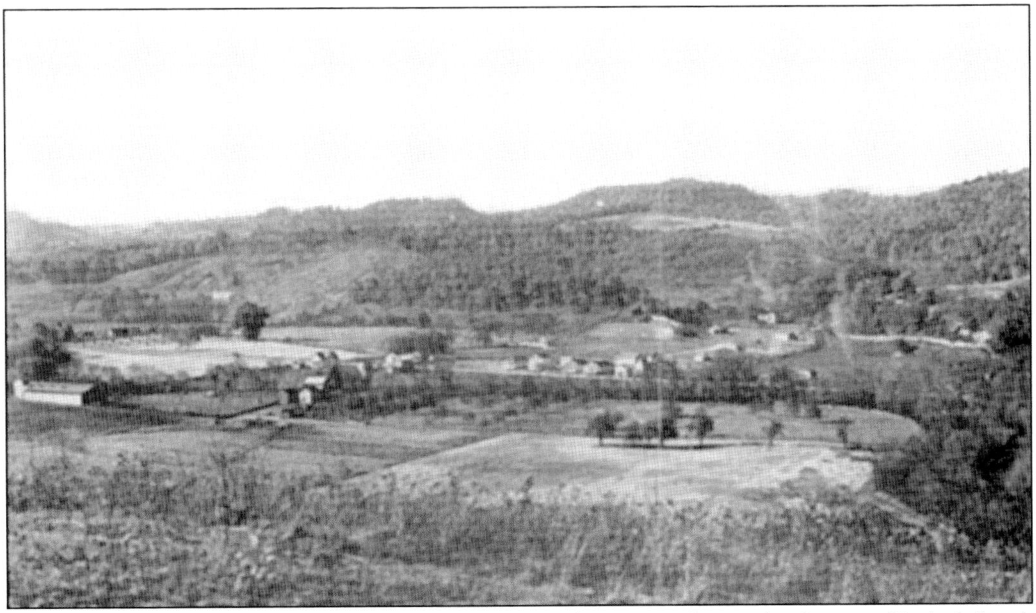

This c. 1910 view of New Hamlin shows the future location of Lincoln County High School. Citing numerous noncompliance issues, officials forced high school consolidation upon Lincoln County in the 2006–2007 academic year after the West Virginia State Board of Education took over the county school system. That body mandated the construction of a single campus at New Hamlin. (MU-Lambert.)

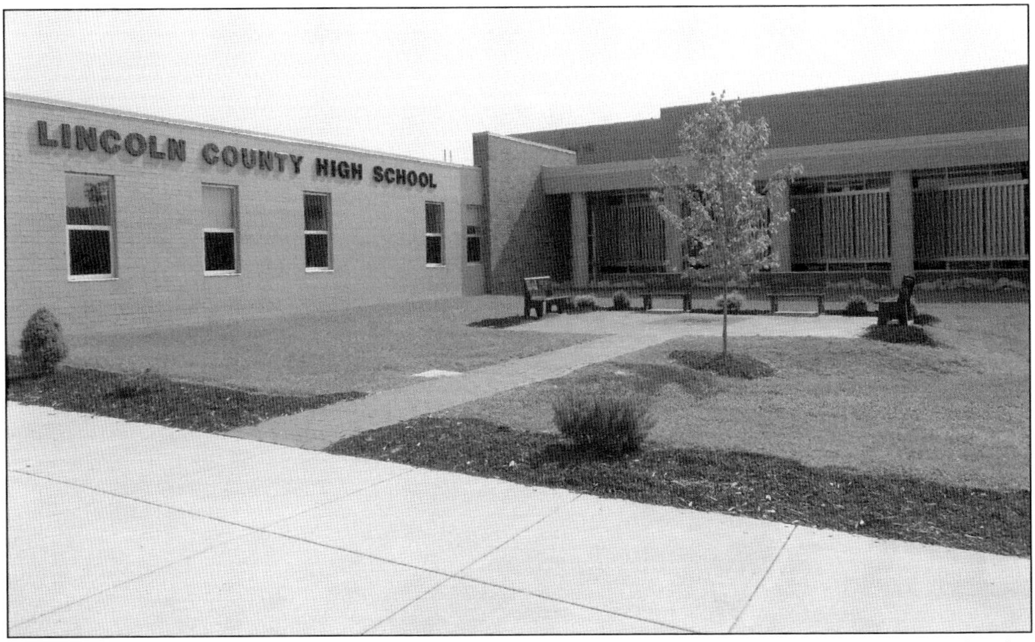

Some hard feelings still exist in the county over what is perceived as heavy-handedness by the state on the school consolidation issue, but most residents have since rallied behind Lincoln County High School. Black, blue, and silver were selected as the school colors, and the nickname "Panthers" was chosen. This courtyard at the entrance of the school pays homage to the four former high schools. (AC.)

Four

Over towards Duval

Guyandotte Valley is to the west. Harts Creek is to the south. Hamlin is to the north. Now the journey comes full circle with Duval to the east. One of Lincoln County's original three townships, it is named for Union Civil War general Isaac Harding Duval. The county's first high school, Duval High, was in operation at Griffithsville from 1914 until 2006. It functions as an elementary and middle school today.

Duval is notable for an oil boom at the beginning of the 20th century. Gushing oil wells resulted in an era of economic prosperity that gave rise to the county's first bank. Besides the high school and bank, Duval can claim several other county firsts: first entry in the National Register of Historic Places, first organized sports team (baseball), first Red Cross organization, first Boy Scout troop, and first 4-H Club. And Griffithsville can be fairly claimed as the county's first organized community. When residents petitioned the Virginia General Assembly in 1860 to form a new county called Letcher, Sugartree (later Griffithsville) was to be its seat of government.

Further east is the former Washington District, created out of Kanawha County when county lines were redrawn in 1869. This area of the county has always been oriented toward Charleston, owing to the location of Alum Creek at the forks of the Coal River. A half-day's journey by boat in the early days, the state capital can now be reached in 15 minutes via Corridor G.

Griffithsville and Alum Creek are the larger towns, but Alkol, Garretts Bend, McCorkle, Sod, Sumerco, Spurlockville, and Woodville are other communities that once fed Duval High School.

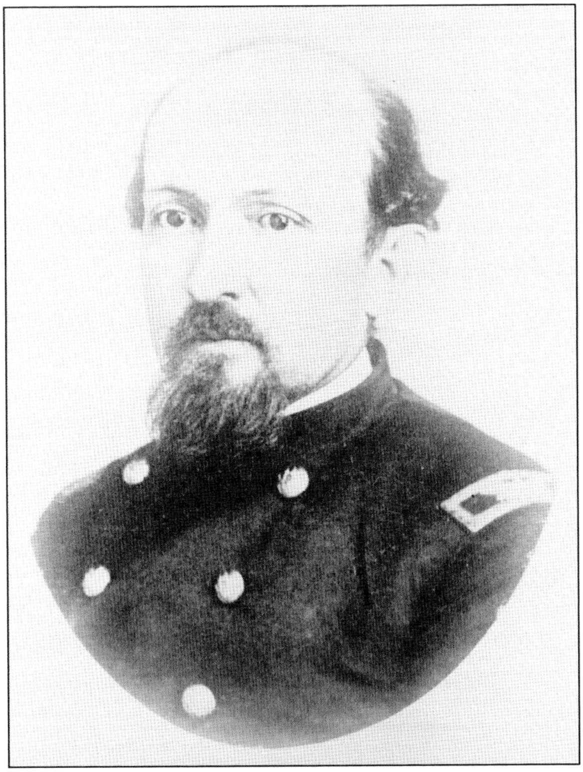

Duval was named for Gen. Isaac Harding Duval (1824–1902), commander of the 9th West Virginia Volunteer Infantry during the Civil War. He had 11 horses shot out from under him during the war. Afterwards, Duval served in both the West Virginia Legislature and US Congress. Duval was from the Northern Panhandle and, other than his name, has no direct connection with Lincoln County. (Courtesy of Library of Congress.)

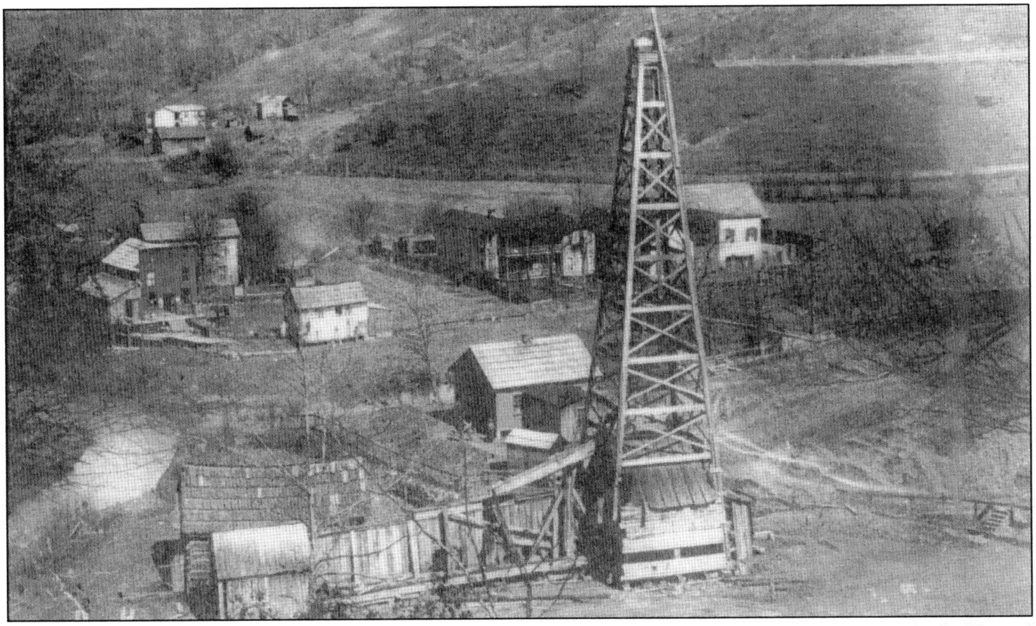

Alexander Griffith founded Eden Baptist Church near the junction of Sugartree Creek (left) and Middle Fork of Mud River in 1848. A post office was established here about 1854 on the star mail route between Charleston and Wayne Court House. Sugartree (now Griffithsville) was selected to be the county seat when residents petitioned Richmond in 1860 to form Letcher County, but this proposal was rejected. (Courtesy of Roger Vickers.)

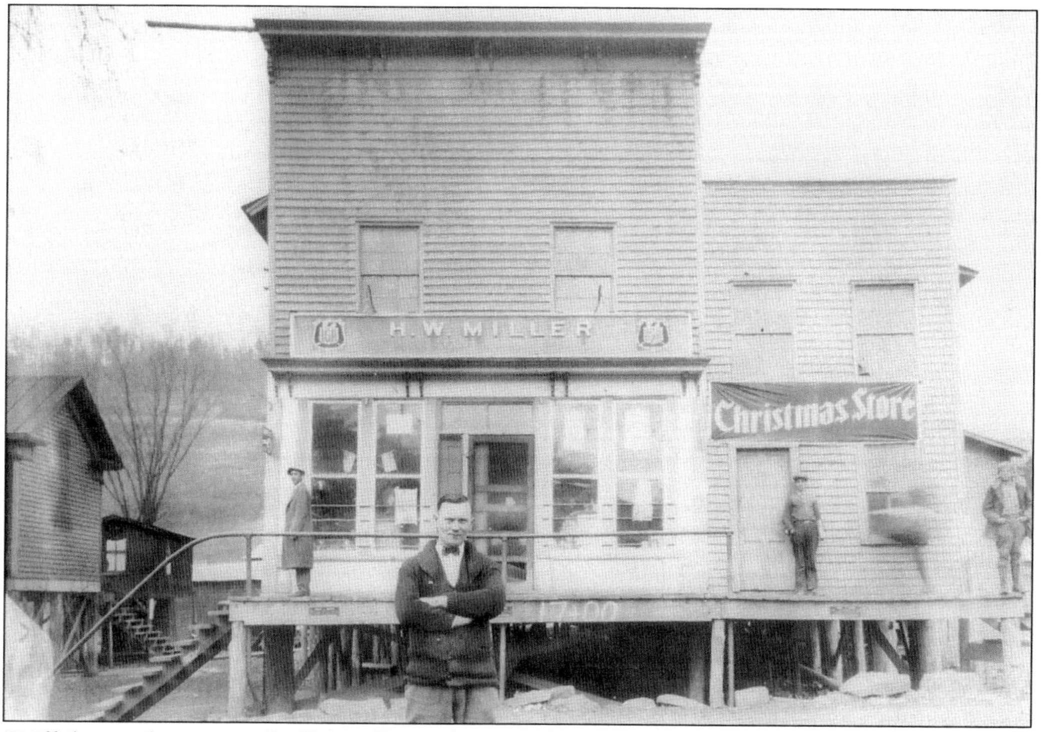

Griffith was also among Griffithsville's earliest merchants and established its first gristmill in 1857. (This relatively late date is "somewhat surprising as Duval was settled at an early date," according to historian Fred Lambert.) Pictured is H.W. Miller's store running a Christmas sale around 1920. This establishment was located just west of Duval High School. (Courtesy of Gary McClure.)

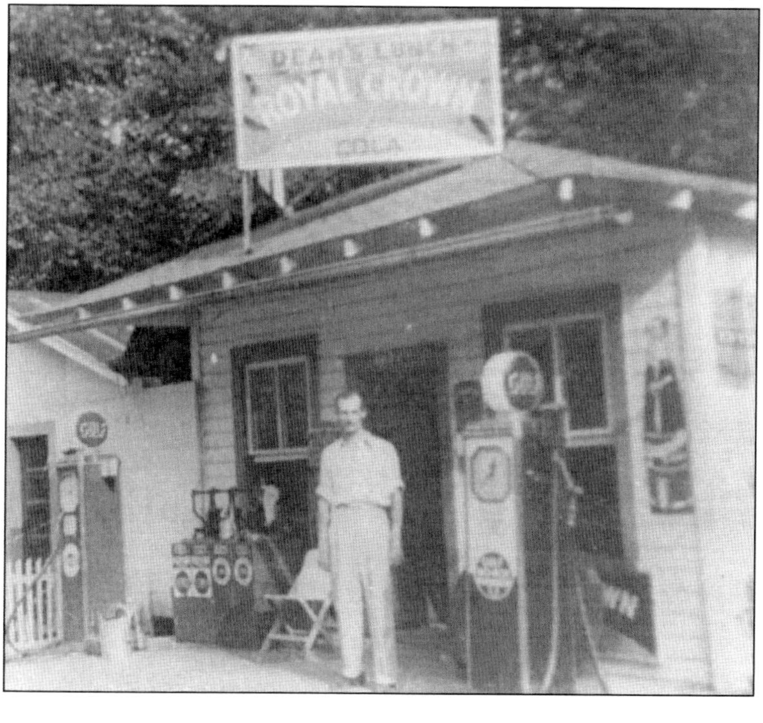

Pictured is Dean's Store at Griffithsville. Other early Griffithsville businesses included the Osborne Brothers General Store, J.L. Carper's Grist Mill, Roberts' Sawmill, and K.T. Spurlock General Store. Numerous schools and churches sprang up in and around Griffithsville during the last half of the 19th century as the town grew into the commercial, industrial, and educational center of eastern Lincoln County. (Courtesy of Gary McClure.)

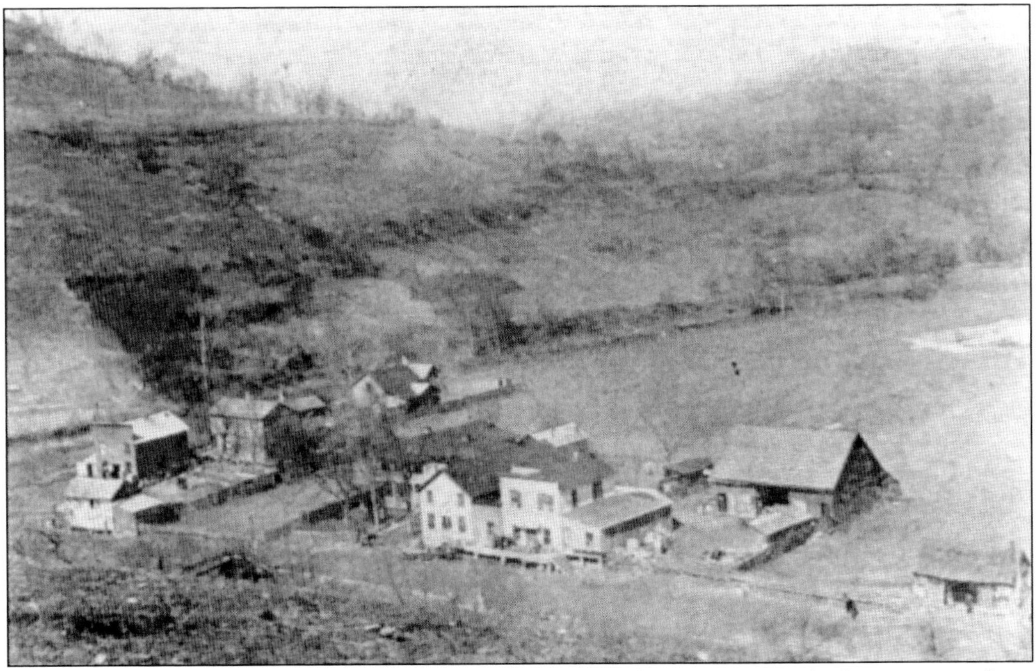

This is another view of lower Griffithsville at the mouth of Sugartree Creek. Coming over from Hamlin, this curve in Route 3 marks the entrance into town. In addition to mail delivery, this road was also important for transporting salt from the Kanawha River works at Malden. Osborne's store is visible in this picture. (HLCPL.)

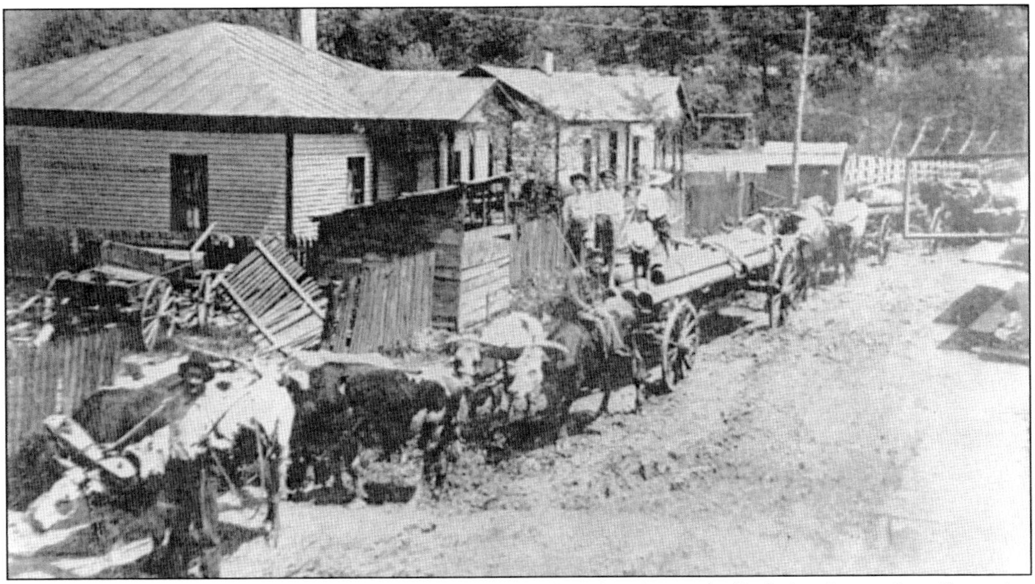

Big Creek Development Company, a Yawkey family subsidiary, drilled the first oil well in the Griffithsville area in November 1906. Only 215 feet deep, it was a gusher nevertheless. Oil production soon became a pillar of the Duval area economy, and the oil derrick became its icon. Here, a team of oxen is shown hauling pipe through Griffithsville in a classic postcard view. (Courtesy of Gary McClure.)

With a booming oil business underway during the opening decade of the 20th century, pipe was everywhere. This pipe yard was at Yawkey, just east of Griffithsville. Yawkey was named for William Clyman Yawkey, a timber baron known as the "richest man in Michigan." Yawkey's Big Creek Development Company owned and developed many of the oil fields here. (AC.)

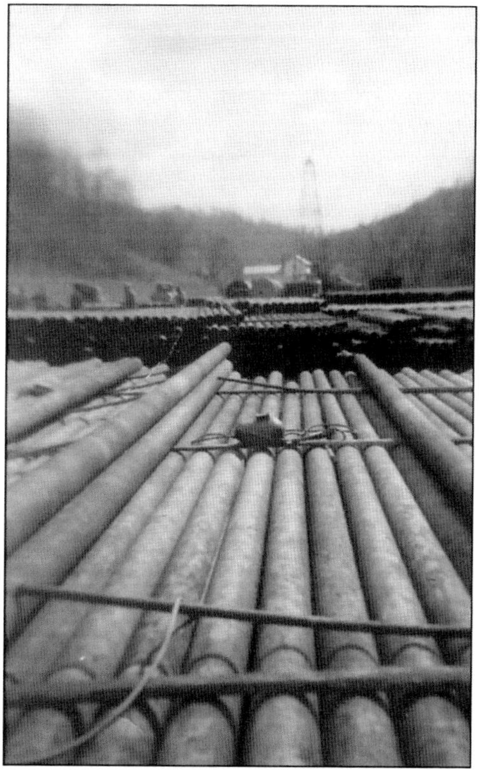

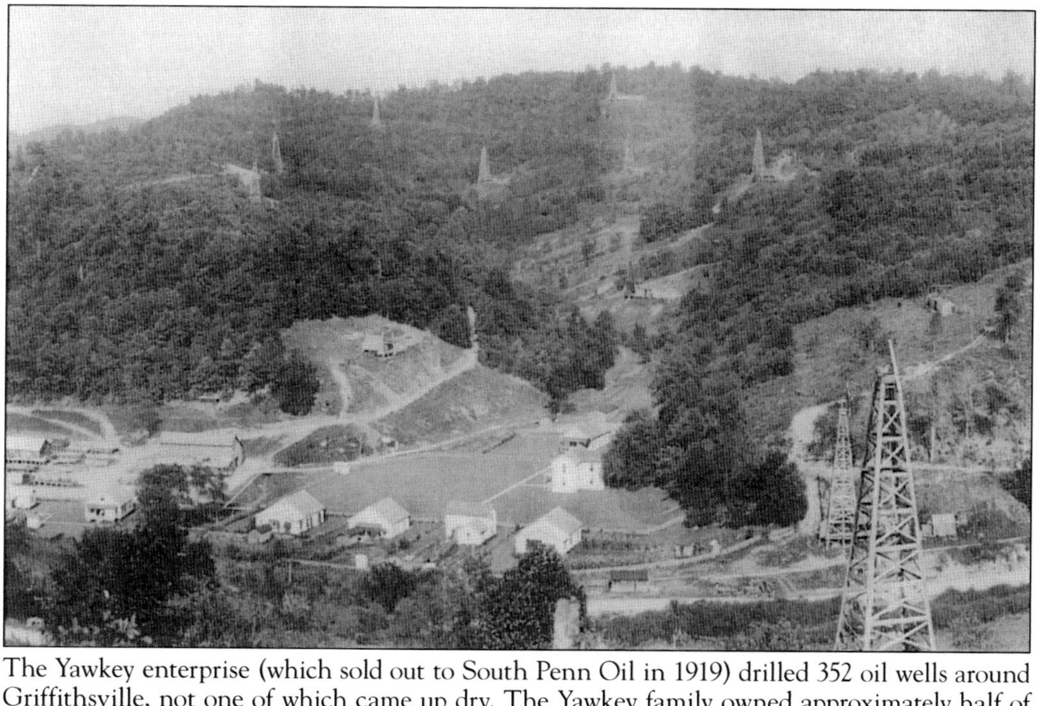

The Yawkey enterprise (which sold out to South Penn Oil in 1919) drilled 352 oil wells around Griffithsville, not one of which came up dry. The Yawkey family owned approximately half of the wells in the field, which totaled about 700. At its peak, the industry employed between 500 to 600 men. Shown here is a panoramic view of the oil fields at Yawkey in 1921. (HLCPL.)

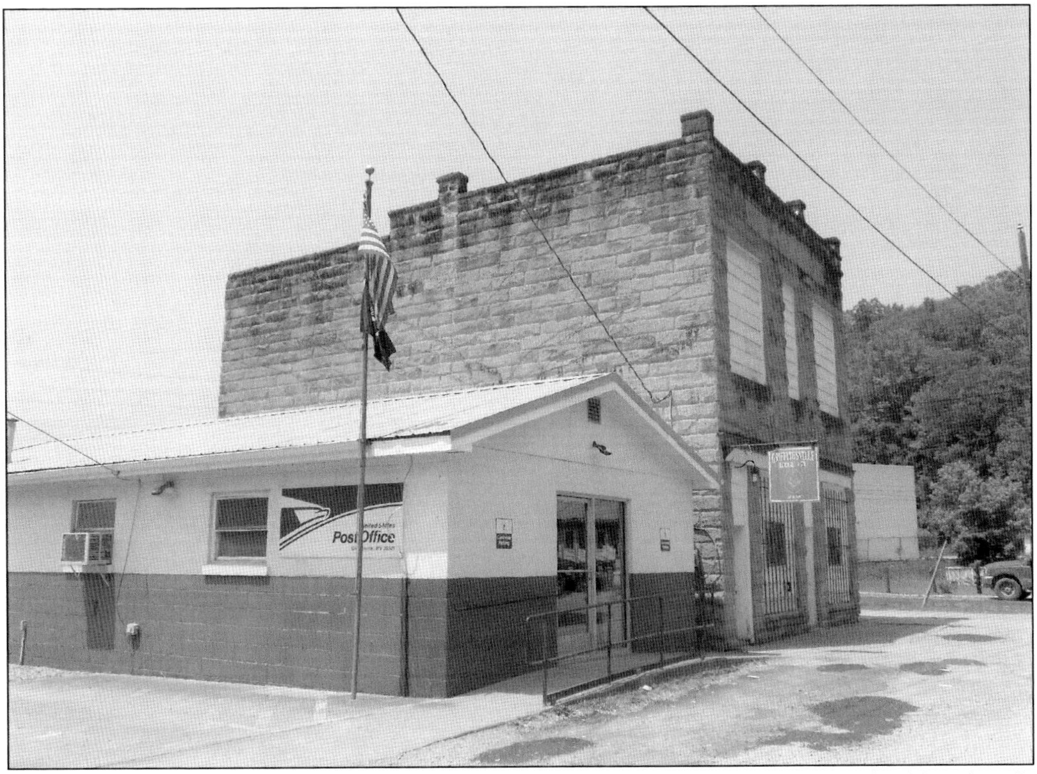

The oil boom precipitated the founding in 1908 of the Oil Field Bank (the stone building beside the Griffithsville Post Office in the photograph), Lincoln County's first bank. The economic prosperity was unprecedented as hotels, mercantile stores, doctor's offices, and company housing sprouted up like weeds amidst the forest of oil derricks. (AC.)

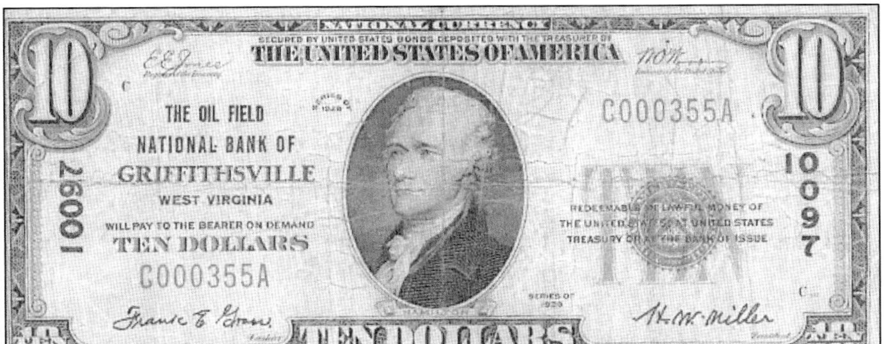

Shown is a $10 note issued from the Oil Field National Bank of Griffithsville, West Virginia. Investors and major depositors in the bank included Standard Oil, South Penn, Union Carbide, Pure Oil, Oil Well Supply, and Acme Tools. (Courtesy of Gary Holden.)

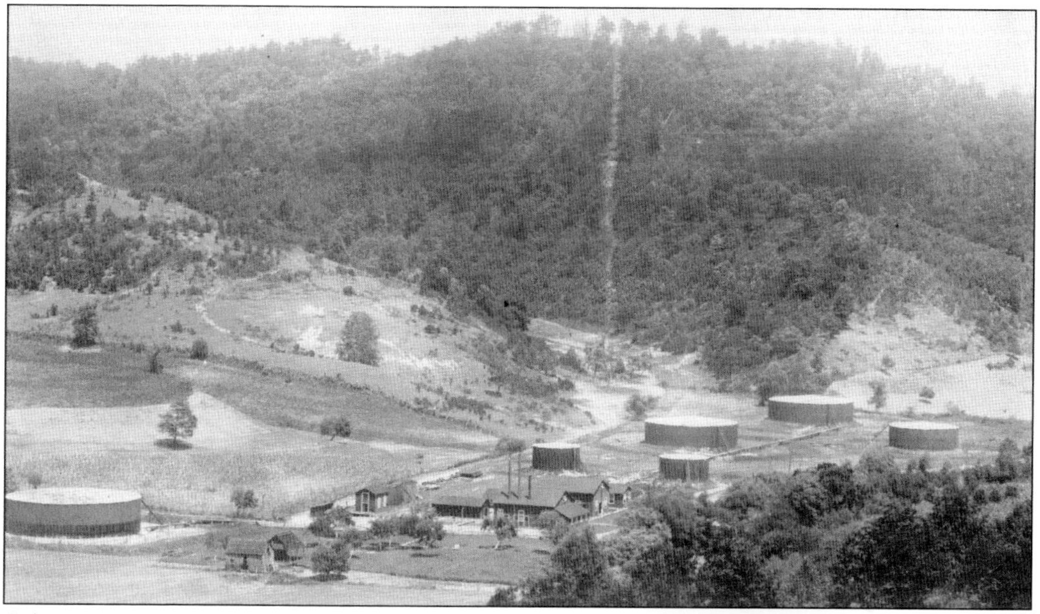

Oil was transported by the Eureka Pipe Line Company via a six-inch pipeline to what were reputed to be the largest storage tanks in America, located at Hamlin. One tank held 60,000 gallons. From there, oil was pumped to terminals on the Ohio River at Eureka in Pleasants County and on the Kanawha River at Poca in Putnam County, where it was transferred to barges for shipment across the country. (MU-Lambert.)

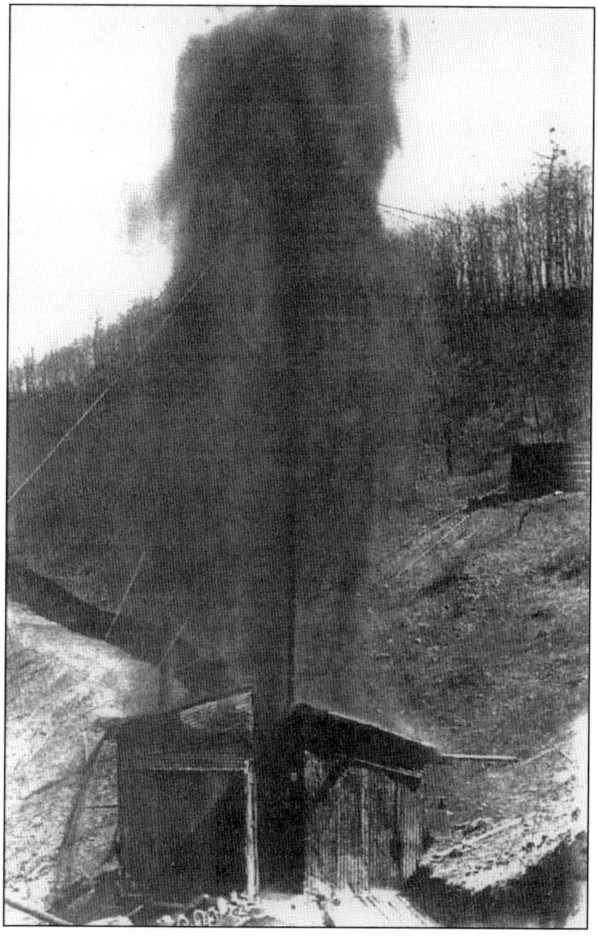

Good wells usually produced between 100 and 125 barrels per day but "blew their tops" on occasion. Gushing oil wells were dangerous to both men and the environment, not to mention the economic impact of destroyed equipment and wasted oil. Fires were also common, as blowout preventers were not developed until the mid-1920s. (HLCPL.)

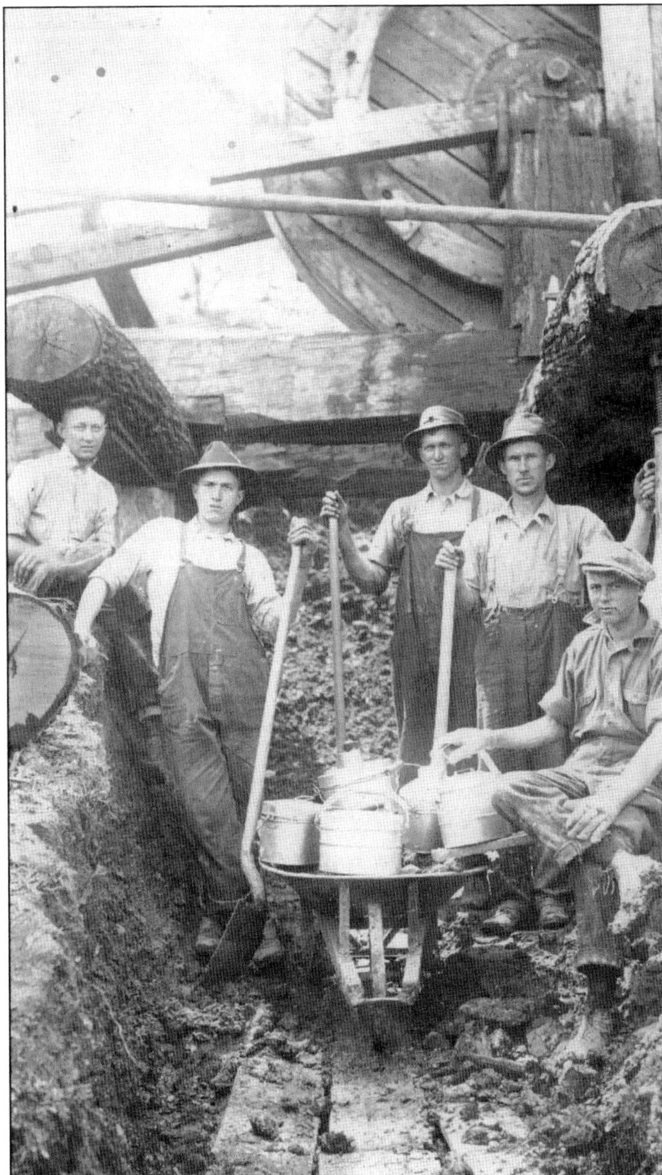

Charles H. Freeman oversaw the business for the Yawkey family, which was being run by William "Bill" Yawkey after the death of his father. When Bill Yawkey died in 1919, his nephew (and adoptive son) Tom Yawkey Jr. inherited the business, but sold out to the South Penn Oil Company. (Both Yawkeys owned major league baseball teams: Bill, the Detroit Tigers from 1903 to 1908; and Tom, the Boston Red Sox from 1933 to 1976.) South Penn Oil had been in Lincoln County from the beginning of the boom and became the dominant local player in the oil business after 1919. Operations were centered at the Bays farm, the largest producing South Penn tract in the field, where offices, tool sheds, equipment warehouses, blacksmithery, company store and boardinghouses were located. Before electricity, oil was pumped out of the ground by gas-powered Bessemer or Reed engines, which required large amounts of cooling water, while derricks supported tons of drilling equipment. Hundreds of derricks once dotted the landscape over towards Duval. (Courtesy of Roger Vickers.)

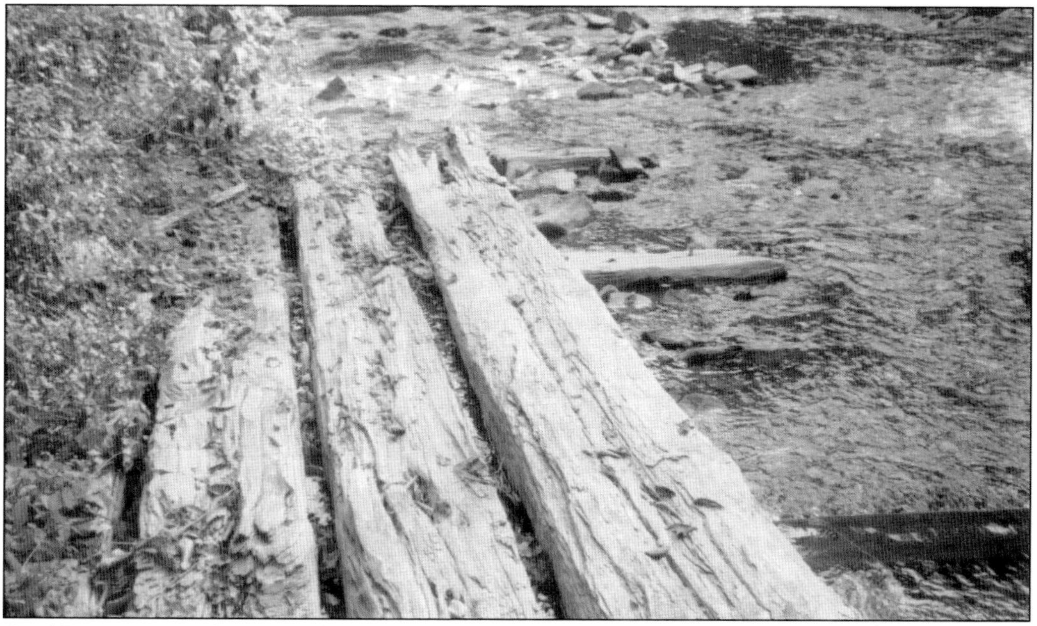

Coal River was made navigable for 35 miles from Peytona in Boone County to the river's mouth at St. Albans by installation of a series of eight locks and dams in the mid-1850s. The project was supervised by future Civil War general William S. Rosecrans. Lock and Dam A extended navigation up Little Coal River. It was abandoned by 1871, and all that remains today are these ruins. (Courtesy of Jim Ryan.)

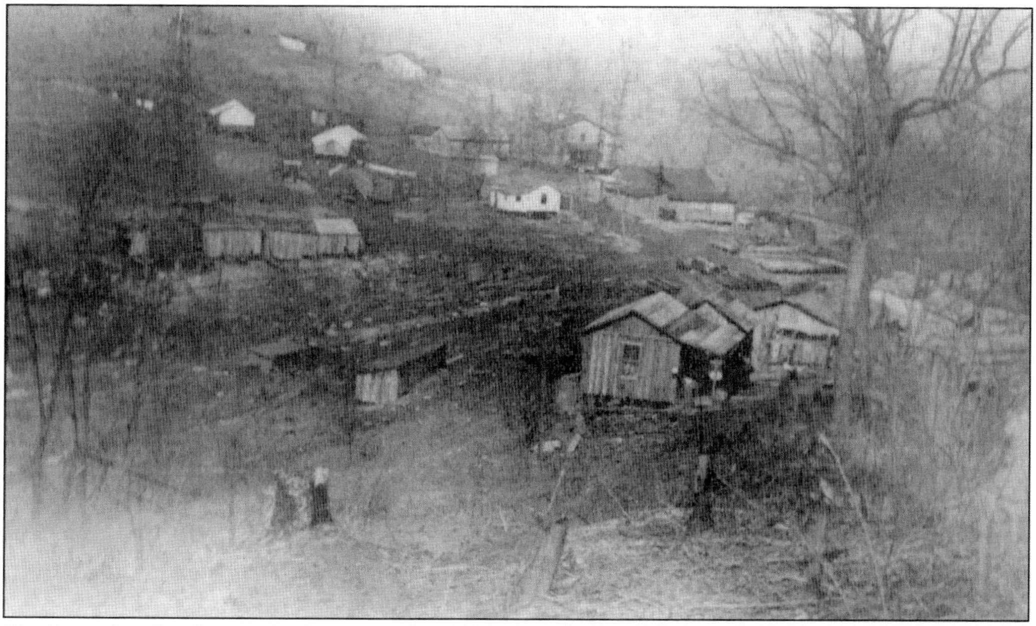

Sited on the dividing ridge between Coal River and the upper reaches of Middle Fork of Mud River, Summit Ridge was a significant transportation barrier during the bustling oil days. The road from Summit Ridge at Sumerco (pictured) down to Griffithsville was made of red mud, and wagon teams that carried equipment in and out of the oil fields sometimes encountered ooze up to the axles. (Courtesy of David McCormick.)

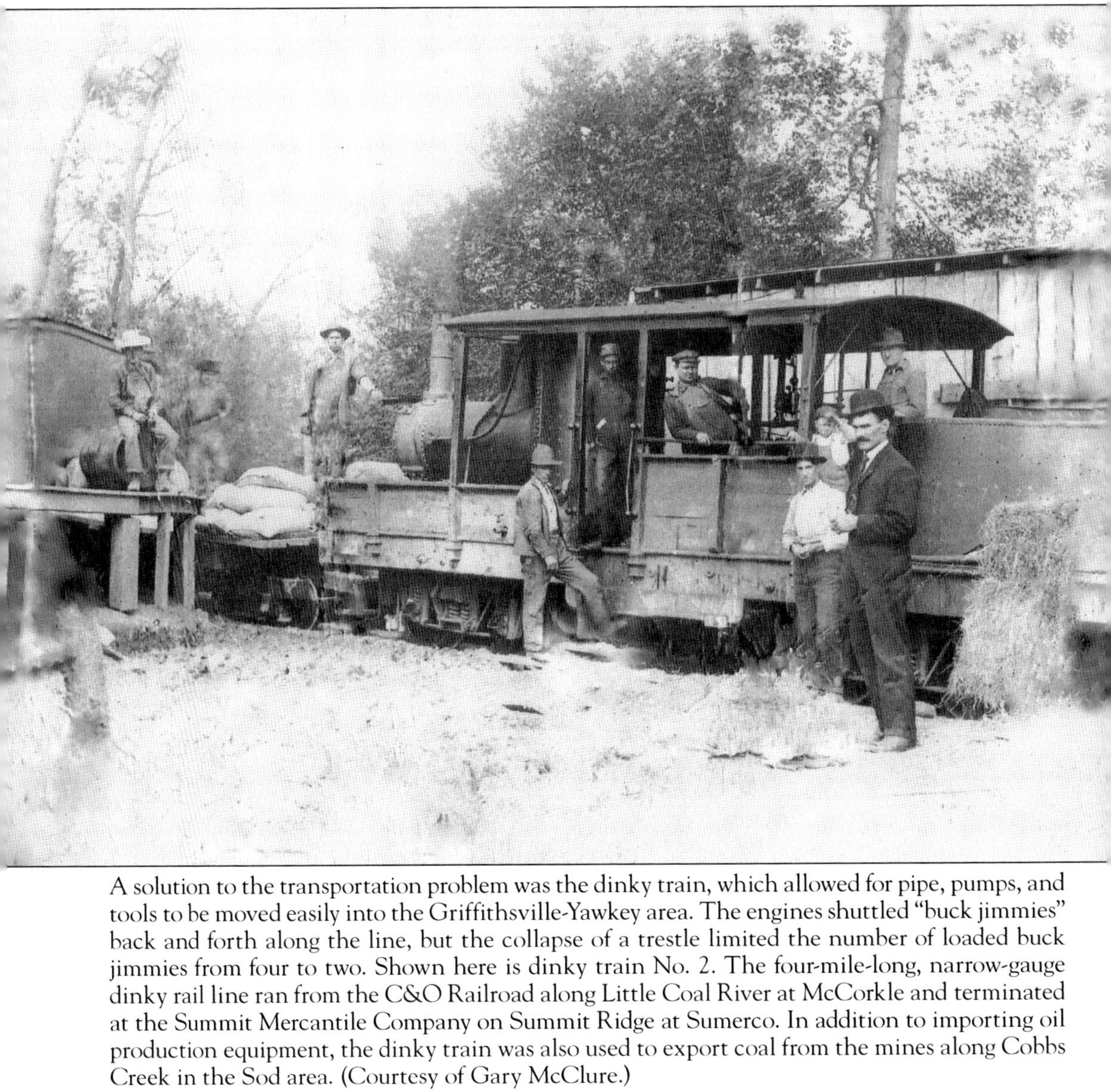

A solution to the transportation problem was the dinky train, which allowed for pipe, pumps, and tools to be moved easily into the Griffithsville-Yawkey area. The engines shuttled "buck jimmies" back and forth along the line, but the collapse of a trestle limited the number of loaded buck jimmies from four to two. Shown here is dinky train No. 2. The four-mile-long, narrow-gauge dinky rail line ran from the C&O Railroad along Little Coal River at McCorkle and terminated at the Summit Mercantile Company on Summit Ridge at Sumerco. In addition to importing oil production equipment, the dinky train was also used to export coal from the mines along Cobbs Creek in the Sod area. (Courtesy of Gary McClure.)

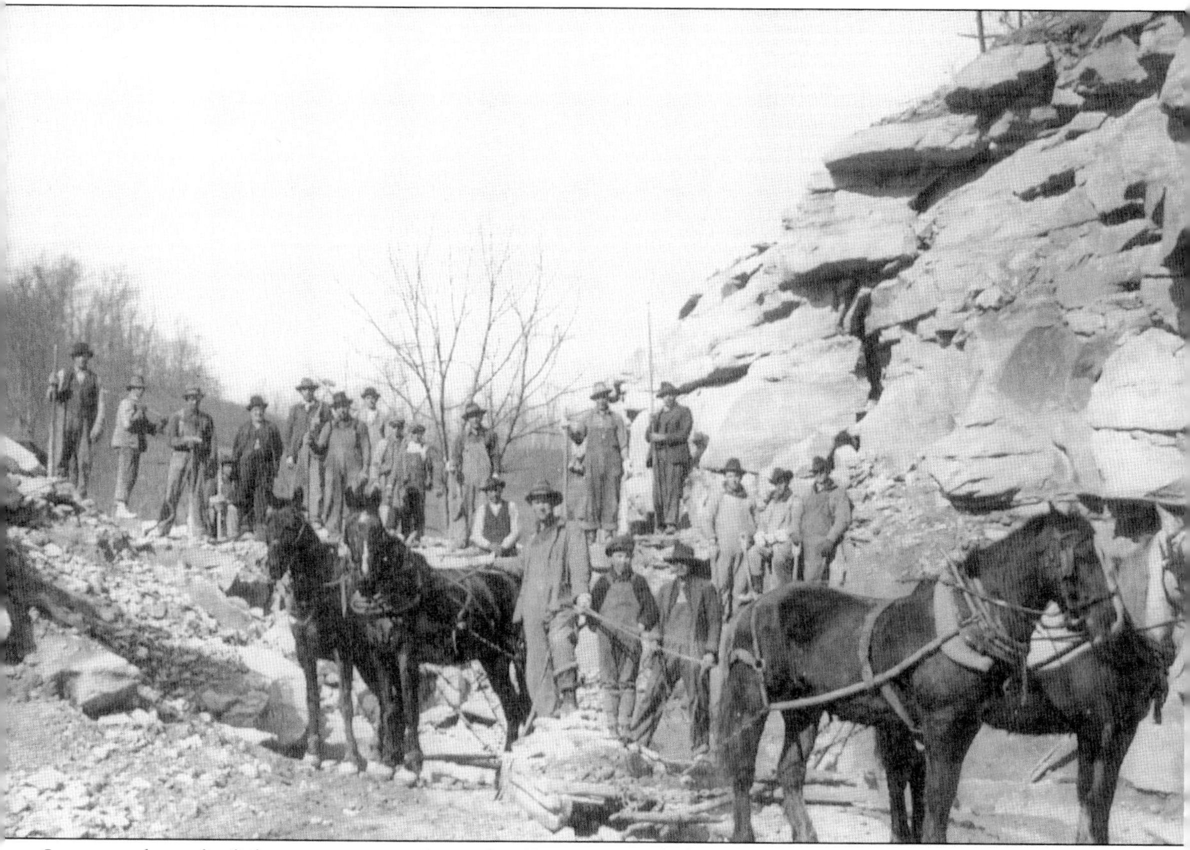

Improved roads did not arrive in Lincoln County until the 1920s. Like Route 10 along the Guyandotte Valley, these highways were built with hand tools using horse-drawn equipment. Blasting was sometimes required to make a cut, like the one shown here at the Kanawha–Lincoln county line during the construction of Route 214. Poor quality highways, coupled with the area's rugged terrain, have hampered the development of the county throughout its history. Recognizing this, West Virginia senator Robert C. Byrd created the Appalachian Regional Commission (ARC) in 1965. One legacy of the ARC was the construction of a system of four-lane freeways or corridors. Corridor G (US Route 119) was built during the early 1980s and clips through the eastern part of the county. Except for this short stretch of Corridor G, Lincoln County's other roads are notoriously twisting and narrow. (Courtesy of Jim Ryan.)

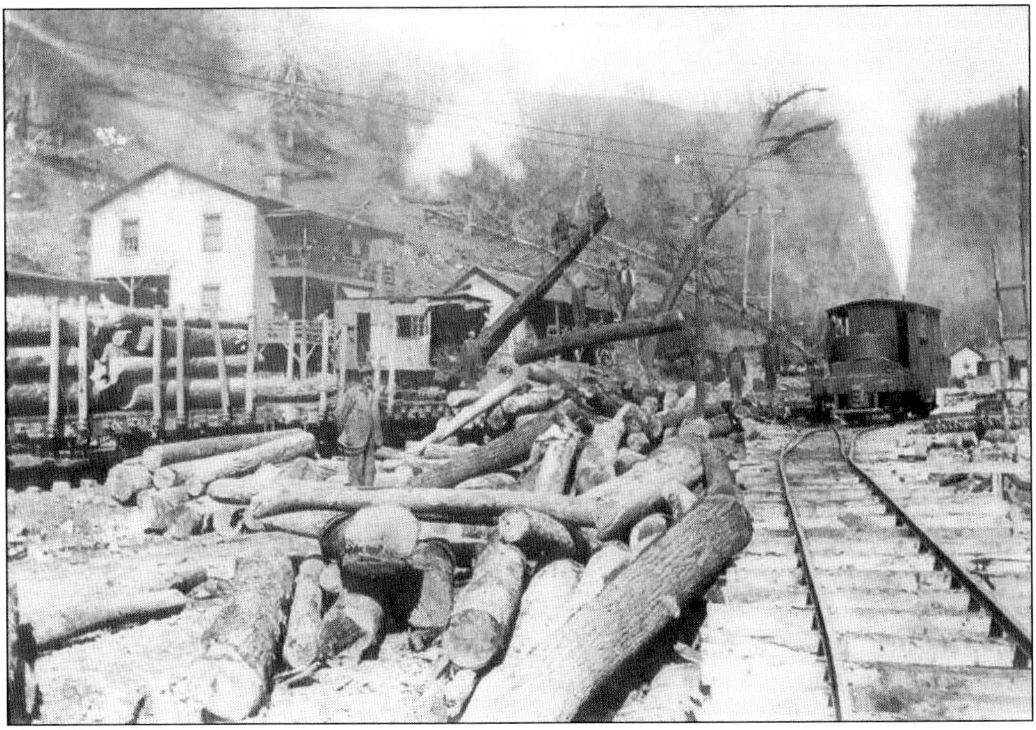

Ivaton was the hub of the local timbering industry. Comparable to similar activity on the Guyandotte, timber rafts were floated down to St. Albans. Some was obviously moved by rail. (Note the logs ties on the rail line.) Coal was the bread and butter of the Ivaton economy, but like Rochester or Eden Park, the place is now largely abandoned. (Courtesy of Gary McClure.)

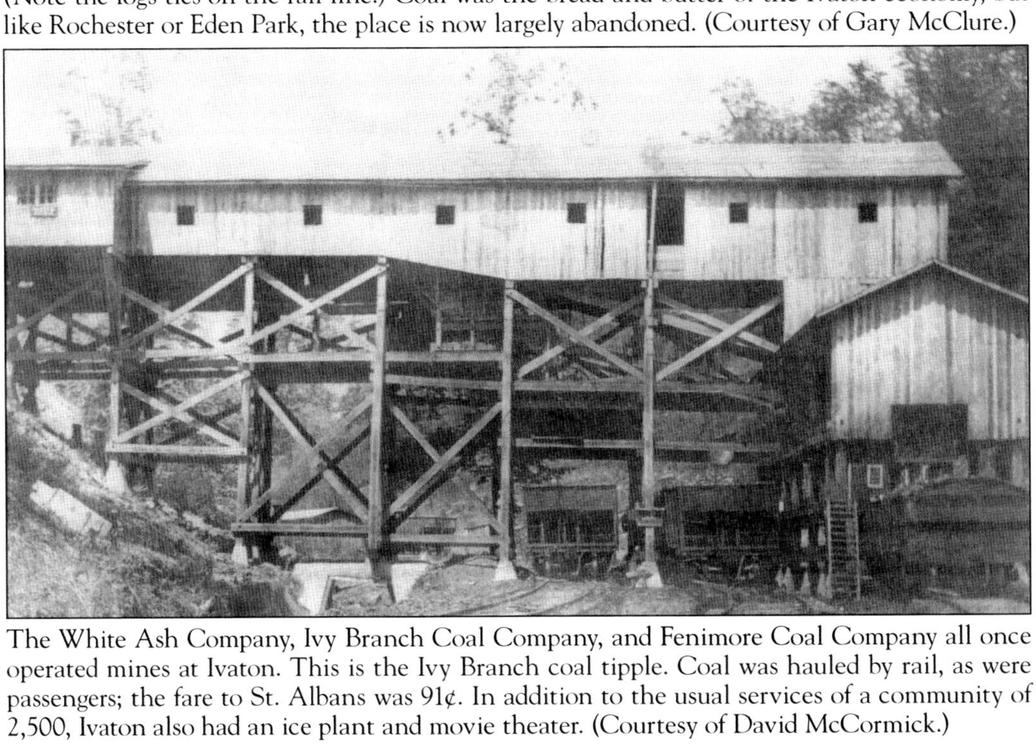

The White Ash Company, Ivy Branch Coal Company, and Fenimore Coal Company all once operated mines at Ivaton. This is the Ivy Branch coal tipple. Coal was hauled by rail, as were passengers; the fare to St. Albans was 91¢. In addition to the usual services of a community of 2,500, Ivaton also had an ice plant and movie theater. (Courtesy of David McCormick.)

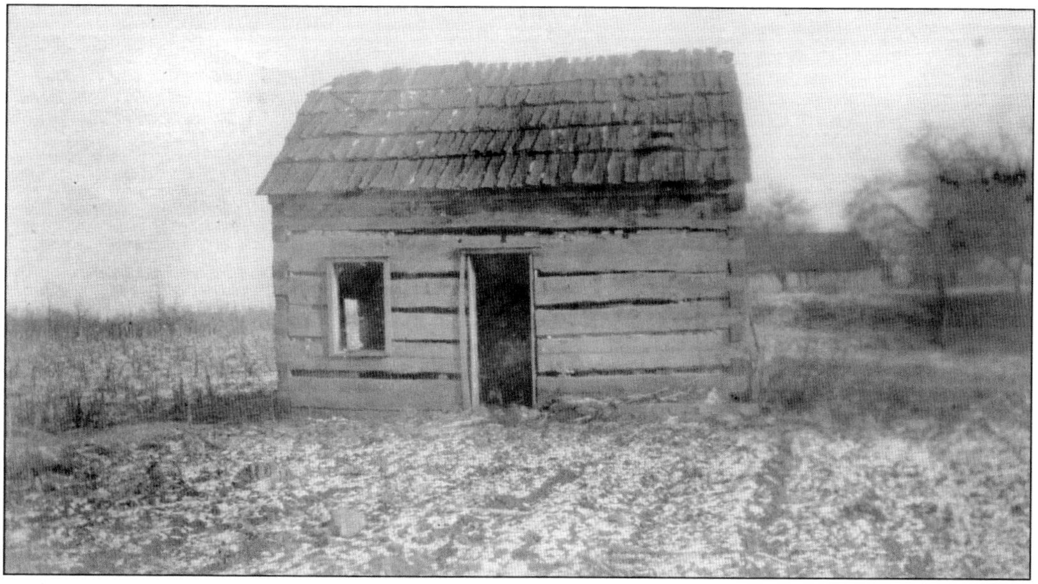

Sod, also known as Scioto, is located under the shadow of Sumerco Mountain in the valley of Cobbs Creek. The community grew up around the Cobbs Creek Church (pictured), which was established in 1855. Samuel Odell Dunlap established a post office here in 1904, and it remains in operation today. Stone quarrying was once a thriving industry in Sod. (MU-Lambert.)

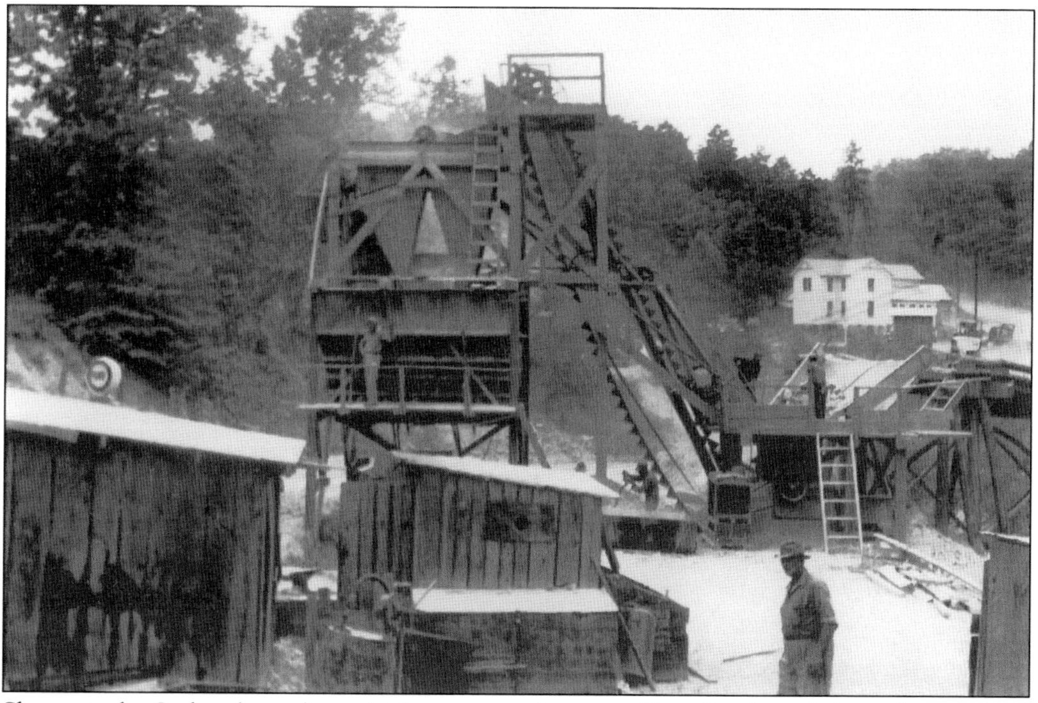

Shown is the Sod rock crusher, which was near the post office. Crushers did just that, turning big rocks into little rocks. Connected to the C&O Railroad and Little Coal River via the dinky train, Cobbs Creek mines also shipped large amounts of coal out of Sod. (Courtesy of Gary McClure.)

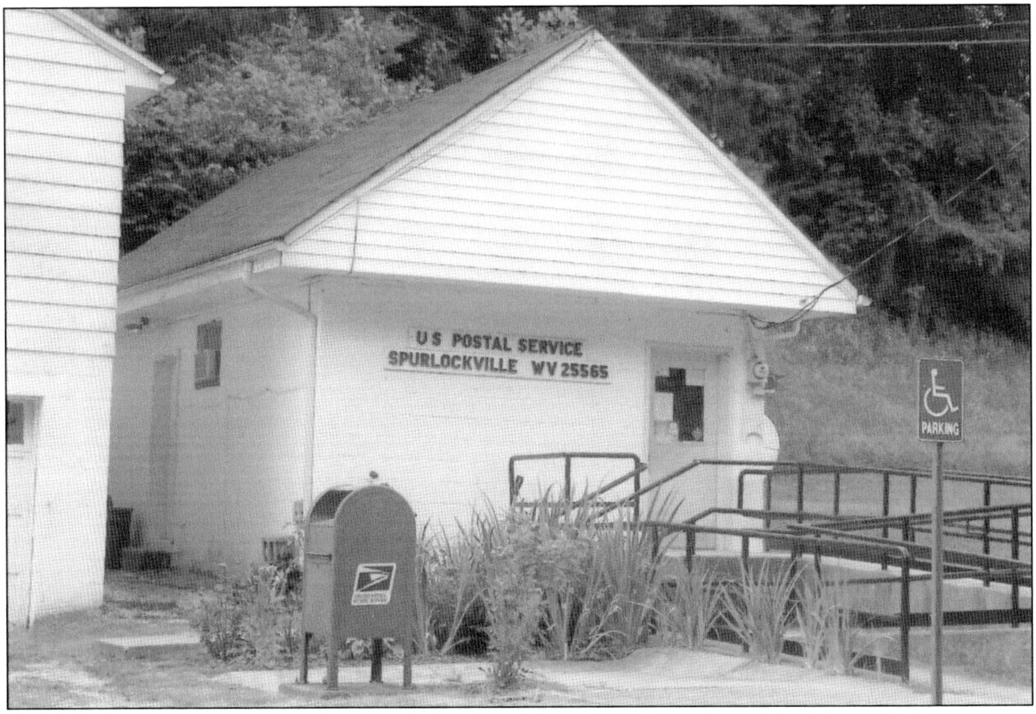

Somehow, the tiny post office at Spurlockville survives. Its zip code is 25565. It probably remains open because of its remote location on the extreme upper reaches of Mud River. Spurlockville is actually closer to Big Ugly, a Harts Creek community, than it is to Hamlin or Griffithsville. (Courtesy of Jim Ryan.)

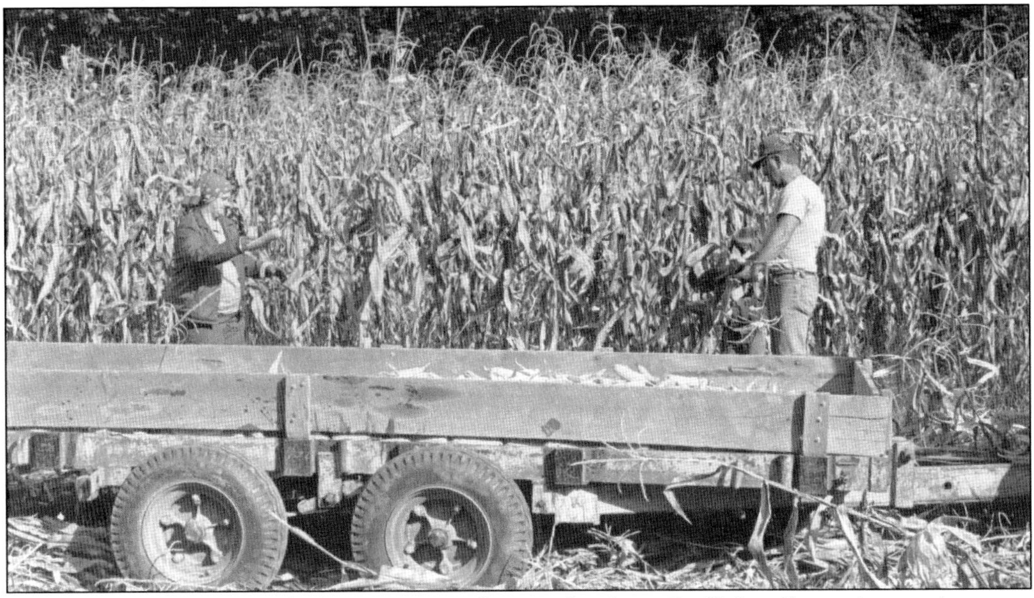

Charles and Mary Burford of Garretts Bend, six miles from Griffithsville in the northeastern corner of Lincoln County, gather up feed corn. Expressing a preference to harvest by hand, Mr. Burford told the *Lincoln Journal* that it was too difficult to maneuver a corn picker along with a wagon and tractor. (Courtesy of *Lincoln Journal*.)

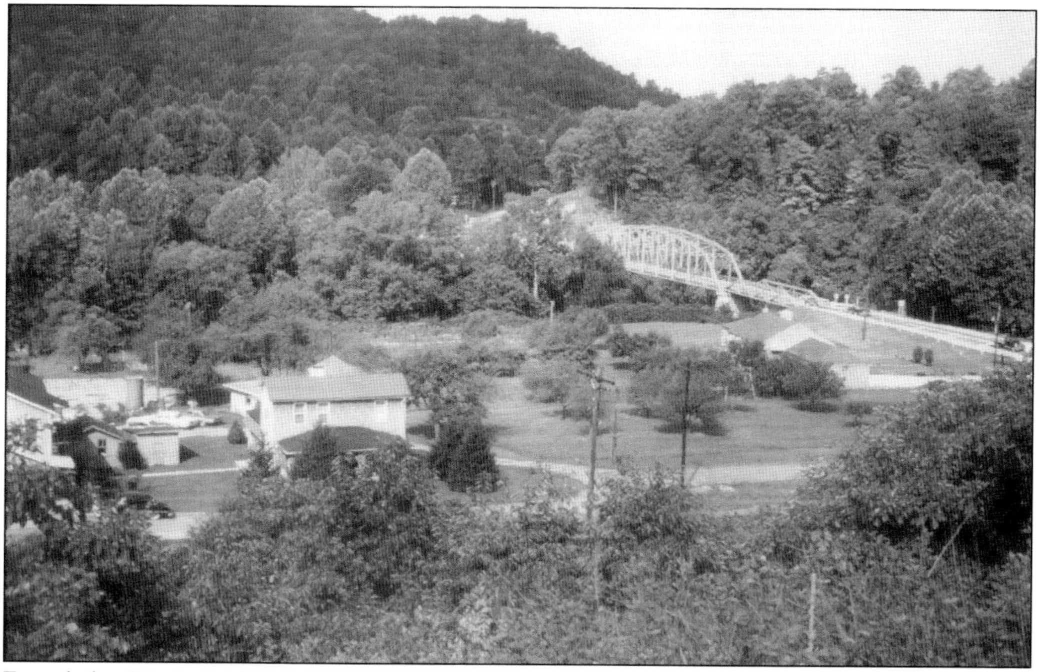

Founded as Rome in the 1890s, this town's name was changed to Alum Creek in 1910. It straddles the Lincoln–Kanawha county line at the strategic forks of the Coal River (named for pioneer scout Benjamin Cole but later changed to Coal). Alum Creek's flag depicts two connected stars, which represent both Alum Creek communities, while a diagonal stripe symbolizes the river that divides them. (Courtesy of Jim Ryan.)

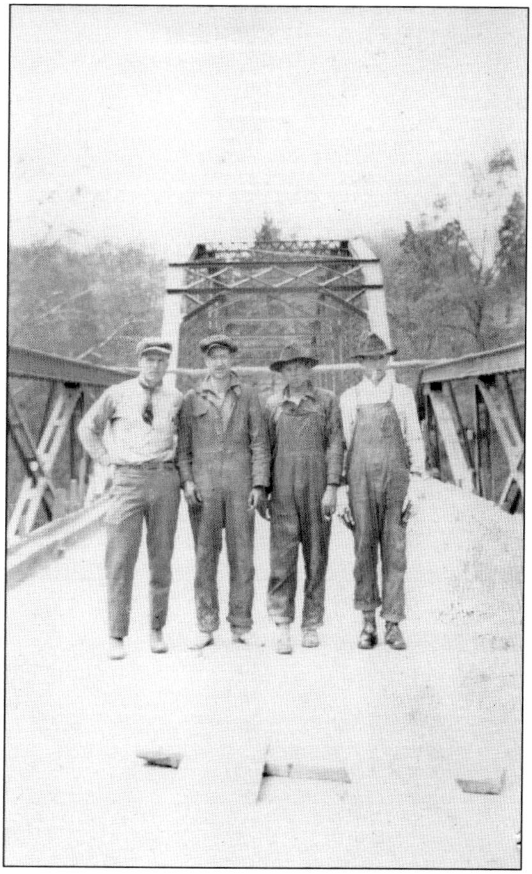

The first bridge joining the divided community of Alum Creek was not built until 1919. It served the area for 67 years until being torn down in 1986. Prior to construction of the bridge, this was the site of Henry Ramsey's ferry. It crossed the Coal River between Lincoln and Kanawha Counties, just below the junction of the Big and Little Coal Rivers at the forks. (Courtesy of Jim Ryan.)

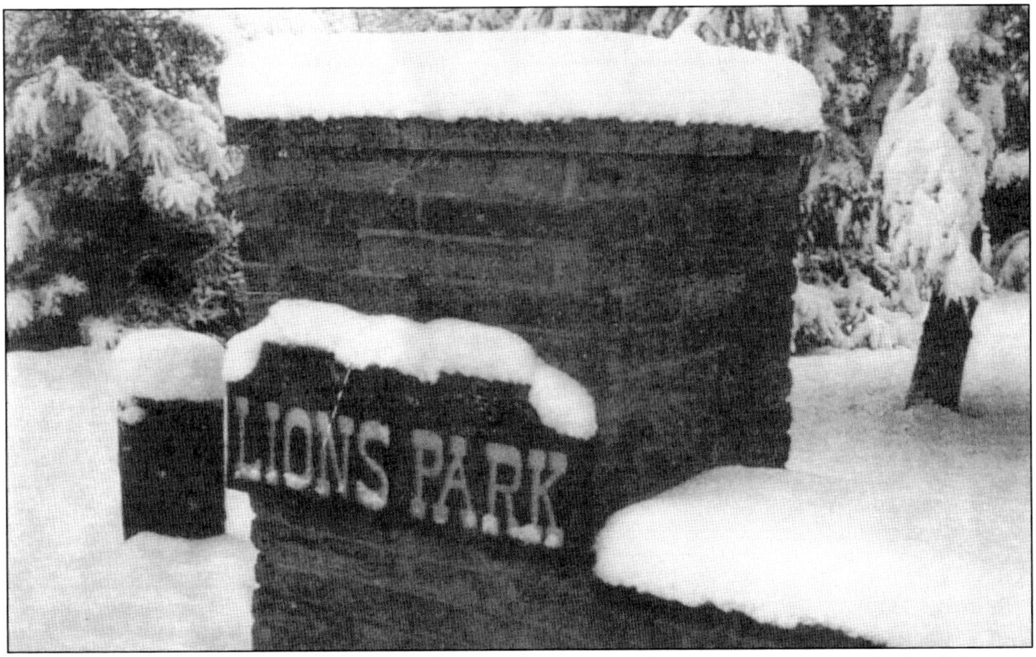

Members of the Alum Creek Lions Club have demonstrated active community leadership over the years. One such example is the 1972 purchase of land for the establishment of a town park. Lions Park is home to Ernie Turley Memorial Field and the Bill and Erna Miller Memorial Walking Path. (Courtesy of Jim Ryan.)

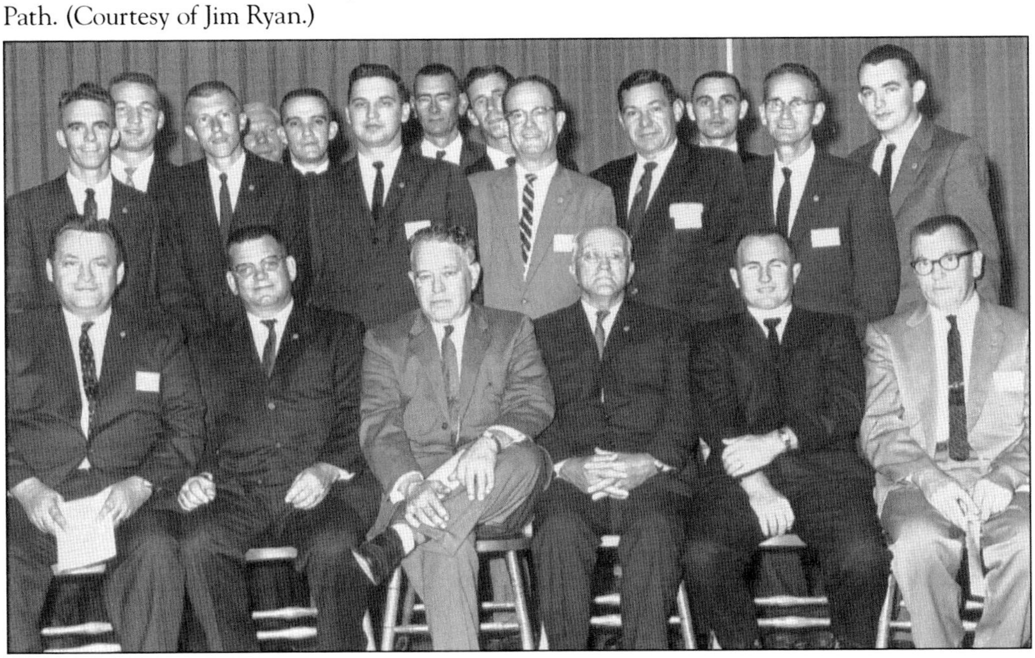

Charter night for the Alum Creek Lions Club was October 20, 1961, at Humphrey's Pine Room in Charleston. Roger Wheeler (sixth from left in back) was the first president. Besides Lions Park, some other Lions Club projects have included establishing the Alum Creek Public Library, buying the town's first fire truck, constructing the community center, and sponsoring a bicentennial parade. (Courtesy of Jim Ryan.)

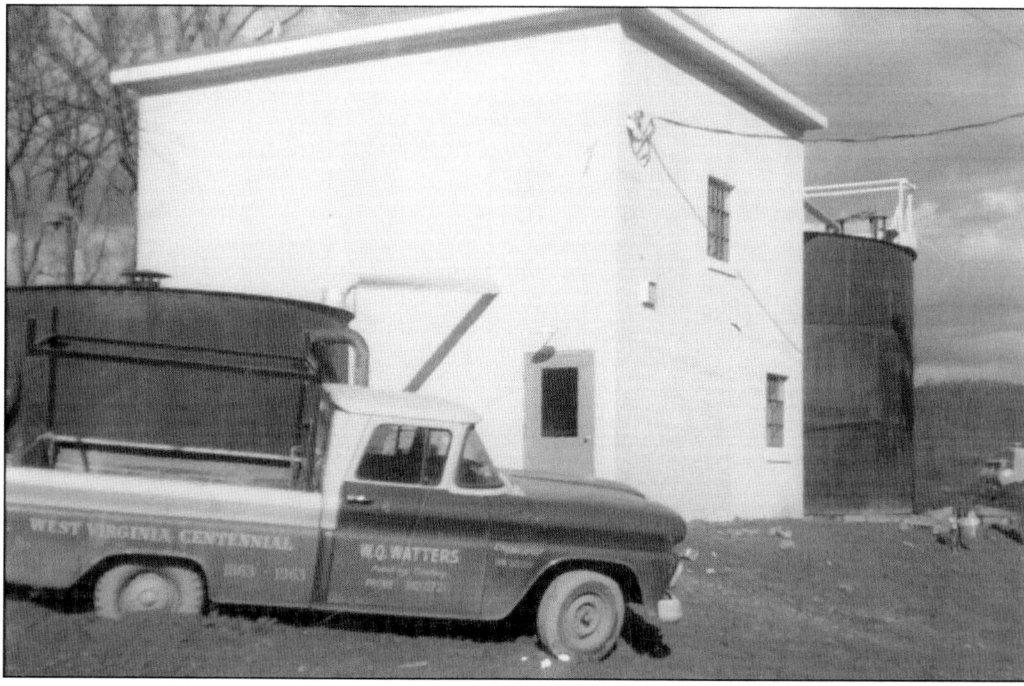

Organizing the Lincoln Public Service District was the very first project of the Alum Creek Lions Club. The West Virginia Centennial water truck dates this photograph to around 1963. Rates at that time were $2.20 per 1,000 gallons of water used. The line was run from Alum Creek to near Midway Elementary School. (Courtesy of Jim Ryan.)

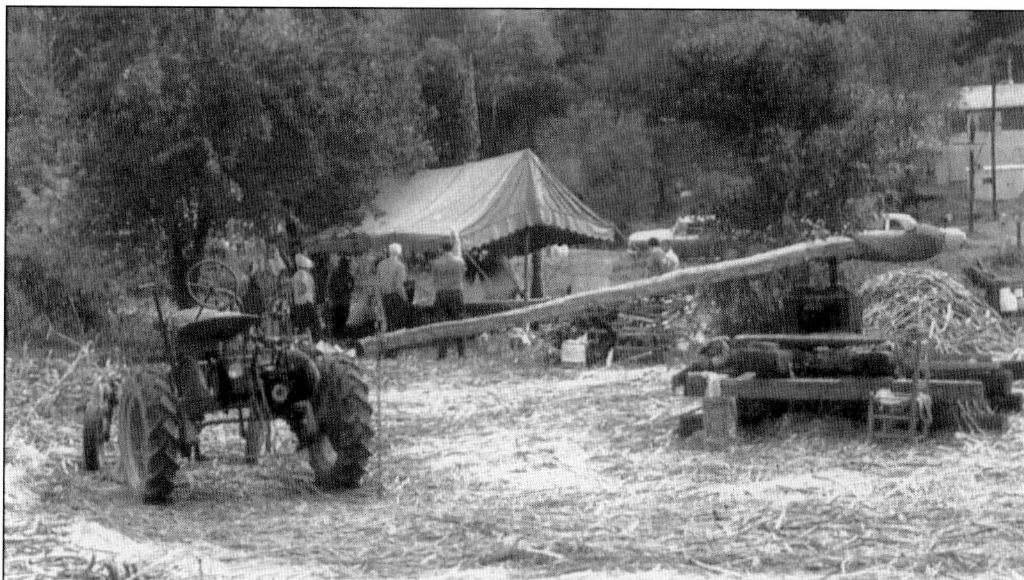

Yet another of many community activities organized by the Alum Creek Lions Club was this molasses-making demonstration, which took place around 1970. Cane sugar was grown on the future site of the Ernie Turley Memorial Field at Lions Park. The process involved stripping sugar plants, extracting juice from the stalk, and boiling the juice to crystallize the molasses. (Courtesy of Jim Ryan.)

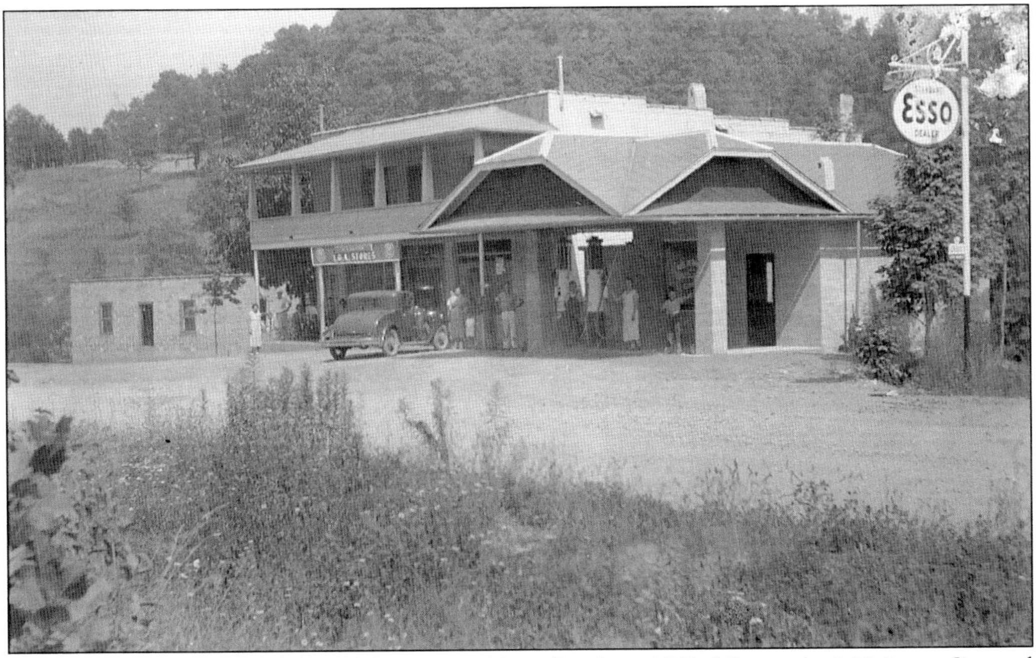

Walter G. Adkins opened this IGA store at Alum Creek in 1929. Like at the L.T. Jones General Store at Harts, an Esso station was added later. The store also functioned as a restaurant. Other notable Alum Creek food-related businesses included the Childress Superstore, Forks of Coal Store, Lincoln Lunch, Riverside Inn, and Roundtable Restaurant. (Courtesy of Jim Ryan.)

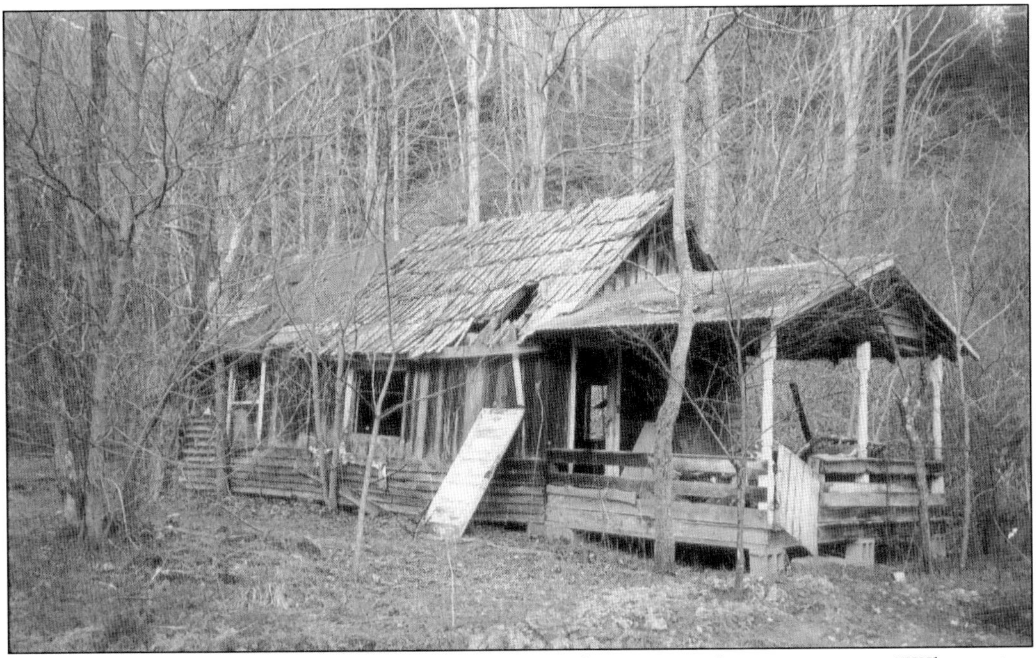

Big Ugly does not have a monopoly on unusual Lincoln County place names, as a "Whispering Pine aka Booger Hole" sign greets visitors who turn off of Route 214 just west of Alum Creek. Bill Trent once occupied this c. 1900 cabin at Booger Hole. Not to be topped, Branchland lays claim to a Slipper Gut Hollow. (Courtesy of Jim Ryan.)

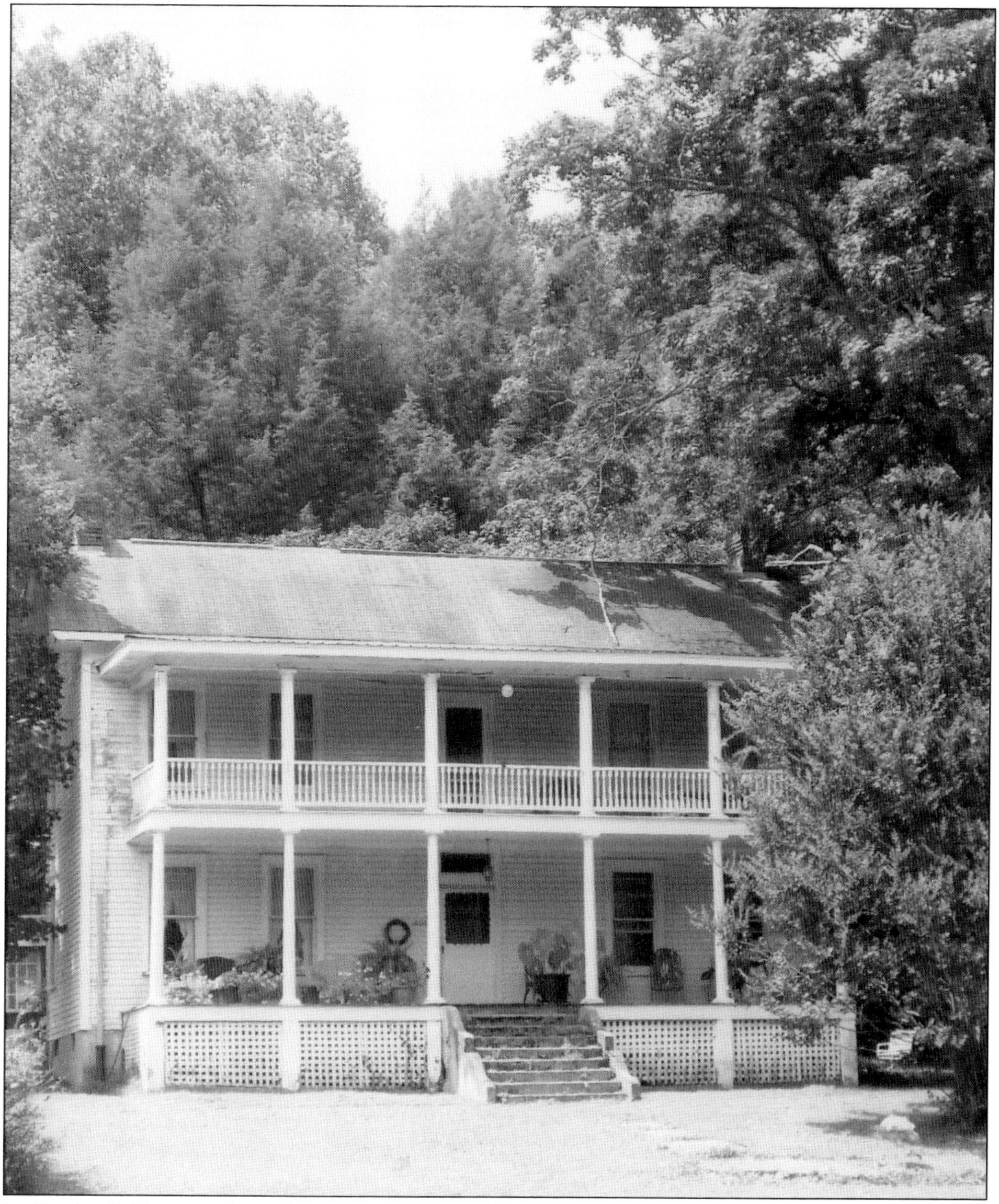

Holley Hills Estate is Lincoln County's first and only entry in the National Register of Historic Places. Featuring a Greek Revival–style main house and six outbuildings (including a toolshed, cellar, grain storage facility, and barn), it is located on a 296-acre farm along the Little Coal River south of Alum Creek. Built around 1885 by James Avis Holley Jr. (whose father had bonded the Lincoln County Board of Supervisors $2,000 when the county was founded in 1867), the main L-shaped farmhouse has a two-story front porch with five bays and was originally constructed with an oak frame, poplar lap siding, and a hip roof. Lumber was harvested on the farm, shipped by river to St. Albans for sawing, then sent back upriver to Holley Hills. The National Register application states: "The grandeur of the Holley Hills farm is majestic and serene. No photograph can accurately reproduce this setting." It is now a private residence. (AC.)

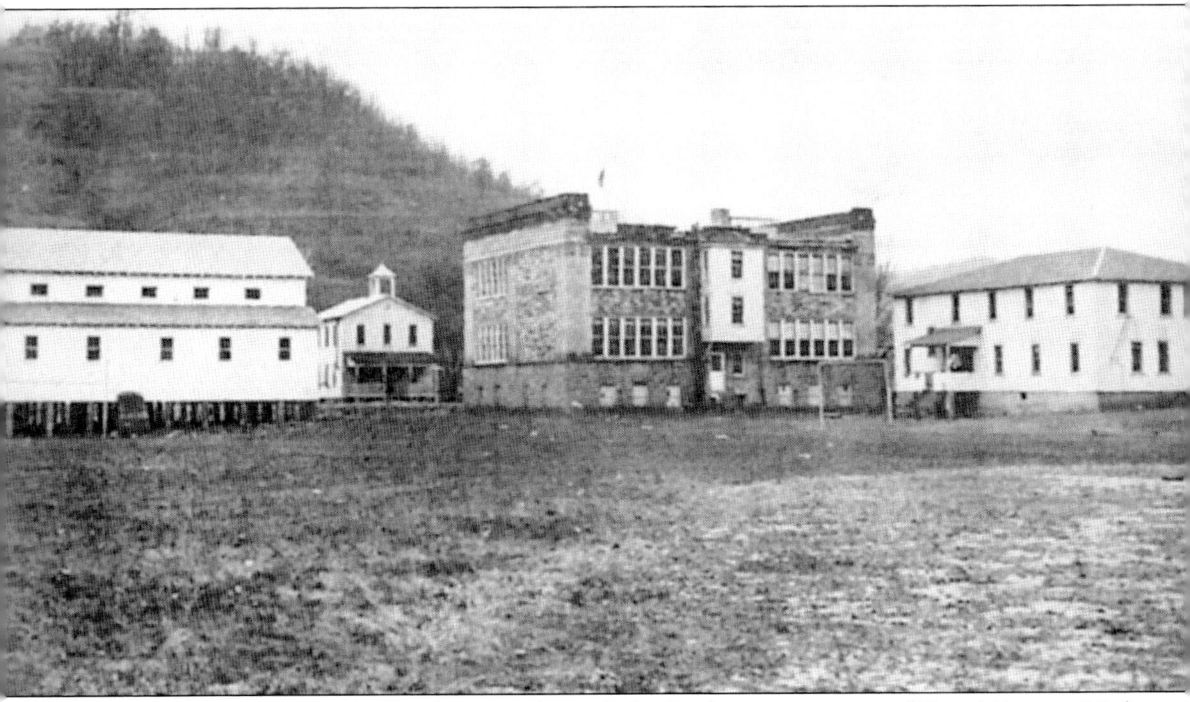

Spearheaded by school official James Blaine Coberly, the construction of Duval District High School in 1913 was overwhelmingly approved by citizens in a vote of 323 to 85. The school opened a year later in the basement of Griffithsville's IOOF Hall with an enrollment of 13. The high school building (center) was dedicated on October 21, 1915. George W. Hawkins was Duval's first principal, and William Ezra Williams was its first graduate. Duval grew to 61 students and 5 teachers by the 1915–1916 academic year. As it was Lincoln County's only high school, continued development was rapid. Construction of both a dormitory (right) in 1925 and gymnasium (left) in 1926 created a college-like campus environment. By 1934, "District" was dropped from the school name as students from Jefferson and Washington Districts were offered bus service. A new high school building was built in 1952. (Duval High School yearbook photograph, courtesy of Bev Johnson.)

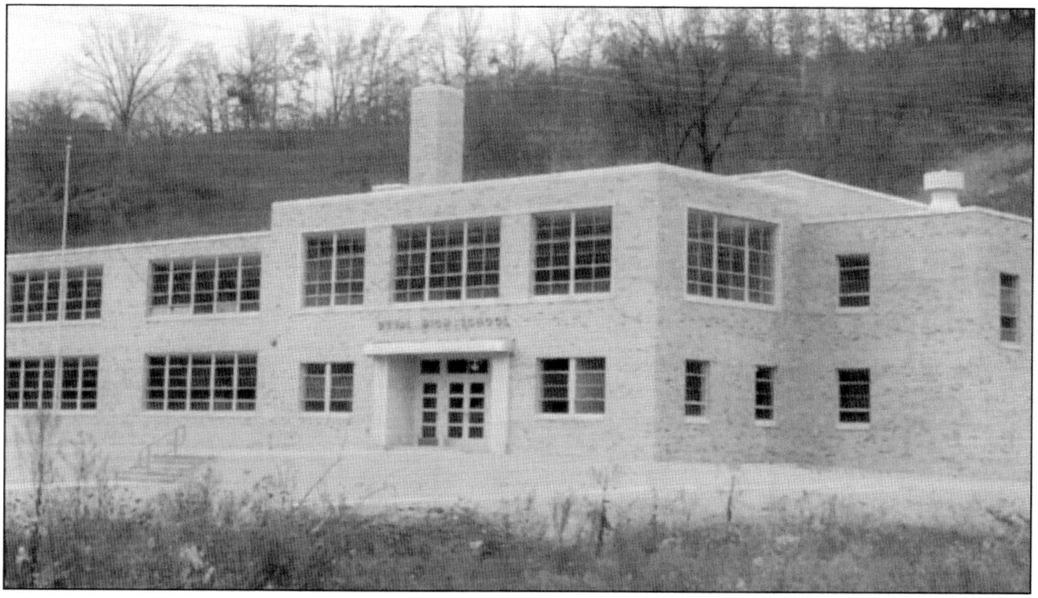

The last Duval High School building at Griffithsville (now serving as an elementary and middle school) was constructed in 1952. Three new classrooms and a cafeteria were added in the early 1960s. Further expansion followed in 1980 when a band room and 10 classrooms for the junior high school were built. Enrollment at Duval High School, which closed in 2006, peaked around 500. (Duval High School yearbook photograph, courtesy of Bev Johnson.)

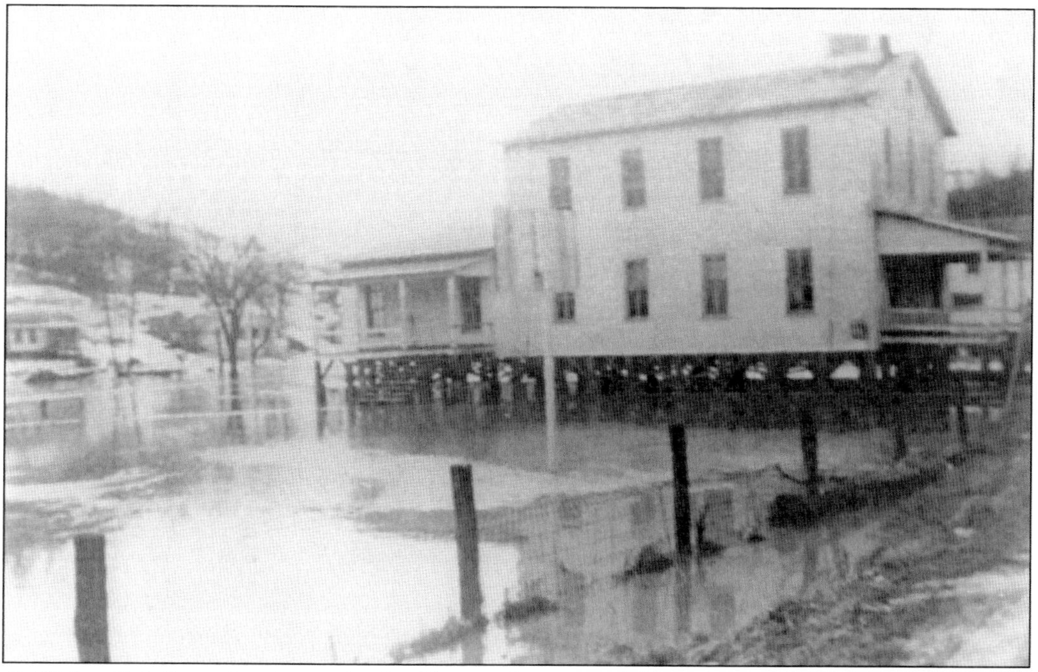

Griffithsville's first school was a log building at the mouth of Sugartree Creek, around the time of the Civil War. Ohioan Adam Hinchman taught "readin', 'ritin', and 'rithmetic" there until classes were moved to this two-story frame building in 1901. (Duval High School yearbook photograph, courtesy of Bev Johnson.)

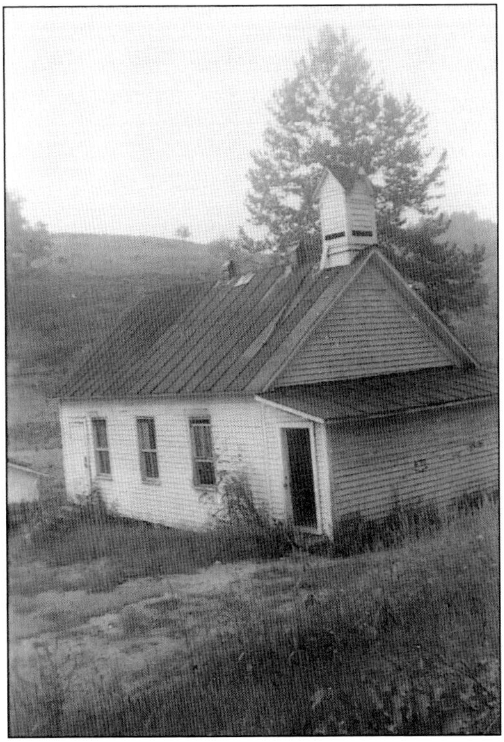

At the end of the 1940s, there were 134 elementary schools in Lincoln County. Midway (pictured in 1940) is one of only six that remain. The landmark Recht decision had its origins at nearby McCorkle Elementary. West Virginia Supreme Court judge Arthur Recht ruled in *Pauley v. Bailey* that the school funding formula was unconstitutional because students in poorer counties received unequal funding, a decision that led to widespread reforms. (Courtesy of Jim Ryan.)

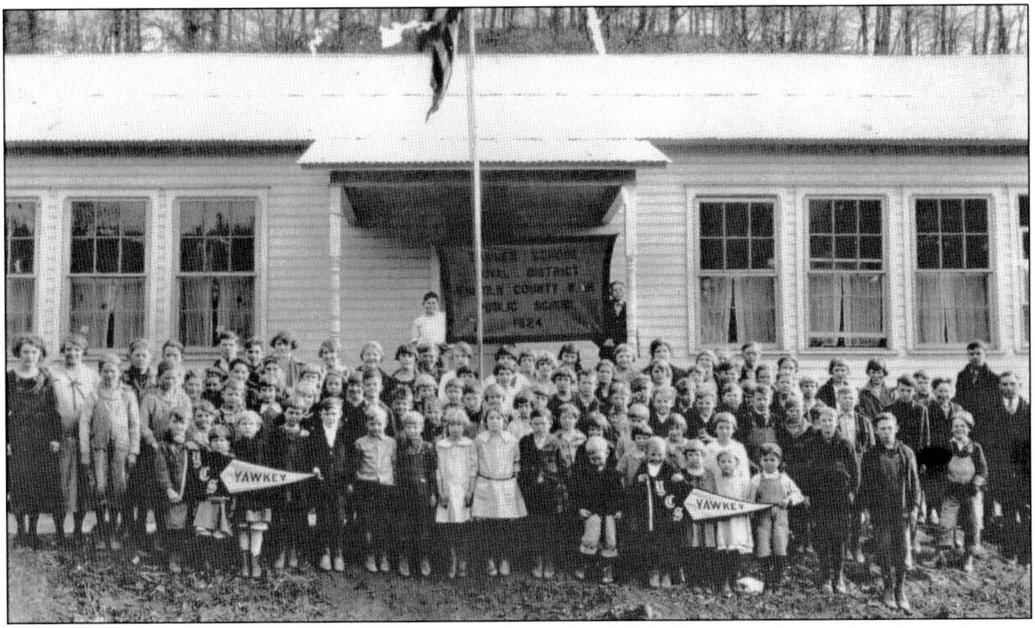

Students at Yawkey show off their banner awards in this 1924 photograph. A select list of former grade schools that once fed into Duval includes Angel Branch, Berry Branch, Brushy Fork, Buckeye, Cobbs Creek, Conley, Eli, Fairview, Flat Creek, Garretts Bend, Huckleberry, Island Creek, Ivaton, King Creek, Martin, McCorkle, New Hope, Parsner, Pea Ridge, Porter Fork, Slab, Snowden, Spurlockville, Sunnydale, Stinson, Summit, Tango, Whitten, and Woodville. (Courtesy of Gary McClure.)

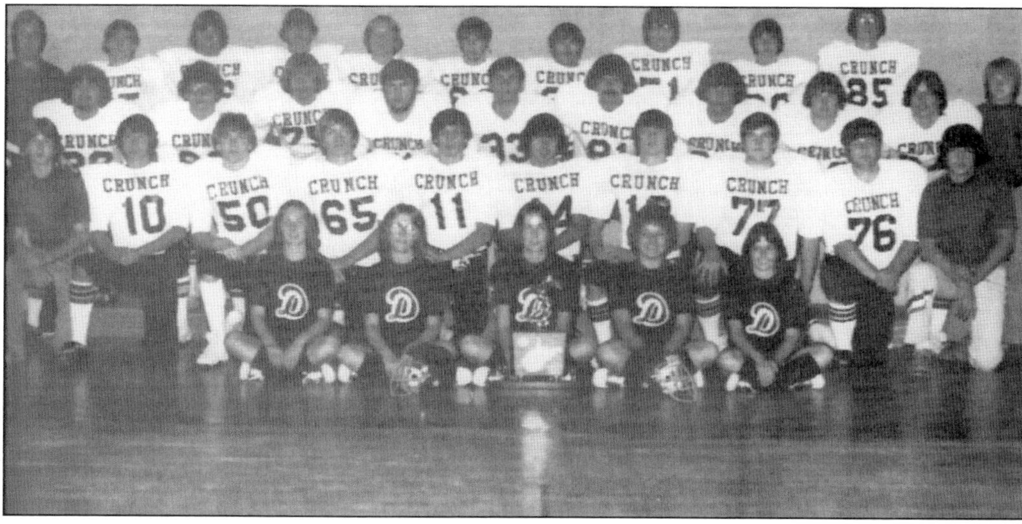

Duval's Yellow Jackets claimed a proud football tradition. The school fielded its first undefeated squad in 1933, and more recent editions won West Virginia Class A championships in 1978 (pictured), 1982, and 1990. Trademarks of those championship teams included a bruising running game and a hard-hitting defense nicknamed the "Orange Crunch." (Duval High School yearbook photograph, courtesy of Bev Johnson.)

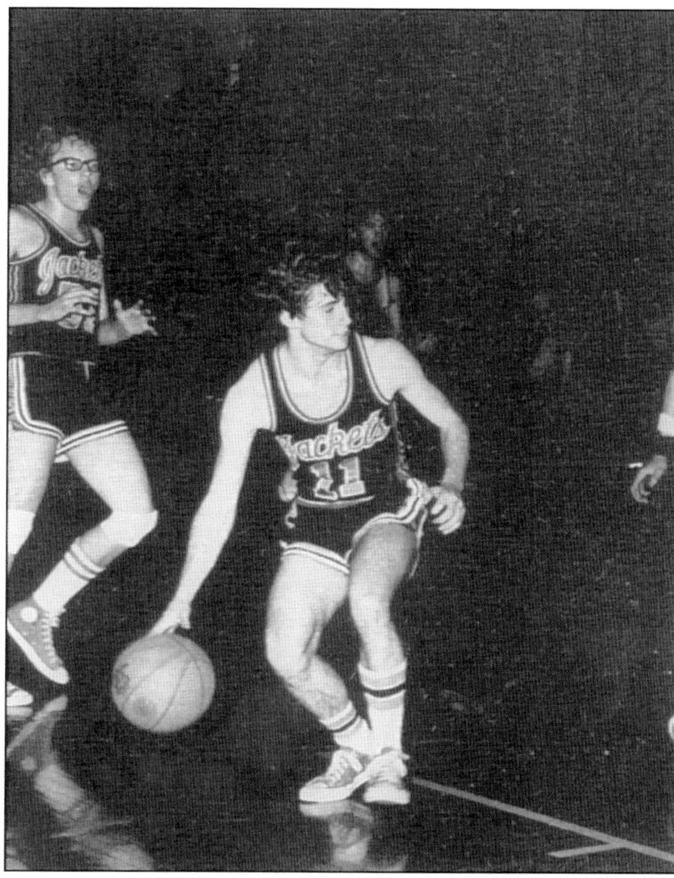

While Duval is better known for its strong football teams, a basketball player wearing the black and orange of Duval set the county single-game scoring record on January 8, 1974, when Randy Hill scored 62 points against Guyan Valley. The school retired Hill's No. 11 jersey to honor this accomplishment. (Courtesy of Jim Ryan.)

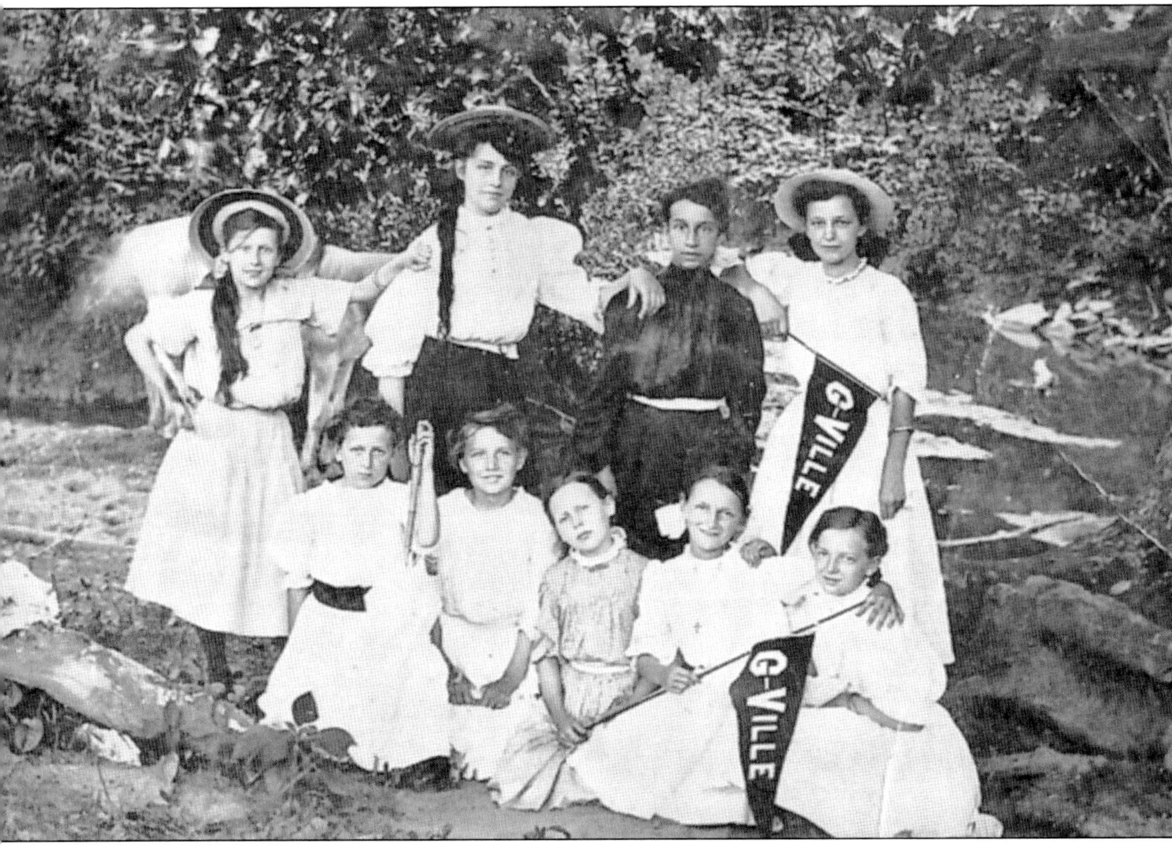

Lincoln County's first organized baseball team was fielded at Griffithsville in 1910. The team even had its own cheerleading squad. Identified members of the Griffithsville Belles include, from left to right (first row) Mable May, daughter of Francis E. and Laura May; Sylvia Wilson, daughter of Henry F. and Carrie Wilson; Myrtle Grass, daughter of Albert G. and Martha Grass; Helen Osborne, daughter of Harvey C. and Emma May Osborne; and Anna Markham (Osborne), daughter of Lee and Jennie Markham; (second row) Verna Grass, sister of Myrtle Grass; Goldie Wilson, sister of Sylvia Wilson; Mayme Spurlock, daughter of Albert and Rebecca Spurlock; and Glenna Osborne, sister of Helen Osborne. Most of the cheerleaders had fathers on the baseball team. (Courtesy of Sue Grass Parsons.)

The Griffithsville Nine (for some reason, only six men are pictured here) was an amateur traveling squad that played games all over the region. Comprised of local oil field–workers and merchants, turn-of-the-century teams like this one operated as clubs. Such organizations typically played informal games in which ground rules were sometimes improvised on the fly. (Courtesy of Sue Grass Parsons.)

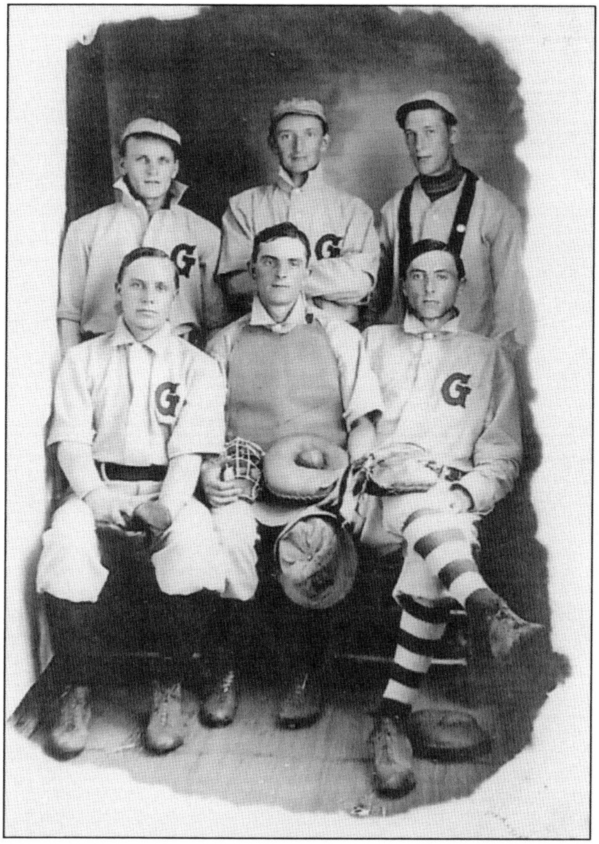

Clearly, the Griffithsville baseball team was a tremendous source of community pride, and games were major events. Scribbled as a caption on this photograph is "Yawkey, W.Va. '11." Several hundred spectators attended this ball game, and a row of automobiles may be seen along the first base line. The towers are not light stands, but oil derricks. (Courtesy of Fred and Alice Triplett Miller.)

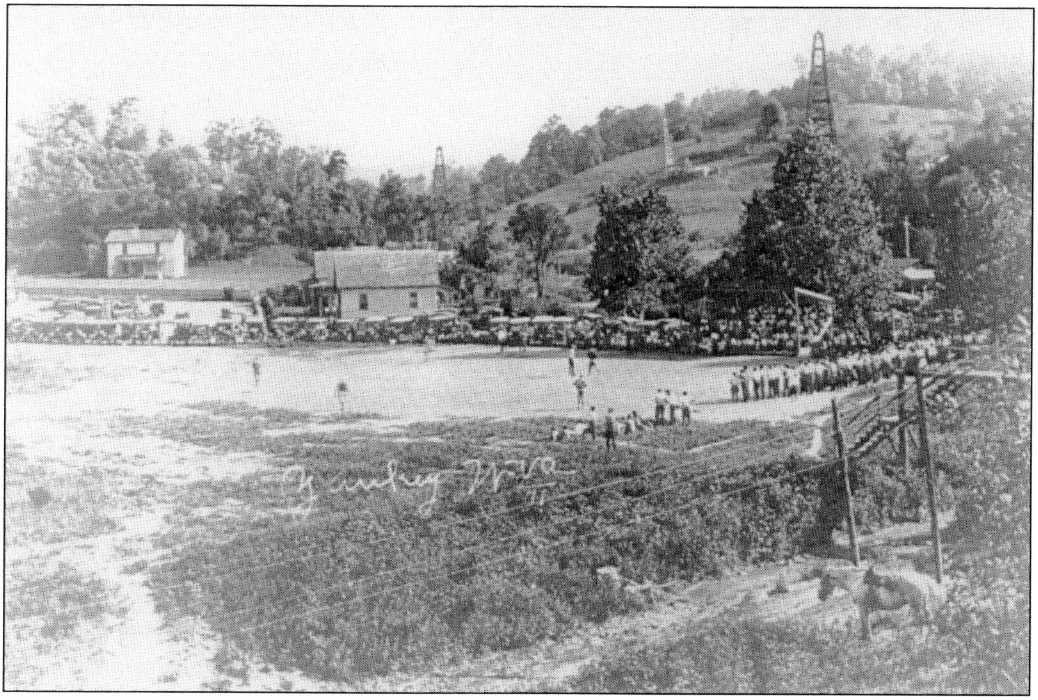

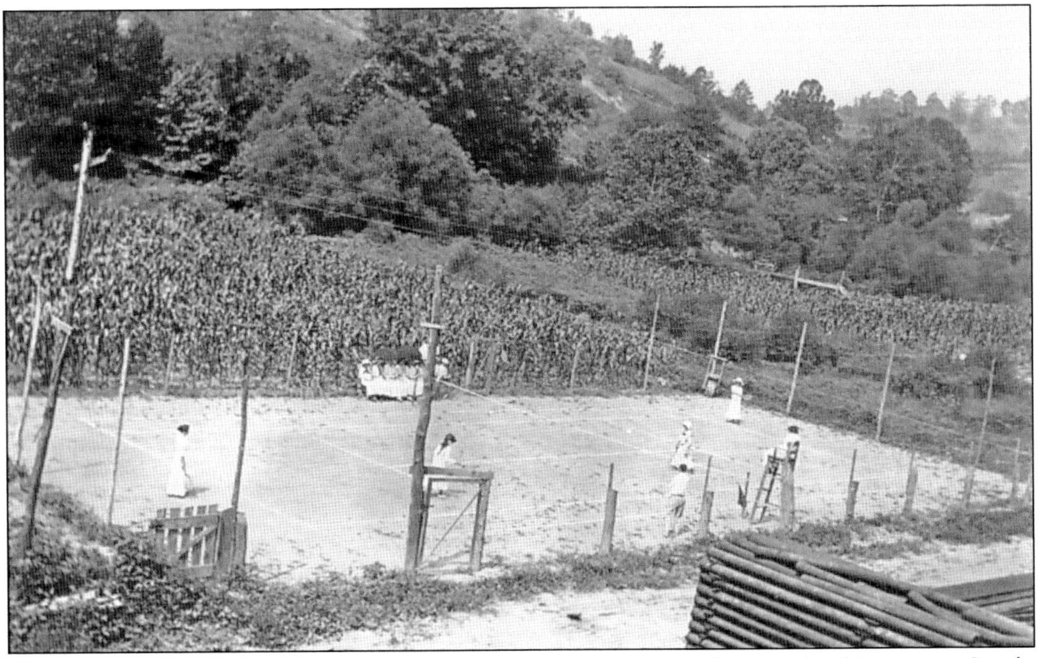

Members of the Osborne family, who operated a general store at the mouth of Sugartree Creek, were avid sportsmen. Participants on the local baseball team, they also liked to play tennis and built courts at Griffithsville for that purpose. These courts were widely acclaimed for their smooth clay surface. (Courtesy of Sue Grass Parsons.)

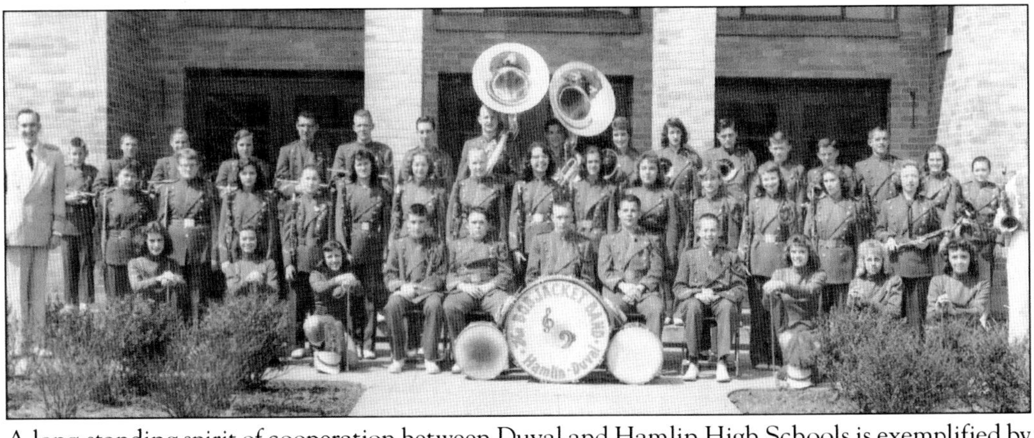

A long-standing spirit of cooperation between Duval and Hamlin High Schools is exemplified by the Bob Jacket Band, photographed here in 1960. Voters had the opportunity in the late 1990s to approve construction of a consolidated Lincoln East High School at Sweetland (a Guyan Valley–Harts merger called Lincoln West was to be built at Ranger), but the proposal was defeated. (Hamlin High School yearbook photograph, courtesy of LCFOA.)

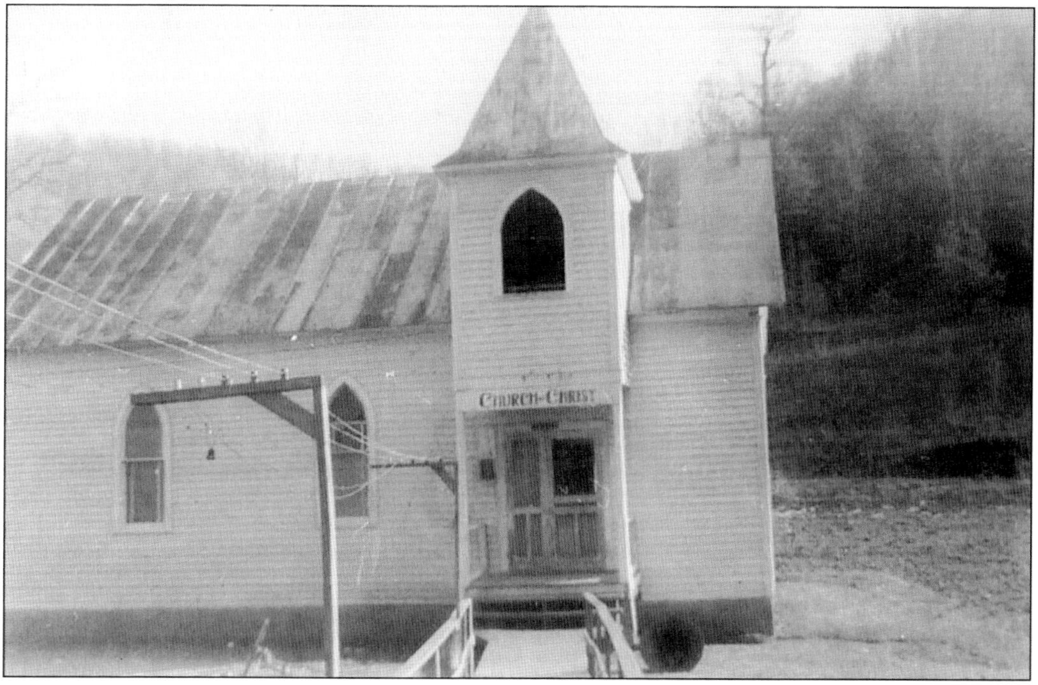

Organized around 1878 by James Chafin, the Griffithsville Church of Christ held services here until 1960. Before construction of this building at the beginning of the oil boom in 1906 or 1907, the congregation held meetings at Valley Fork School. The Osbornes, who operated the nearby general store and tennis courts, provided land for construction of the church. (Courtesy of Gary McClure.)

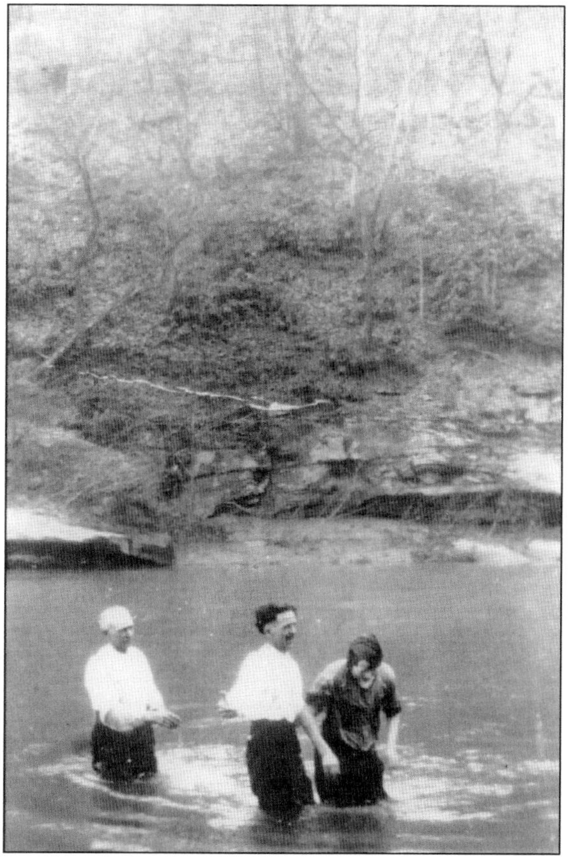

This baptism took place at Alum Creek near the Forks of Coal Missionary Baptist Church. Established in 1834, Forks of Coal may be Lincoln County's oldest continuously operating church. The original building was a log structure, which was replaced with a white-frame building. A new brick church was erected in 1949 and was extensively remodeled in 1980. (Courtesy of Jim Ryan.)

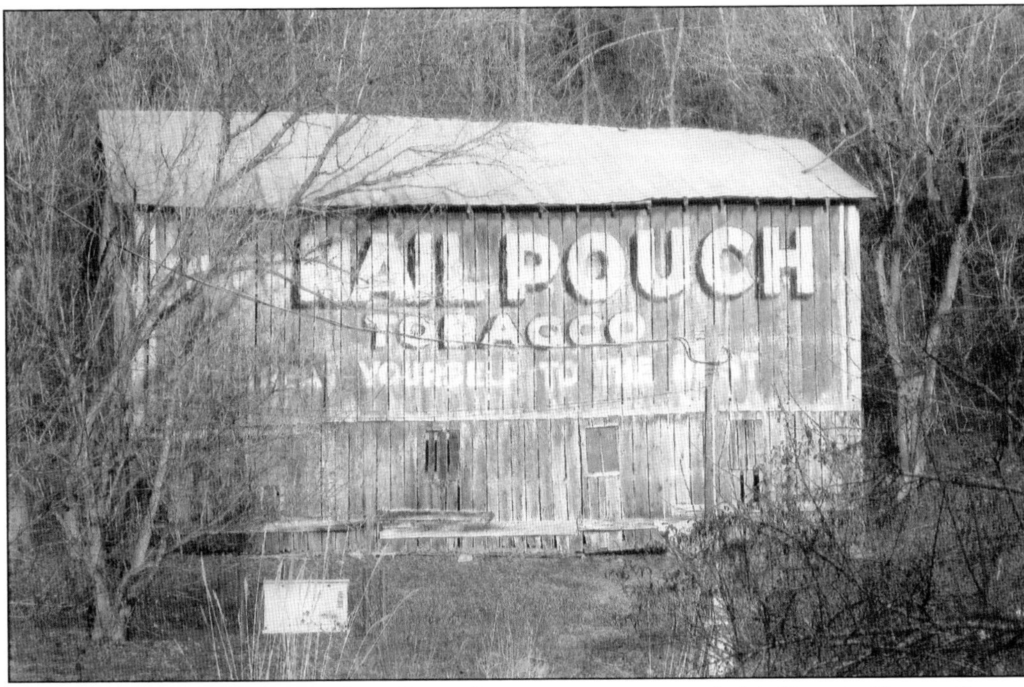

Yawkey is a crossroads town, where Route 3 continues on towards Madison in Boone County while Route 214 (Yeager Highway) heads to the state capital, Charleston. It is also the site of this rare red Mail Pouch barn. Pews at the nearby Yawkey United Methodist Church were provided by former Boston Red Sox owner Tom Yawkey. (AC.)

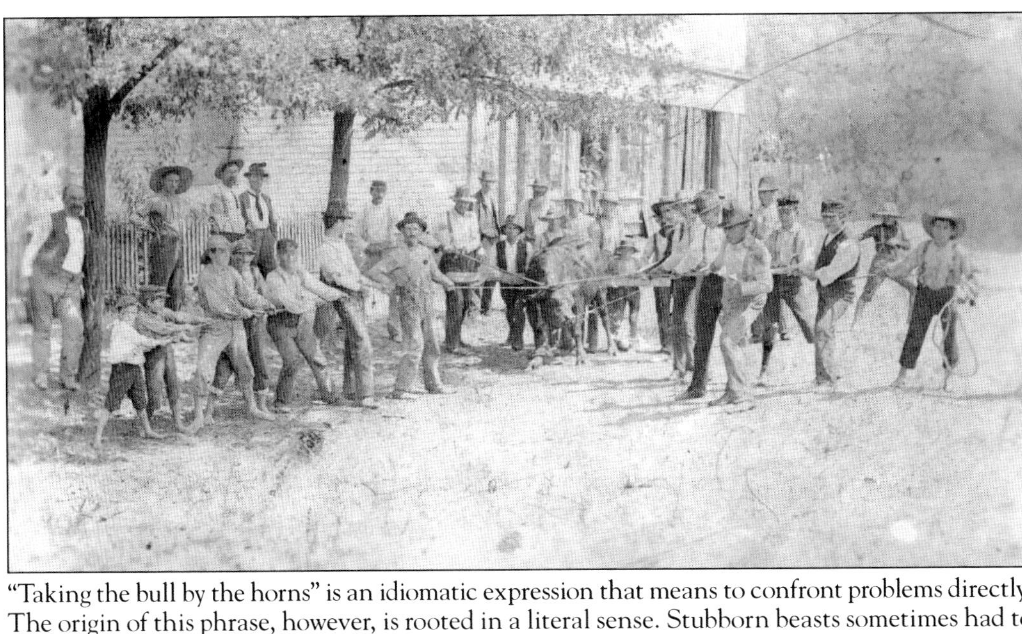

"Taking the bull by the horns" is an idiomatic expression that means to confront problems directly. The origin of this phrase, however, is rooted in a literal sense. Stubborn beasts sometimes had to be taken by the horns, but the relaxed expressions in this photograph indicate that it was also done for sport. (MU-Lambert.)

Pinnacle Rock is set in a loop of Little Coal River alongside Corridor G (US Route 119) between McCorkle and Julian in Boone County, and is characterized by a CSX railroad tunnel, which runs underneath. The popular Hatfield and McCoy ATV Trails network is planning to construct a trailhead near the rock. (Courtesy of David McCormick.)

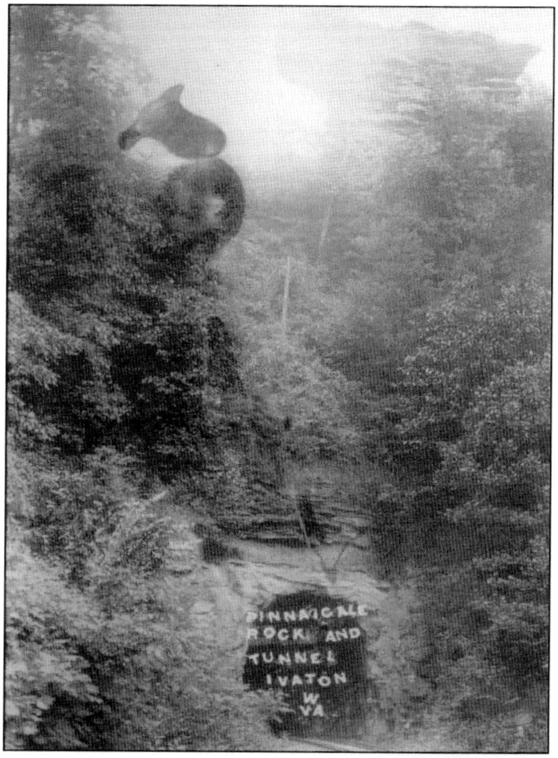

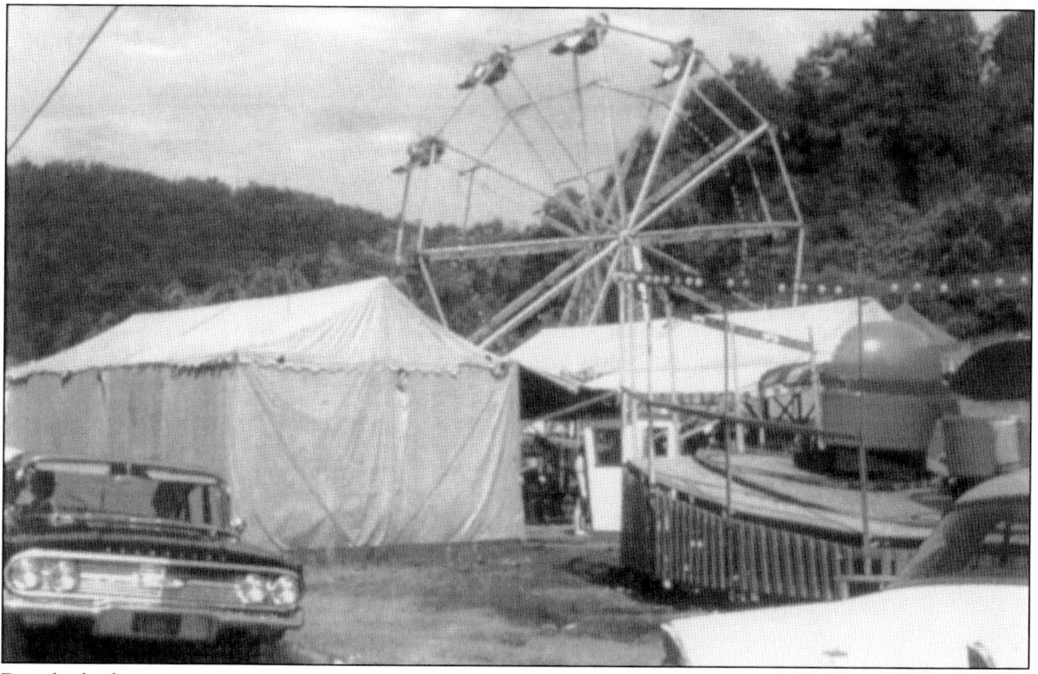

Roadside fairs were once a common sight around the county, and they still set up occasionally with Ferris wheels and Tilt-A-Whirls. This one operated near Midway Elementary School in 1962. Not surprisingly, the carnival was sponsored by the ever-active Alum Creek Lions Club. (Courtesy of Jim Ryan.)

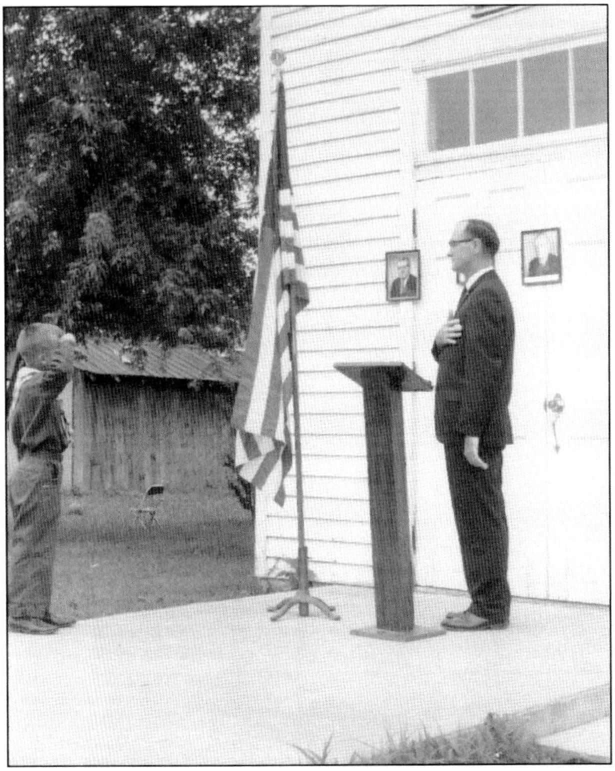

Duval can claim Lincoln County's first Boy Scouts of America troop. In this image, Elba Davidson administers the oath to a young scout: "On my honor, I will do my best / To do my duty to God and my country / and to obey the Scout Law; / To help other people at all times; / To keep myself physically strong, mentally awake, and morally straight." (Courtesy of Lucian Isaacs.)

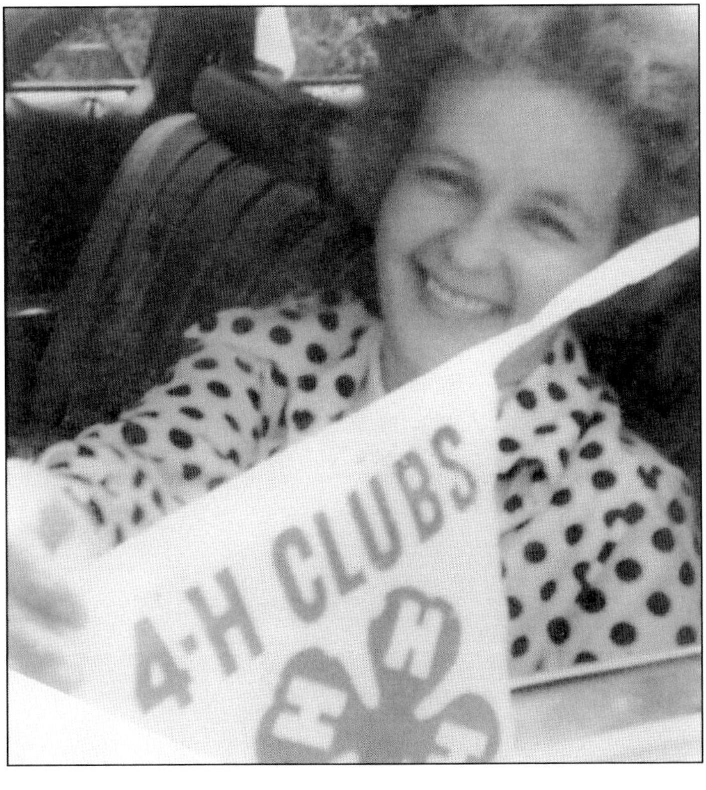

Another Duval first is the establishment of a 4-H Club in the county. Trilba Hill of Sod was a champion for this organization. She also served on the board of directors for the Alum Creek Library and was active in several other area youth groups. The four Hs are head, heart, hands, and health. (Courtesy of Jim Ryan.)

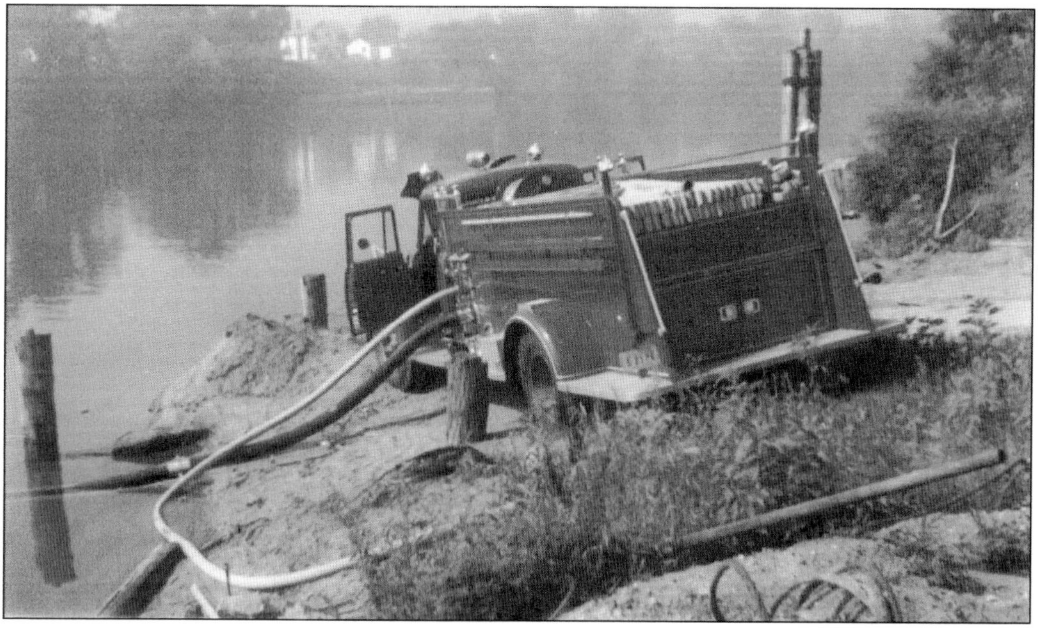

Eastern Lincoln County residents have traditionally led the way in the area of helping others. Lincoln County's first American Red Cross Organization was established at Griffithsville, where fire brigades grew up around the oil drilling industry. Shown here, Alum Creek's first fire truck, "Big Red," undergoes a series of tests (on the Kanawha River in 1964) in order to be qualified by the state. It passed. (Courtesy of Jim Ryan.)

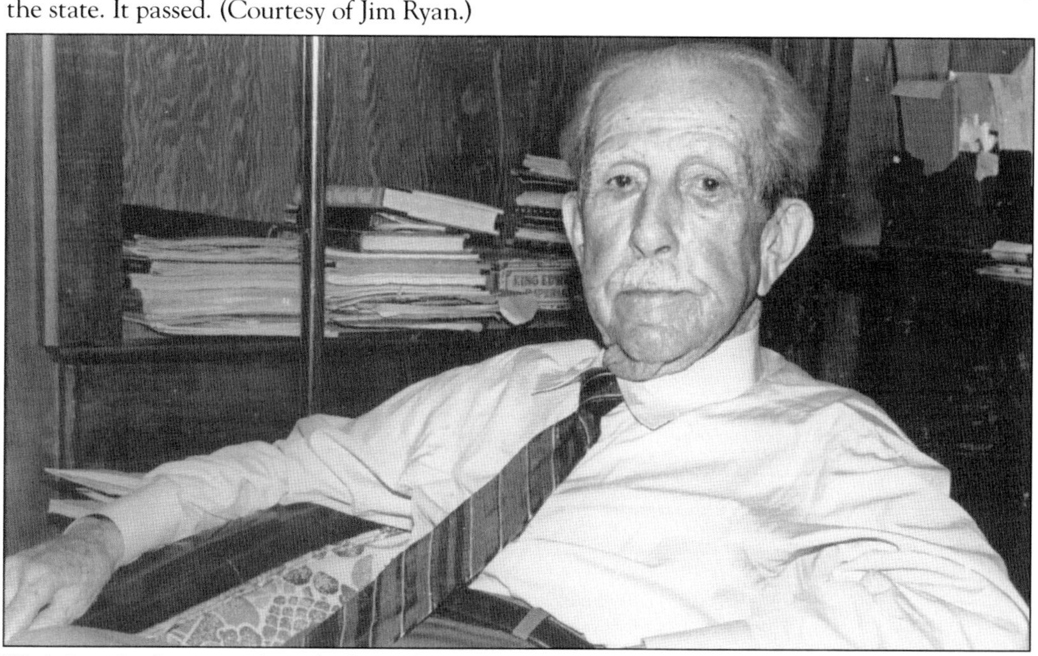

With hundreds engaged in the hazardous occupation of drilling, many doctors immigrated to Griffithsville during the oil boom era. Early physicians included Drs. J.H. Walden, Chauffins, Craig, Henson, and McLwain. Pictured is Dr. George Walden, who operated an office at West Hamlin. The Waldens played a key role in establishing both the Lincoln Primary Care Center and the Marshall University School of Medicine. (Courtesy of *Lincoln Journal*.)

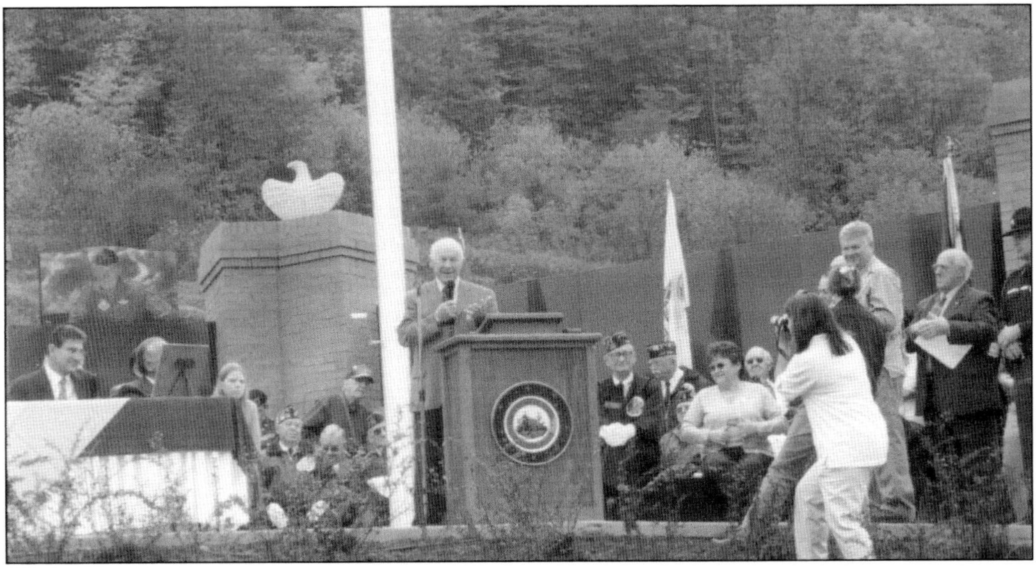

General Yeager made his most recent visit to Lincoln County in 2006 to dedicate a "Welcome to Lincoln County" sign. He was greeted by a large and adoring crowd. Shown in this photograph are two governors of West Virginia: Joe Manchin and Earl Ray Tomblin. (Courtesy of Jim Ryan.)

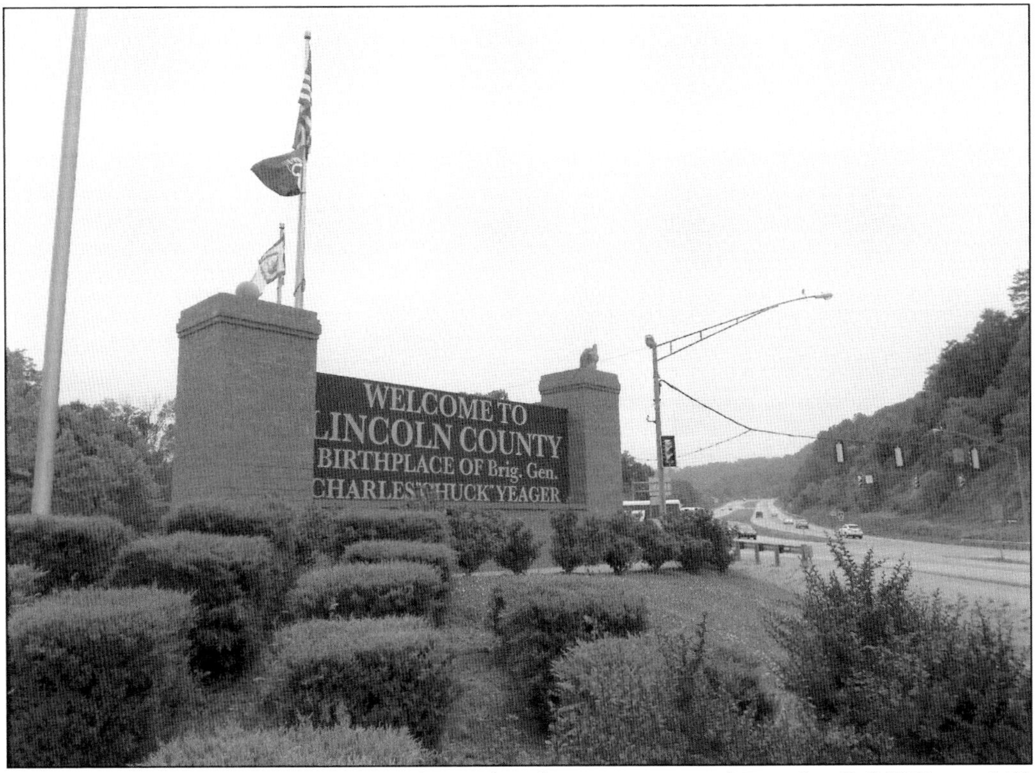

Lincoln County's unofficial gateway is located at the intersection of Corridor G (US Route 119) and the Charles E. "Chuck" Yeager Highway (Route 214) in Alum Creek. This short section of Corridor G between Charleston and Madison is the only four-lane freeway in the county. It is also the location of Lincoln County's only traffic signal (back right). (AC.)

Bibliography

Hardesty's Historical and Geographical Encyclopedia: Special History of the Virginias, Maps and Histories of Wayne, Lincoln and Cabell Counties, West Virginia. New York: H.H. Hardesty and Company Publishers, 1884.

Johnson, Leland R. *Men, Mountains, and Rivers: An Illustrated History of the Huntington District, U.S. Army Corps of Engineers, 1754–1974.* Washington, DC: Superintendent of Documents, US Government Printing Office, 1977.

Lambert, Fred B. *The Llorrac: Sketches of Lincoln County History.* Hamlin, WV: Carroll District High School, 1926.

Lincoln County Genealogical Society. *Lincoln County and Its People.* Hamlin, WV: Lincoln County Genealogical Society, 1989.

McCormick, David. *First 200 Years of Cobbs Creek History.* Sod, WV: Self-published, 2004.

Muller, Heidi, ed. *Patchwork Dreams: Stories, Songs and History from Big Ugly Creek and Harts Creek, West Virginia.* Harts, WV: Step by Step, 2007.

Ryan, Jim. *The Barber of Bonami.* Charleston, WV: Printing Press, Ltd., 2010.

Smith, Harold Ray. *Civil War Veterans of Lincoln County, West Virginia.* Ranger, WV: Self-published, 2008.

Then and Now at Duval, 1914–2006. Griffithsville, WV: Community-published compilation of Duval High School yearbook photographs.

West Virginia Department of Environmental Protection. *An Ecological Assessment of Lower Guyandotte Watershed.* Charleston, WV: Watershed Assessment Section, 2004.